D0615515

Drawing on Trollope's unpublished notes on seventeenth-century drama and bringing to light many instances in the novels of direct borrowings from old plays, Herbert reveals Trollope carrying out a steady critique of the Victorian subversion of pleasure, and doing so by means of a subtle and almost recklessly inventive deployment of comic materials. Herbert emphasizes the tension between Trollope's allegiance to comic pleasure and his strain of moral earnestness, a tension that is symptomatic of strains in Victorian culture at large but here pays rich dividends, yielding much of the novelist's richest and most suggestive and problematic writing.

Thematically organized around such aspects of Trollope's work as his investigations of sex, his formal structures, and his principles of "realism," Herbert's study includes detailed readings of two of the nineteenth century's most ambitious exercises in comedy: *The Way We Live Now* and Trollope's neglected masterpiece, *Ayala's Angel*.

CHRISTOPHER HERBERT is associate professor of English at Northwestern University.

For information on books of related interest or for a catalog of new publications, please write:

Marketing Department
The University of Chicago Press
5801 South Ellis Avenue
Chicago, IL 60637
U.S.A.

Trollope
and Comic Pleasure

Hablot Knight Browne ("Phiz"), "Edgehill," illustration for the 1864–65
edition of Trollope's *Can You Forgive Her?*

Trollope
and Comic Pleasure

Christopher Herbert

*The University of Chicago Press * Chicago & London*

CHRISTOPHER HERBERT is associate professor of English at Northwestern University.

The University of Chicago Press, Chicago 60637
The University of Chicago Press, Ltd., London

© 1987 by The University of Chicago
All rights reserved. Published 1987
Printed in the United States of America

96 95 94 93 92 91 90 89 88 87   1 2 3 4 5

LIBRARY OF CONGRESS CATALOGING-IN-PUBLICATION DATA
Herbert, Christopher, 1941–
  Trollope and comic pleasure.

  Bibliography: p.
  Includes index.
  1. Trollope, Anthony, 1815–1882—Criticism and interpretation.   2. Trollope,
Anthony, 1815–1882—Humor, satire, etc.   3. Comic, The, in literature.   I. Title.
PR5688.C56H47   1987   823'.8   86-11367
  ISBN 0-226-32741-8

ECC/USF Learning Resources
8099 College Parkway, S.W.
Fort Myers, Florida 33907-5164

For my mother and my father

Contents

Acknowledgments

It is a pleasure to preface this study of pleasure with thanks to several friends who read portions of the book in earlier stages and gave me valuable suggestions and encouragement: Elizabeth Dipple, Gerald Graff, Stephen Greenblatt. Herbert F. Tucker, Jr., read the whole MS in a busy season and almost at a moment's notice, and made many a shrewd comment, from which the book has greatly benefited, although it still falls well short of the book that he could have written on the same subject. I need especially to express my gratitude to the University of Chicago Press's two readers, one of whose identities is known to me, the other not. James R. Kincaid's thoughtful, detailed suggestions erred only in their tendency to value my work beyond its merits; I was indeed fortunate to get advice from such a distinguished Trollopian, whose work I have long admired. The other, anonymous, reader lavished on my MS a vast amount of attention, keen critical judgment, and generosity. I hope that he or she will have occasion to observe how much the book has been improved by those meticulous comments, and will find the finished product satisfactory, even in occasional places where I failed to follow his or her advice.

Northwestern University provided leave time for work on this project, and awarded me a travel grant enabling me to study the Trollope materials at the Folger Shakespeare Library in Washington, D.C. During the profitable week I spent at the Folger in May 1984, I accumulated a large debt of gratitude to Laetitia Yeandle, Curator of Manuscripts, and to numerous members of the library staff. A debt spread over a longer period of time is the one that I owe to my colleague Barbara Shwom, who spent hours guiding me through the arcane mysteries of WordStar and resolving one near computer meltdown after another in the course of preparation of this MS. Of all my debts, the most important is to my wife, Bernadette Fort, who has read chapters insightfully, shouldered various domestic burdens, and given me confidence that this project would come to something worthwhile in the end. Sophie and Stéphane, finally, get my thanks for kinds of help hard to put into words.

A Note on References

In the absence of a uniform critical edition of Trollope's novels, I refer to them in this study by chapter number only. References to Trollope's handwritten annotations in his copies of the works of early dramatists, which are housed in the Folger Shakespeare Library in Washington, D.C., are identified by the heading *Marginalia* followed by the appropriate Folger call number and volume and page numbers.

Introduction: Fictional Duplicity and Comic Vocation

Here is a writer who seems to represent the apotheosis of normality.
Bradford A. Booth, *Anthony Trollope: Aspects of His Life and Art*

I know nothing in literary history to match the divided opinion on Trollope's novels.
Ibid.

The current revival of interest in Anthony Trollope's fiction (which so often has been dismissed as unworthy of critical attention) suggests at least a half-conscious awareness that what has come to be called "the Trollope problem" is a manifestation not merely of one writer's stylistic peculiarities, but of deep-running issues in the interpretation of nineteenth-century imaginative literature. The "problem" has various facets, but at its core is what the two incongruous statements in my epigraph, taken together, suggest: Trollope's unique ability to baffle critical analysis, to foster conflicting opinions, and by so doing, as we are bound to feel, to throw our methods of scrutiny and our standards of judgment into question. In the mid-nineteenth century, everything about the writing and interpretation of novels was full of anomalies radiating out from the central one, as Trollope himself analyzed it, that the primary literary form of the age had never attained full respectability and was unsure, as a result, of its status, its audience, and its functions (*Autobiography*, 216–17). But Trollope's pedestrian-seeming fiction and the history of its vexed reputation are problematical to an unusual degree, and it is with this factor, it seems to me, that any significant attempt to gauge the importance of his work needs to begin.

One judgment about him has seemed axiomatic and has long dominated critical perception of his work: the one asserting (usually though not always in negative terms) his deep-dyed conventionality. With regard to his attitudes and moral values, it has often been stated, he stands as "the most typical representative of the Victorian [bourgeois] spirit" (Praz, 265), the writer defined above all by his "general conformity to everyday, middle-class ideals" (Skilton, xiii);[1] and his artistic technique, likewise, has been declared by many readers unsurpassably conventional. "With Trollope we were always safe," Henry James maliciously remarked; "there were sure to be no new experiments" (Smalley, 527). For George Levine, likewise, Trollope's great failing as a novelist is that "he accepted the conventions and limitations of his art quite comfortably." "Technically," he concludes, "Trollope is profoundly uninteresting; his work . . . points to no changes in fictional art" (pp. 187, 185).[2] The persistence of this image of Trollope is hardly surprising, for it is the one that he deliberately, indeed ostentatiously, presented to the public—in the famous likening of himself to a diligent shoemaker, for instance. What *is* surprising is to observe, as Donald Smalley's collection of Trollope reviews in the *Critical Heritage* series makes it easy to do, the sharp discrepancy between this view of Trollope and the one held by many of his contemporaries. For them, he seemed a recklessly innovative writer whose career was a series of "hazardous experiments" (Smalley, 466), and he had the reputation of being an inveterate enemy of all the most sacrosanct conventions of popular novels, especially those calling for strongly structured plot, for dramatic tension and climax, and for the idealization of character. One phrase echoes in a series of different formulations through decades of reviews of this "almost perversely prosaic" fiction: "Nobody but Mr. Trollope would have dared" (ibid., 523, 218). The unorthodox conception of *Miss Mackenzie*, says a typical reviewer, was "a bold undertaking . . . but Mr. Trollope revels in risk, and delights in surrounding himself with difficulties and dangers" (ibid., 228).[3] By the same token, so far from being seen as the epitome of the conventional bourgeois mentality, he was once widely criticized for his perverse, offensive breaches of taste, notably his supposed addiction to the vice of "vulgarity"; in fact, as David Skilton has shown, he was regularly denounced by reviewers as morally suspect, as "repellent" and "dangerous" (Skilton, 58–59).[4] What kind of a conventional bourgeois novelist can it be who scandalizes so many of his original readers, and whose work is open to being described in such contradictory terms?

Insight into this question begins with the realization that "the Trollope problem" was a deliberately manufactured one, the guiding principle of Trollope's strategy for the conduct of his career. The motive of this strategy was Trollope's intuition that the modern novelist's most urgent subject was the ambiguity of the novelist's calling itself, particularly with reference to his or her relations to the popular audience; and the main practical expression of this strategy, as the present study seeks to show, was Trollope's lifelong devotion to the mode of comedy—an artistic choice bound to ensure a precarious relation at best with readers of his own day and ours. I need to stress this point, for much of what follows revolves around it. Comedy in mid-Victorian England was an anachronistic literary type deeply foreign to contemporary taste and sensibility, and no writer could have practiced it with impunity. It is true that more than one scholar has represented the nineteenth century in England as "one of the most fertile periods of comic literature . . . the time of Dickens, Thackeray, Lewis Carroll, Meredith, and Wilde" (Henkle, 5). This depends on what one means by "comic literature," and in any case is a potentially misleading claim, for comedy had only the most equivocal status in nineteenth-century England and offers, in fact, a principal exhibit of the period's anxious instability of taste. Even taking the loosest possible definition of comedy as "amusing literature," it is striking, by contrast with the two preceding centuries, how very unfertile the nineteenth is in this respect, especially in the genre of the novel, governed as it powerfully is (in spite of the partial but gigantic exception of Dickens) by Carlylean seriousness, by tragic themes of loss and biblical ones of redemption, and by puritanically severe moral teaching. Typically, much Victorian theory about comedy in this loose sense of the term, as Robert Bernard Martin has shown, "hovered uneasily between the extremes of proclaiming its virtues and worrying that it was inappropriate for serious persons" (p. 7). To emphasize the erosive effect of this worry is not to claim that the comic spirit was extinct in Victorian literature and everyday life: the popularity of burlesque theater, of a magazine like *Punch*, of nonsense writing, and, always, of Dickens, testifies to the contrary. But the marginal and ephemeral quality of many of the most prominent instances of Victorian literary humor, and the half-lunatic mode in which it often appeared, go to reinforce the point that comic sensibility (that is, the sensibility keyed to amusement) had no clear charter, was not normative and central, in Victorian culture, but played at best an erratic, eccentric, destabilizing role, and had difficulty articulating itself in substantial literary form. Few "serious persons" could have doubted that the humorous point of view, if not actually illegitimate, was fundamentally incommensurate with the most significant functions of literature. The assumption that comedy's opposite, tragedy, defines the standard of literary seriousness and worth was taken for granted by Victorian readers, as David Skilton, again, has shown (pp. 40–45); and it is still taken for granted today.[5]

If, moreover, we take a stricter view of comedy—Trollope's view and the one underlying this study—as a distinct literary type based upon the formal patterns of standard stage comedy and possessing a traditional thematic structure, then the Victorian period can only be judged an historic nadir of comic writing. Original stage comedy was to all practical purposes extinct in England in Trollope's lifetime,[6] though in the fifteen years or so following his death it had a limited renascence in figures like Arthur Wing Pinero, Wilde, and G. B. Shaw. Nor did Victorian novelists often try to write genuine comedies. Dickens, deeply attuned as his imagination was to fairytale, melodrama, dream, and myth, wrote none, though sometimes (most notably in *Pickwick Papers* and *Martin Chuzzlewit*) he deployed a spectacular array of comic machinery. *Vanity Fair*, though far more deeply rooted in Bunyanesque allegory and in realistic drama than is usually compatible with the comic mode, might be styled a comedy; to it we can add a handful of titles like *The Egoist*, *Under the Greenwood Tree*, Elizabeth Gaskell's *Wives and Daughters*, possibly one or two others. Leaving Trollope out of consideration, this short list to all intents and purposes exhausts the record of significant Victorian comedies and bears out the verdict of a writer in 1869 that "the age of comedy is past" (Martin, 38).

The near eclipse of traditional comedy in the nineteenth century is easy enough to understand, if only because the frivolous and impudent character of this mode was so obviously antagonistic to the Victorians' powerful cult of earnestness. Worse yet, much—virtually all—traditional English comedy deals in openly indecent materials that even urbane Victorian gentlemen with a taste for comic literature like Thackeray and Trollope, as we shall see, were bound to find morally obnoxious. To legitimize comedy as a genre meant incurring the dangers of the scandalous ribaldry of Fletcher, Wycherley, and Etherege. Thus, Meredith in his 1877 essay on comedy dwells on the need to purify comic writing of what he euphemistically calls "realism" and more pointedly calls "the gutters of grossness" (pp. 9, 31), and his very insistence on this point raises the fear that the taint of indecency and licentious morality may go too deep in comedy's weave ever to be fully cleansed. His solution to the problem is to equate comedy with Molière, but even this maneuver fails to dispel the mood of moral anxiety that pervades his essay. Victorian readers were necessarily alienated from traditional stage comedy, too, by its deeply ingrained quality of stylization and artificiality, which could not fail to offend a middle-class public whose cardinal principle for evaluating literary works was that of direct, faithful representation of reality, a principle expressing a Wordsworthian tradition based on ideals of naturalness, sincerity, and deep feeling—and that left little room for the preposterous artificialities of traditional comedy. For these reasons and others, comedy in anything like its full-fledged form was bound to be taboo or at least severely inhibited in nineteenth-century England.

Trollope's gravitation to this dubious mode seems designed, I have said, to highlight certain contradictions inherent in the nineteenth-century writer's relations to the public and to the literary materials that he or she tries to shape. Modern writers do not so much strive to resolve such contradictions as to aggravate them and to draw their creative impetus from precisely this source; and this is what we shall see Trollope doing. Comedy enabled him to focus in particular on a phenomenon of which he was almost obsessively aware: the appearance of a rapidly deepening split in the field of literature between the popular and the serious, a development that introduced a new dimension of ambiguity in a writer's vocation—especially in the case of novelists, practitioners of a mode of doubtful respectability to begin with. The origins of this fragmentation of literary culture lay fairly plainly in "the democratizing of reading" (Altick, 8), the emergence of a half-educated mass reading public unknown to Richardson, Jane Austen, and Scott, and in strains of anxiety running deep in bourgeois society, causing cultivated readers and writers to feel an increasingly urgent need to distinguish their own taste from that of the uncouth. As almost its defining function, it has been said, "modern art divides the public into two classes, those who understand it and those who do not understand it" (Ortega y Gasset, 12).

Reinforcing the distinction between the popular and the genuinely literary became a central nineteenth-century project. The eventual triumph of this paradigm is exemplified, for example, in Gissing's *New Grub Street* (1891), which systematically maps the reformed institution of literature, portraying the choice to practice one or the other type and to address one or the other audience as elemental in any novelist's career and as informing every aspect of the works that he or she produces. The most highly idealistic novelist in this book, the saintly (if somewhat absurd) Mr. Biffen, has totally abjured the goal of writing for the public; in fact, he boasts of working on a novel so barren of entertainment values as to render it for "the ordinary reader"—a very distinct category in his eyes—"unutterably tedious" (p. 120). This emergent principle, crucial to modernist culture, that the serious writer must be "antipopular" (Ortega y Gasset, 5), seemed to Trollope to generate much of the endemic unwholesomeness of the fiction of his age. His discussion in the *Autobiography* of the error of polarizing realism (the acknowledged mode of serious fiction) and "sensationalism" (the popular mode *par excellence*) bears directly on this point: the best fiction, he asserts, will collapse such false distinctions (*Auto-*

biography, 226–29). He attacks the ideal of the "antipopular" writer, among other ways, by parodying it in his own noisy pretense of indifference to literary values apart from providing popular entertainment, inculcating proper morality, and achieving commercial success: an ethic set forth most brazenly in the *Autobiography* and constantly intimated in the novels themselves. But his attempt to preserve the imperiled ideal of a serious popular literature centers primarily on his determination to anchor his career in comedy.

We shall focus throughout this study on the equivocal, unstable quality that this determination inscribed in Trollope's fiction, given his concurrent devotion to the dogma of realism, the main premise of which is the disallowing of literary artifice in all forms. Walter M. Kendrick has particularly stressed this implication of Trollope's realist creed. Trollope, he says, defines literature at the outset as being inferior to life, and therefore "[calls] into question any literary inheritance, just because it is literary." His novels are in fact "antiliterary," denying all kinship with other literary works (Kendrick, 75, 80, 84). However, Trollope's theory and his practice, as we shall see at length, are in this respect sharply at odds, and it is a discrepancy that powers much of his creative work. So far from disavowing a literary heritage, he in fact deeply immersed himself in his own, as is shown, for example, in his never-completed project of writing a scholarly history of English prose fiction (*Autobiography*, 215–17), and, more to the point, in his extensive research, carried out over a period of twenty years, into sixteenth- and seventeenth-century drama, chiefly comic drama. By the time of his death he had studied and carefully annotated at least 257 early English plays, many of which, as his dated entries testify, he had read repeatedly. These unpublished notes, generally impressionistic and judgmental in character, are of uneven interest as criticism, but they leave no doubt that the profundity of Trollope's knowledge of early drama was such that academic specialists in the field might envy. His personal library included, besides such extensive collections of early plays as Dodsley's (twelve volumes) and Dilke's (six volumes), sets of the collected works of at least thirty-seven playwrights, among them post-Jacobean comic writers such as Farquhar, Wycherley, Etherege, Vanbrugh, and Congreve. Nor was his reading of such writers a mere erudite hobby detached from his work as a novelist, for he drew heavily and directly upon these plays for materials for his own comic fiction.

It comes as a surprise to discover just how pervasive are the archrealist Trollope's borrowings from the artificial and extravagant world of Jacobean (and also, to a lesser degree, Restoration) comedy. Following clues carefully left for them in the *Autobiography*, scholars over the years have brought a handful of such borrowings to light, but without gauging the full extent of this practice in Trollope's work, without remarking on the equivocal quality that it imparts to his fictional world, and without attempting to understand its origins.[7] We will have occasion to discuss in detail a number of Trollope's borrowings, including some especially significant Shakespearean ones, in the following chapters, so I shall not load this introduction with examples: for instance, the evident linkage between *Orley Farm* and Middleton and Rowley's comedy *A Fair Quarrel*,[8] between *The Claverings* and Vanbrugh's comedy *The Provoked Wife*,[9] or between *Phineas Finn* and Fletcher's tragicomedy *The Mad Lover*.[10] In some of Trollope's most significant and most original works, the process of derivation from early comedies is especially pronounced. *The Way We Live Now* would be a striking case in point, seeming as it does to owe much to such plays as (among a number of others) Jonson's *Every Man in His Humour*, Massinger's comedies *The City Madam* and *A New Way to Pay Old Debts*, and Fletcher's comedy *The Beggars' Bush*.[11] Whatever Trollope's exact indebtedness to these plays may be, the whole dramatic structure of *The Way We Live Now*—the profligate baronet cynically courting the naïve daughter of the rich swaggering magnate, the flamboyant speculator Fisker conceiving fantastic swindles, the honorable country gentleman haranguing all and sundry on the moral degeneracy of the present age—all this bears the distinct imprint of Jacobean comedy, an influence so deeply ingrained in Trollope's story that no number of specific correspondences could sum it up. To be aware of it is to see that the realism proclaimed in the novel's title is in fact of a dissembling or oblique kind at best: *The Way They Wrote Then* would be an equally eligible title for this book. The same is true, to mention only one more example, in *Mr. Scarborough's Family*, a novel that Bradford Booth shrewdly associated long ago with comedies by Jonson, Massinger, Middleton, and Beaumont and Fletcher (Booth, 130–31). Booth in fact overlooked the two most direct sources for much of Trollope's story, George Wilkins's comedy *The Miseries of Enforced Marriage* (1607) and another comedy of Fletcher's, *The Spanish Curate*.[12] "The reader . . . is constantly struck with wonder," Trollope remarks in his manuscript notes, "by the ingenuity used [by Jacobean playwrights] in combining two or more of these old stories together."[13] It seems that he took from the early comic dramatists not only a wealth of ideas for particular stories but a whole technique of composition, one based on ingenious adaptation and revivification of a body of stories whose familiarity was somehow the secret of their effectiveness as fiction. A nineteenth-century realist writer could not have endorsed this method in so many words, and in fact Trollope perjures himself by expressly rejecting it in the *Autobiography*, [14] but plainly it formed the basis of much of his practice as a novelist.

To become aware of the extent of such borrowing is to see Trollope's fiction ever more distinctly as formed in two separate strata: the visible upper stratum, the realm of the realist verisimilitude that many of his readers have found to be uncannily realer-seeming than life itself and that historians now confidently draw upon for information about Victorian social structures; and the submerged stratum with its dense network of allusions to old plays and, more generally, its elaborate deployment of the artificial comic code. One is tempted to use a Freudian metaphor to suggest the dynamics of the way archaic story materials from below are transmuted into the manifest content of the stories in forms that allow them to elude the vigilance of the realist censor. The transmutation is never really complete, however, and as a result Trollope has long been belittled for all the elements in his work that proclaim its illicit link to comedy (stereotyped love stories, formulaic happy endings, stress on social conventionalities at the expense of depth psychology) and that have always been taken as so many devices for ingratiating himself with a popular readership. He at times goes out of his way to foster precisely this impression, as though to draw down upon himself the wrath of serious-minded readers who worship strictly in the church of tragic realism. "The end of a novel," he declares, for example, in the last chapter of *Barchester Towers*, "like the end of a children's dinner party, must be made up of sweetmeats and sugar plums." If such a gesture is designed, as it seems to be, to give offense by portraying the novelist as a shameless flatterer of his public, it and others like it have certainly succeeded. [15]

But to look closer is to see that far from "capitulating" to public taste (Booth, 164), Trollope used comic strategies to take seditious liberties with it, promoting all along an ambivalent, potentially antagonistic relationship with his readers—the relationship inherent, as he understood, in the incoherent vocation of novelist in the mid-nineteenth century. As I have suggested, his method of cunning indirection focused on his great device—the boldest invention, and also the foundation, of his career—of posing as a bland mediocrity with no literary vocation at all, a writer, in a word, wholeheartedly "conventional." Using the liberty that this pose afforded him, he used the instruments of comedy to dissect various conventional attitudes (and their correlatives in literary style) that other modes of Victorian fiction everywhere collaborated with. In his fixation upon the comic mode, he thus sets the terms of "the Trollope problem" by plotting his own career as comedy, casting himself in the role of wily comic dissembler, assiduously pretending (in the face of much evidence to the contrary) to be "the apotheosis of normality" just as Wycherley's Horner pretends to be impotent, or Falstaff valiant, or Tartuffe pious, or Don Giovanni sincere. All such comic impostures imply contempt for their audiences (only a fool could be taken in), and Trollope's is no exception. How could readers' responses to him, in view of this pattern, have failed to be full of ambivalence?[16]

In order to track this complex, sometimes erratic and inconsistent, artistic method of Trollope's, we need to have before us—if only to clear a working space amid the morass of existing theories of comedy—a definition of comedy itself as close as possible to his own. This study opens, therefore, with a chapter aiming not to provide an exhaustive or a prescriptive definition of comedy, but rather to highlight factors of traditional comedy that have particular relevance to understanding the shape of Trollope's fiction and its subtly stressful relations to its cultural surroundings. This approach yields a working theory of comedy that emphasizes those features of comic imagination that threaten Victorian decorum, and that is in important respects at odds with the ones that have sometimes been invoked by Trollope's critics. Each of the next five chapters analyzes a major principle of comedy as it is developed in his fiction, focusing for illustrations, usually, on two or three selected novels per chapter; and the last two chapters closely examine comic structure in two novels that embody two poles of comic imagination and develop comedy's logic with special complexity, *The Way We Live Now* and *Ayala's Angel*. The argument focuses throughout on the paradox that I take to be the heart of "the Trollope problem" in its different manifestations: that the most anachronistic-seeming element of his fiction turns out to be basic to its most riskily modern lines of thought and its most inventive artistic experimentation. My goal in exploring this puzzle is by no means to make Trollope seem less problematic at last—if anything, the reverse is true—or to pretend that he ever achieves perfect command over his volatile materials. On the contrary, to read him carefully is to see his texts (as we shall) as honeycombed with fissures, irregularities, signs of disequilibrium. But these are precisely the rifts that he loads with his most valuable ore.[17]

1

Comedy: The World of Pleasure

ALGERNON: How are you, my dear Ernest? What brings you up to town?
JACK: Oh, pleasure, pleasure! What else should bring one anywhere?

The Importance of Being Earnest

To say, in the words of a recent essay, that "no coherent theory of comedy has yet gained wide critical acceptance" (Slights, 13) is to give only a faint idea of the perplexed state of current comic theory. Depending on which authorities one consults, comedy may be identified either with principles of practical worldliness (Heilman) or with vitalist metaphysics (Langer) and religious transcendence (Polhemus, *Comic Faith*); with conservatism, order, the golden mean (Cook), and what Northrop Frye calls "the integration of society" (p. 43), or, alternatively, with revolutionary anarchy (Gurewitch). There is a moralized and sentimentalized model of comedy defining it as an agency of humanistic benevolence, bestowing "the gift of sympathy, understanding, love" along with "faith in ultimate mercy" (West, 136, 141); another school of thought posits "the cruelty inherent in comedy" (Sypher, 209). Comedy in fact subsumes all these antinomies and others besides, but theories of comedy, however productive they may be of particular insights, have failed to show how this could be. Without any thought of aspiring to an absolute or conclusive theory of this mode, we can only judge the inability to reach even the beginnings of a consensus as to the nature of comedy one of the striking failures of modern literary criticism—as well as a sign of the equivocal position of comedy itself in an age attuned to tragic realism.

If, however, there is one point on which modern theories do significantly agree, it is the determination to portray comedy as totally *serious*. So doubtful a proposition has needed to be asserted with unusual frequency and peremptoriness. To be reputable is to be serious, that is, to offer reasoned philosophical commentary upon a reality de-

fined from the outset as no laughing matter:[1] from this axiom flow, for one thing, the compulsive-seeming attacks on laughter that are central to modern comic theory. Genuine humor, declares W. S. Landor in a typical passage approvingly quoted by George Meredith (p. 19), can only come from "grave" minds; "Comedy is essentially a serious activity," insists L. C. Knights, "pre-eminently serious" (pp. 433, 438); many of the greatest comedies, agrees L. J. Potts, "have a rather sobering effect" (p. 19).[2] These persistent, always futile attempts to force the dangerous genie of comic hilarity into a bottle of grave respectability all bear witness to comedy's mischievous gift for arousing anxiety, and they remind us insistently, too, of the ambiguity of the term *serious* itself, on which so much rests. In one of its two senses it is the antonym of "trivial"; in its other, very distinct sense, it is the antonym of "playful" or "lighthearted." In critical discourse on comedy, the first sense has been silently but with momentous results compressed into the second, thus prescribing, in effect, a "grave" and "sobering" attitude—the attitude appropriate to tragedy—as the precondition of literary worth. This significant episode in the history of taste is one outcome of a broad modern presumption that the experience of pain, sorrow, and constraint is permanent and engages the individual self at its deepest levels (is *real*, in a word), while experiences of pleasure and freedom can only be fleeting and superficial, essentially illusory.[3]
"All laughing comes from misapprehension," thinks that allegorical figure of modern consciousness, Father Time, in Hardy's *Jude the Obscure* (272). The campaign against comic levity thus lends credence to Johan Huizinga's thesis that a "fatal shift toward over-seriousness" forms the key phenomenon—and the disabling, impoverishing flaw—of modern European culture since the mid-eighteenth century (p. 198). It also, I believe, marks with precision the point where the disablement of modern discussion of comedy occurs.

In making comedy out to be unimpeachably serious, many of its interpreters have presented it as the vehicle of an ideal of social order and harmony.[4] "The establishment of community, after all, is the basis of comedy" (Kincaid, 53). This premise, so gratifying to moral sensibilities, assigns a major role to the therapeutic function supposedly performed by comic ridicule of socially deviant behavior. It commits one, too, to a scheme of overriding emphasis on the events of the last act in stage comedies: on attainment of clarity, on patterns of reintegration and reconciliation, on the expulsion of scapegoat troublemakers. According to Northrop Frye, comic action symbolically enacts through such patterns the emergence of "a new society" (p. 44). It would be impossible to dispense with the major insights contained in this approach to comedy, which of course is compatible with complex and subtly differentiated readings of particular comic texts. But the view of comedy as aimed at the perfecting of social order fails to account for some of the chief features of this mode. More than anything else, perhaps, it precludes a thorough discussion of comic laughter, and makes it impossible to see why comic writers, given the quasi-didactic function ascribed to them, employ an idiom full of preposterous artificiality and typically seem bent not at all on creating a mood of sobering gravity but, rather, on advertising the frivolousness of their materials with every means at their disposal. If comedy is "serious" in the ways that have been claimed for it, where does it get its predilection for so unsuitable a style? That comedy ridicules deviancy in order to sanitize society is a dubious conjecture at best. The idea of comedy as the guarantor of social order and the repressor of excess makes it incomprehensible that this same mode has consistently been denounced by moralists, and not just puritan fanatics, as an agency of damnable depravity, lewdness, disorder, and obscenity.[5] It cannot explain why spectators and readers of comedy should so frequently be drawn into a feeling of collusion with rascals and even with monstrous grotesques. Nor does it provide us with a coherent vocabulary with which to analyze the society whose order is supposedly being glorified: is order itself the all-sufficient merit of comic society? A different original premise may help to address these and other deeply ingrained problems in comic theory.

In the last line of *Twelfth Night*, Feste defines comic rhetoric in the form of a pledge or compact between performers and audience: "We'll strive to please you every day," he says. This passage and others in Shakespeare[6] confess what I take to be the sovereign principle of comedy: that it strives above all to *please*. I say "confess," for it has never been an innocuous matter to acknowledge comedy's nearly all-absorbing concentration on the production of pleasure. Such a premise is bound to seem an affront to critics with vested interests in one or another conception of "seriousness," whether this conception be embodied in sophisticated technologies of interpretation or, more traditionally, in codes of moral propriety. For example, when Dryden declared that "the chief end of [comedy] is divertisement and delight" (p. 357), he knew that he was uttering a heresy, affronting the traditional view of comedy as moral corrector and making it seem dangerously frivolous. His view was sharply rebutted by polemicists like Jeremy Collier and Thomas Shadwell. "I must take leave to dissent from those who seem to insinuate that the ultimate end of a poet is to delight without correction or instruction," said Shadwell. "Methinks a poet should never acknowledge this, for it makes him of as little use to mankind as a fiddler or a dancing master" (quoted in Morreall, 17). In a word, it calls his seriousness into question, an imputation never to be tolerated.

However, to claim that comedy is fixated upon pleasure need not imply that it is limited to the functions of "mere" entertainment or is devoid of philosophical structure; nor need it imply that terms like "amusement" or "pleasure" stand for simple, self-evident, or histori- cally uniform things. Nor does such a principle enable us to construct a paradigm or set of ordinances to which individual comic works are bound to conform in all respects. The pure or ideal comic script is a hypothetical abstraction that may be inferred in a tentative way from a collection of actual texts but is fully manifested in none of them; even those comedies that adhere most faithfully to classic patterns con- stantly invest these patterns with novelty. Yet the principle that I have set forth does imply that in order to trace the special dialectics of comic literature, we need to begin by recognizing the chief conven- tions of comedy for what they primarily are, an array of potent figures of pleasure: the abundance of fooling and laughter; the obligatory happy ending; the chastisement of the culpable; the overturning of feared authority; and especially the continual glorification of wish- fulfillment figures gifted (like Falstaff or Don Giovanni) with preter- natural capacities for carnal and worldly enjoyment. "The joys of many I in one enjoy," cries the hero of George Chapman's comedy *The Blind Beggar of Alexandria* (1598), who, thanks to a series of brilliant disguises, is able to seduce four prospective wives simultaneously (3.155). Belinda the temptress in James Shirley's *The Grateful Servant* (1629) strikes just the same note as she attempts to seduce Lodowick by claiming to have the power of magical metamorphoses. "If this presence / Delight you not," she says, "I'll wear a thousand shapes / To please my lord" (4.5). This fantasy of multiplied, of virtually bound- less, pleasure, in which imagery of protean limberness is fused with the idea of voluptuous gratification, is the heartbeat and the *idée fixe* of the comic. The above examples point directly, also, to the scandalous implications of such a mode as this, a theme to which we shall often return.

THE PLEASURE PRINCIPLE

Are not all literary modes, not just comedy, almost by definition gov- erned by the necessity of giving pleasure? It is safe to say that a liter- ary type that fails to do so will quickly become extinct. But in other modes (tragedy, lyric, romance, realistic fiction, history) pleasure is formally subordinated to functions that claim precedence: moral edi- fication, the arousing of lofty emotion, or the depiction of unadulterated truth, for example. It is by no means clear how it is possible to reconcile such objectives as these with the almost disreputable one of giving pleasure. The deeply problematical status of pleasure in the theory of tragedy, in particular, is a conundrum that many writers over the centuries have tried to unravel.[7] By the same token, if the premise of the realist novel as practiced by Trollope and his contemporaries is that it present a strictly truthful depiction of reality, it seems inescapably contradictory to admit that such depictions must at the same time conform to the statutes of aesthetic pleasure: Thackeray in *Vanity Fair* mercilessly belabors this crucial anomaly in the doctrine of realism.

In comedy, the pleasure principle is given a kind of emancipation, for in this mode alone the endorsement of pleasure is direct, explicit, and primary, unentangled (at least potentially) from contradictory motives. The clearest index of this principle lies in comedy's insistent imagery of entire worlds or ways of life keyed to pleasure: the worlds of festivity presided over by Falstaff or Sir Andrew Aguecheek and Sir Toby Belch; the Forest of Arden, where the exiles "fleet the time carelessly, as they did in the golden world" in *As You Like It* (1.1.107–9); the "court of flourishing pleasure, where delight, in all her shapes, and studied varieties, every minute courts the soul" that Lodowick promises to establish in *The Grateful Servant* (2.1); the world of libertinism in Restoration comedy; the aristocratic world of Bath in *The Rivals*; the world of rural "Bunburying" in *The Importance of Being Earnest*. Taken together, these coeval worlds define the specific imaginative locale of the comic: comedy is where pleasure reigns. Hence the predominance of the theme of erotic relations in comedy—this of all fields of human action being the one most urgently motivated by the attainment of pleasure. (Of course, the comic perspective is also an excellent one from which to observe the many pitfalls that the quest for erotic and other pleasures entails.) Comedies focus on and glorify youth for the same reason: because in the eyes of the grownup audience for which comedy is intended, the young embody, above all their other characteristics, a triumphant capacity for pleasure. Even the much-overemphasized strain of mockery in comedy is more immediately a function of the sheer stimulation and pleasure, generally repressed by social politeness, of mockery than of the alleged intent of improving society, something that no comedy has ever demonstrably done. In short, the paramount feature of comic style, the one from which all the others radiate and to which whatever "seriousness" that comedy generates is subject, is its orientation toward pleasure. Such at least is the proposition to be tested at length in this book, not by logical extrapolations but by showing its use as an instrument of practical criticism.

To recognize comedy as first and foremost a crystallization of the will to pleasure is to glimpse the relationship between modern comedies and the ancient ritual antecedents, from the *komos* of Dionysian fertility rites to pre-Elizabethan May Day revels, from which they are conjectured to have sprung.[8] The literary institution of comedy comes into focus, that is, as the residue left by these festivals once their original religious or magical motive has decayed and all the festive ritual apparatus of erotic invocation, wine drinking, feasting, and sacrifice has become a vehicle purely for pleasure itself; it is at this stage that the comic spirit properly so called comes into being. Frazer's *Golden Bough* offers scores of instances of this process by which sacred ceremonies dwindle "into mere shows and pageants" (p. 162) for which new rationales must be elaborated by later generations. Having evidently emerged from a degenerative cultural cycle of this kind, comedy takes as its task not to invoke fertility any longer—though in some comedies strong traces of this function may linger—but to show the now-enfranchised libido ramifying expansively into a constellation of carnal and worldly pleasures and at least implicitly (but often in so many words) to impel us to reflect on the complex interrelations of various types of pleasure, some of which couple together synergistically, others of which prove deeply incompatible. Thus, although erotic pleasure and its vicissitudes are central to comedy, scarcely less important are all the other kinds of pleasure that rarely are absent for long in comedies: drinking, eating, singing, dancing, joking, sociability, and especially the form of libido most intimately related to the motive of dramatic spectacle itself, playful make-believe, "the dear pleasure of dissembling," "the pleasure of a masquerade," as it is called in Etherege's *The Man of Mode* (3.1.128–29) and Congreve's *Love for Love* (4.1.851), respectively. Needless to say, it is the prevalence of such themes that accounts for the aura of moral danger that has always surrounded comedy, which can so easily seem not to dissipate disorderly urges harmlessly within the *cordon sanitaire* of the theater, but rather to exacerbate them and cause them to spill over dangerously into civic life.

The whole formal structure of comedy presupposes glorification of the manifold varieties of pleasure that it focuses upon, but this originating will takes on an equivocal and unstable character as the price of its historical unfolding. Thus the impulse to proclaim the supremacy of the libido is inseparably joined in true comedy to the literary will to *thematize* pleasure, which is to say, to embody judgments of various kinds upon it. In a society whose moral culture is permeated with puritan asceticism, as that of England has been from an early date, these judgments cannot fail often to be negative. The tension between these two motives of glorifying and of evaluating pleasure can well be seen, therefore, as the mainspring of comic imagination, which tirelessly explores pleasure as a locus of moral uncertainty. Is pleasure legitimate? What are its allowable forms and limits? How can the radical egoism of the pleasure principle be reconciled with an ethic of duty and unselfishness? Does pleasure degrade or enhance character? Here is the complex of issues that articulates itself wherever we turn in comedy, and here is the reason that the word "pleasure" itself, charged with tension, reverberates throughout comic literature.

Comedies, therefore, almost always incorporate in some explicit form the motif of a disputation (in the words of a Jonson masque) "'Twixt Virtue and her noted opposite / Pleasure" (*Pleasure Reconciled to Virtue*, ll. 169–70). There is no formal law that they must, but the pattern is so strongly implied by the essential function of this mode— the function, that is, of a cultural institution for the venting of libidinal energy—that comic writers return to it incessantly. One of the central comic figures, consequently, is that of the ascetic and killjoy, the determined enemy of pleasure: King Ferdinand of Navarre in *Love's Labour's Lost*, Malvolio, Molière's misanthropic Alceste, Wycherley's Pinchwife, or Gilbert and Sullivan's Mikado, who

> decreed, in words succinct,
> That all who flirted, leered or winked
> (Unless connubially linked)
> Should forthwith be beheaded.
> (Act 1)

These repressive figures have so central a role to play in the generation of plot in comedy as to be almost indispensable, though in the most festive romantic comedies, like Trollope's *Rachel Ray*, where it is the effortless ease of pleasurable experience that is stressed, their influence is slight. In all types of comedy, the most natural pattern is for suppressors and defamers of pleasure to be found perverse or hypocritical, and to be suitably chastised. But often a far more complex and ambivalent argument develops, testifying to the necessary precariousness of a mode of literature that sponsors pleasure within a culture professing values of duty, sobriety, and self-restraint—a culture where the prevailing psychic structure, as Freud teaches us to recognize, is repression. Consider for example the long declamation in Sir Richard Steele's comedy *The Conscious Lovers* (1722), a work expressly written to reform the dissolute comic stage, where the hero argues at some length that true pleasure (as opposed to the baser kind) lies not in "sensations" but, rather, in the consciousness of virtue. Leaving nothing to the imagination, this paragon lists the kinds of false pleasures he has in mind, suggesting by the very particularity of his catalog the psychic tension involved in his ideology of strict repression: horses, dogs, cards, dice, "bottle companions," and "loose women" are all singled out for condemnation (and repressed longing). "If pleasure be worth purchasing," he intones to his enraptured fiancée, "how great a pleasure is it to him, who has a true taste of life, to ease an aching heart . . . ?" (2.3.155–57). The strained argumentation of this scene, centering as it does on a farfetched redefinition of "pleasure," suggests the difficulty of preserving comedy once Huizinga's "fatal shift toward over-seriousness" has begun to occur; yet it only reflects in extreme form the compromise typically effected in comedy between the antagonistic principles that propel comedy's argument, the pleasure-drive and its noted opposite, virtue.

Where compromise cannot be reached, comedies may work sharply at cross purposes with themselves by creating comic pleasure-worlds only to betray their own creations by sponsoring outright denunciations of pleasure itself. This self-contradicting pattern is probably the dominant one in English comedies of the early seventeenth century, where puritanism (operating as it did again in the world of Victorian England) heavily contaminated even this mode so foreign by its nature to the puritan temperament. It imprints itself distinctly, for example, upon *Eastward Ho* (1604), by Marston, Chapman, and Jonson, where all of the play's dramatic vitality lies in the machinations of a band of roguish pleasure-seekers, and where nevertheless the pleasure ethic is constantly assailed. At one point in this comedy, for example, the high-minded goldsmith Touchstone, the play's spokesman for ascetic virtue, states the puritan moral calculus as succinctly as it can be stated. "Of sloth cometh pleasure," he declares; "of pleasure cometh riot, of riot comes whoring, of whoring comes spending, of spending comes want, of want comes theft, of theft comes hanging" (4.3.286–89). Such a discourse would suit a somber killjoy like Malvolio—but here the speaker is a touchstone, not a comic grotesque. Or in Shirley's comedy *The Lady of Pleasure* (1637), to cite only one more example of comic self-division, the protagonist, Sir Thomas Bornwell, intending to cure his wife of her ruinously extravagant taste for pleasure, pretends to plunge into dissipation himself, and in the process gives a hyperbolic vision of the destructiveness of pleasure that sums up the puritan streak running through the comedy of the period. "If I live," he declares to her,

> I will feast all my senses, and not fall
> Less than a Phaeton from my throne of pleasure,
> Though my estate flame like the world about me.
> (5.1)

That there is room in comedy for this jaundiced vision of worldly and carnal pleasure as a consuming fireball testifies to the spaciousness and ideological complexity of comedy: comedy is no monolith, but a dynamic system charged with contradictory tendencies. But if my analysis is at all valid, we can anticipate that the greatest or at least the most coherent comedies will be those in which the pleasure principle is in some way made triumphant at last. The agents of this more unified comic pattern are the champions of pleasure, prodigals, profligates, reprobates, voluptuaries, and ne'er-do-wells who with varying degrees of self-awareness espouse the pursuit of pleasure even if need be in the teeth of moral prohibitions: Falstaff, Mercutio (a comic refugee in a tragedy), Wycherley's Horner, Tom Jones, and a host of others. The annals of comedy are punctuated by their fervent declarations of allegiance to the creed of pleasure, which is the creed of comedy itself. "I hold it as commendable to be wealthy in pleasure," says the libertine Mirabell in John Fletcher's excellent comedy *The Wild-Goose Chase* (1621?), "As others do in rotten sheep and pasture" (2.1). Archer, one of the two debonair rogues in a play important to Trollope, Farquhar's *The Beaux' Stratagem* (1707), is a keen theorist as well as a devotee of pleasure, which when richly and expertly cultivated ought, he explains, to stimulate and energize character rather than debase it. He argues that the great danger is in becoming so fixated upon one form of pleasure—eating, fine dress, sex—that other pleasures atrophy. "Give me a man," says Archer, "that keeps his five senses keen and bright as his sword, that has 'em always drawn out in their just order and strength, with his reason as commander at the head of 'em, that detaches 'em by turns upon whatever party of pleasure agreeably offers" (1.1.213–17). This belief in the humanizing power of pleasure, a belief forever reiterated in comedies, lies at the heart of comic thinking. So does the chief corollary of this belief, the identification of pleasure with a personal ideal of flexibility and keen responsiveness.

Characters like Archer and Mirabell testify to comedy's insistent glorification of rebellious egoism and of personal gratification; yet the comic argument has little room for Romantic ideas of autonomous or introspective selfhood (and even less, though theorists persist in making such claims, for mystical or religious transcendence). This is because comedy defines all experience as social experience; individu-

ality itself, even in the recklessly iconoclastic forms that it typically
takes in comedy, is profoundly a communal phenomenon that is made
legible by virtue of its relations to social norms and its effect on the
community. Comic writers explore the logic of pleasure, therefore, as
a means of exploring that of a whole system of civilization—not from
a neutral, detached perspective, but from one with a distinct ideological bias. The nature of this bias (at least in its most optimistic phases)
is strongly to qualify the Freudian view of a war waged inevitably between civilized order and the libido. Comedy begins from the proposition that the sole *raison d'être* of society—of sophisticated society, at
least—is to foster pleasure, and that affirming pleasure therefore is
tantamount to affirming social order. We cannot inquire here into the
legitimacy of such a proposition, but it is hard to doubt that the perennial appeal of the comic model of society is based on a sense that it
holds at least potential relevance to real social life. One of the most
eloquent passages in Malinowski's classic of anthropology *Argonauts
of the Western Pacific* touches on just this point, identifying "cherished
diversions, ways of enjoying life, and social pleasures" as the fundamental organizing forces of human society and even the sine qua non
of individual existence. "Without diversion and amusement a culture
and a race cannot survive," declares Malinowski (pp. 465, 466). Comedy gives hyperbolic expression to such a thesis; yet comic writers are
also acutely sensitive to the fragility of social order, given the rampant, potentially disruptive forces of libido that operate within it.
Here again is the axial problem of comedy, which, far from enacting
over and over a reassuring fable of the resolution of differences and
the expulsion of troublemakers, perpetually leaves us with the sense
of unresolved, indeed of unresolvable, danger. A society that generates a flourishing growth of pleasure is bound to be hazardous, comedy usually tells us.

Danger is everywhere, for example, in Etherege's great comedy *The
Man of Mode* (1676), where the focus falls unceasingly upon the self-
contradictions of the pursuit of pleasure, upon the way the ethic of
rampant self-indulgence in licentious Restoration society has led to a
grotesque denaturing of pleasure itself, and upon how "the freedoms
of the present" (1.1.137) have turned in fact into a system of bond-
age—a system that Etherege names "affectation." The principal image
of danger in *The Man of Mode* is that of the predatory rake Dorimant,
whose libidinal appetites have all been channeled into sadism and
narcissism, and whose only real pleasure now appears to lie in parading his cruel "ill nature" (2.2.240) for all to see. Hence the significance
of the play's title character, the absurd Frenchified dandy Sir Fopling
Flutter, whose leading trait is his singular, indeed outlandish, capac-

ity for pleasure, which causes all his efforts to mimic fashionable malevolence to fail utterly. Going about London dressed, like the very
effigy of comedy, in masquerade costume, Sir Fopling makes us perceive all the more clearly how little gaiety survives in the libertine
world ruled by Dorimant, where a cultural pathology attacks pleasure
at the root like a disease and renders all social life perverse as a result.

The unbridled pursuit of pleasure may often seem in comedy, as it
does in *The Man of Mode*, inimical to the preservation of social order,
but a central insight of comic imagination is that pleasure, even in its
most outrageous forms, is intrinsically tied to order itself, that pleasure and disorder are opposites. One implication of this principle is
the one set forth by Farquhar's Archer in the speech quoted above:
that the keenest pleasures are the prerogative of the man careful to
keep his senses in a harmonious, balanced state, "always drawn out
in their just order and strength." This is not so much a physiological
principle as a reflection of the social basis of all experience in comedy.
Comic hedonists forever attempt to liberate themselves altogether
from the constraints of society by going on binges of lawless pleasure,
but even the most extravagant pleasures turn out in comedy to have
an inescapably orderly, formalized quality, as though the libido could
only express itself after all in the form of ritualized social patterns. No
doubt it is the (supposed) origin of comedy in religious or magic festival that imprints upon comic writing its intense perception of the
ceremonial quality of all social life; in any event, comedy everywhere
gives graphic, entertaining form to Mary Douglas's argument that ritual not only shapes and interprets human experience, but actually
creates it (pp. 63–64). If we may speak of such a thing as comic consciousness, this principle is one of its most important components.
Thus, just as *Love's Labour's Lost* and *As You Like It* lay heavy comic
emphasis on the perception that erotic excitement is largely a function, one could almost say a by-product, of such stylized courtship
rituals as composing sonnets, so Etherege in *The Man of Mode* underlines the fact that Sir Fopling's pleasures are all elaborately conventionalized ones—aping the latest French fashions, singing rhymed
and metrical songs, executing complex dance steps—and that even
the sexual escapades of Dorimant and the other libertines are not so
much instinctual, spontaneous acts as they are rehearsals, again, of
highly formalized social rituals. Libertinism is an *institution*, a discipline, a fashion like the wearing of French ribbons, and in all his pleasures Dorimant the would-be desperado reveals how deeply he is embedded in and loyal to the patterns of his social world. The deepest
dialectic of comedy would seem to lie in this perpetual liberation from
and reaffirmation of social formalities. The institution of comedy is of

course wholly caught up in its own dialectic, generating novelty and pleasure as it does through the medium of a highly formalized set of artificial conventions—conventions that ambiguously evoke order and disorder both.

SCANDAL AND TOLERANCE

If only to allow for comedy's powerful tendency toward giving moral offense, but just as importantly, to register the complex effects that I have touched on, it is apparent that we need to qualify in important ways the traditional idea of this mode as chastiser of vice and folly and as strict enforcer of social order. Many have testified to the scandalous aspects of comedy: Thackeray in his condemnation of the dissolute Congreve, "whose ghastly doctrine seems to be that we should eat, drink, and be merry when we can" (*English Humourists*, 209), and Trollope himself in his disgusted remarks on the "filthiness" of Fletcher and of Jacobean comedy in general (see below, chap. 3), are echoing a long tradition marked by declarations like William Prynne's in 1633 that comic plays gravely threaten morality by arousing laughter at "obscene, lascivious, sinful" things (quoted in Morreall, 87). (Prynne's presumption, we may note for future reference, is that laughter implies delighted solidarity with its object rather than scorn and rejection, as classic comic theory asserts.) The supreme anticomic text, if it is not Rousseau's "Letter to d'Alembert" (1758), is probably Jeremy Collier's *Short View of the Immorality and Profaneness of the English Stage* (1698), where comedies are excoriated for, among other things, "their smuttiness of expression; their swearing, profaneness, and lewd application of Scripture; their abuse of the clergy, their making their top characters libertines and giving them success in their debauchery." In comedy, Collier declares, in a noteworthy phrase, "vice is varnished over with pleasure" and thus rendered morally dangerous (pp. 2, 140). We shall miss something vital in comedy if we dismiss reactions like these as unbalanced, for they accurately identify comedy's tendency to tolerate a dangerously high level of moral irregularity in its pleasure-seekers. Tolerance in a wide sense, in fact, is one of the hallmarks of comedy (though there are intolerant comedians, like Aristophanes), and I suspect that it is for this reason more than any other that Trollope, whose steadiest moral instinct was for generous tolerance, found in comedy, its historical "smuttiness" notwithstanding, his most natural medium of expression.

In a striking 1822 essay that prefigures Huizinga from afar, Charles Lamb sheds light on the crucial bond between comic tolerance and comedy's scandalous-seeming devotion to pleasure, identifying the "detestable coxcombry of moral judgment" as the bane of a proper response to comedy (p. 300). As Lamb saw, the all-important condition of comedy is that readers or spectators be willing at least briefly to suspend their habitual principles of moral judgment, and to lend themselves to what Bergson calls a "relaxation of the rules of reasoning" (p. 181). This hiatus defines precisely the field of comic pleasure, which in large part is nothing but the euphoria of momentarily being allowed to shed our oppressive judgmental responsibility—in other words, of being able actually to shed our habitual selves for the duration of the play. Comedy's radical impulse is thus to show how burdensome our habitual selves really are (which ultimately is why it dwells so insistently on themes of disguise and impersonation, mirroring in its typical imagery of "the pleasure of a masquerade" the liberating experience that comedy affords its spectators). When Dorothy Van Ghent describes Jane Austen's obsequious buffoon Mr. Collins as "a moral monstrosity" (p. 106), she thus nullifies the comic effect in just the way that "over-seriousness" invariably does, instructing us that disciplined readers must never countenance any "relaxation" of judgment. In fact, Collins surges into the world of *Pride and Prejudice* as an image of such gloriously extravagant affectation and impertinence that a reader attuned to comic values is obliged to greet him as a priceless ornament to the story—as the delighted Mr. Bennet does himself. "There is a mixture of servility and pomposity in his letter, which promises well," avers this connoisseur of comic foolishness. "I am impatient to see him" (p. 48). Collins wears his flaws so preposterously open to view as to dissipate moralistic indignation out of hand, clearing the way for what matters most in comedy, pleasure, and also for its surprising correlatives: not exactly "sympathy, understanding, [and] love," but amused detachment, as much magnanimity as circumstances allow, and what might be called moral nimbleness.

Approaching this same point from another slant, and pointing to the next step in our argument, we can speak of comedy's preoccupation with the factor of *charm*. Charm is the peculiarly social dimension of personality; it is personality considered as a function of its capacity for giving pleasure. Bergson truly says that "unsociability" rather than actual vice is the great comic flaw (p. 150); by the same token, if there is one predominant comic ideal it is that of personal charm. Hence comedy's long-standing service on behalf of the cult of wit, which could be defined as intellect focused upon the function of rendering personality delightful. To stress the centrality of charm in the value system of comedy is necessary to make clear the incompleteness of those theories, such as Bergson's own, that declare comedy to be confined to the portrayal of "flat" generalized character types. Charm is the essence of comedy's concern for variegated indi-

viduality (no generalized type can possibly project charm) and it is
what imaginative sympathy in comic poets most readily distils itself
into, in figures like Shakespeare's Rosalind, Etherege's Sir Fopling,
Jane Austen's Emma Woodhouse, or a gallery of Trollope characters
from Mr. Harding to Madame Max Goesler, all of them incarnations of
the deceptively trivial-seeming gift of charm. Such characters are the
distinctive emanations of a world organized around the law of imaginative pleasure; not to focus on their role, and not to inquire into the
exact constitution of charm, is to leave a hole at what ought to be the
exact center of comic theory.

ARTIFICE AND COMIC LIMBERNESS

The ground of all comic conventions and thus the origin of comic
pleasure (as well as the origin of modern antipathy to comedy) is comedy's all-pervading artificiality. Critics attempting to shore up the
questionable seriousness of comedy have sometimes blurred the con-
tours of the genre by identifying it with realism, but comedy's inveterate artifice in fact turns it decisively away from the realistic.[9] As W. P.
Ker says, in one of the finest modern essays on the subject, comedy is
laid in an "imaginary world with laws of its own" (p. 197), though this
world may—indeed must—delusively resemble the ordinary one.
The laws of comedy show themselves with particular brazenness in
the design of comic plots. Rather than seeking to create the illusion of
natural-seeming sequences of events, comedy's repertoire is that of
stylized geometrical patterns and glaringly implausible predicaments
whose very artificiality constitutes, for a spectator attuned to comic
values, the essence of the pleasure they create—though it may not immediately be clear why the invocation of "a symmetry and correspondence seemingly too neat and perfect for true history" (Ker, 205)
should be inherently delightful. Erotic pursuit being the prevailing
subject of comedy, the archetypal comic plot is that of a vexed courtship
ending in joyful union; but in comedy this basic story (which it shares
with various forms of romance) is elaborated into a visibly contrived
choreography, the more contrived the better, of impersonations and
interchanging pairs of lovers, as happens with such a flourish of artifice in *Love's Labour's Lost*, *A Midsummer-Night's Dream*, *Twelfth Night*,
Così fan tutte, or Henry James's *What Maisie Knew*. The paradigm of
symmetrical pairings and substitutions is so fundamental to comedy
that it seems bound to have originated in the structure of some ritual
antedating comedy itself; it is closely related, too, to comedy's stress
on the artificiality of social life in general. In any case, it is the stylistic
signature of the comic imagination.

As Bergson declares, then, sharply severing the comic and the realistic, comedy is "a game" (p. 105); and we may say that the basis of the comic game is its constitutional liberty to *make a joke of its own appearance of representing real life*. Albert Cook remarks that comedies are designed to tell us "Ah, but this is only a play" (p. 45). This seminal joke, from which comedy's mood of exhilarating playfulness largely flows, takes many forms: in Beaumont's *Knight of the Burning Pestle* it is implicit in the whole conceit of the play within the play; in *The Way of the World* it breaks out in a character's exclamation, seeing everyone assembled onstage in act 5, that the cast is "all got together, like players at the end of the last act" (5.1.573–74); and more broadly it is the essence of the highly formalized patterns of all comedy. These patterns give *pleasure* by evoking a world of guaranteed symmetry and order where ordinary possibilities have been peremptorily set aside and where disruptive or dangerous circumstances will be allowed to exist only so long as they remain enjoyable and provide the entertainment we came for. Their whole *raison d'être* is to be swept away at last. (Thus one of the central figures of comic plot is that of the ever-compounded difficulties that in the last act suddenly unravel and vanish, or of the tremendous emergency that just as it becomes excruciatingly imminent evaporates as if by magic.) At the same time, this effect, implicit in the whole formalized design of comedy, acquires much of its force by the way it inevitably becomes contaminated in significant comedies (which tend for this reason always to be "problem" plays full of anomalous, incongruous materials) by surging impressions of serious real life. This double effect in comedy merely follows that of all play, which, as Huizinga says (p. 8), has an inherent tendency to run away with the players: the boundary between play and seriousness is always a fluid, ambiguous one. Trollope's many playful interjections on the artificiality of his highly realistic fiction are thus by no means so eccentric as they first appear, but give expression to a twofold effect lying near the heart of the comic imagination.

The philosophic prank of comedy seems at first glance to be at the expense of the characters who earnestly career about the stage in their tortuously involved patterns, unaware that they are merely pinballs in a machine designed for the amusement of a voyeuristic audience whose presence they are weirdly and even disturbingly oblivious to. One might guess that the impression of a basic element of cruelty in the comic stems only incidentally from episodes like the harsh punishment meted out to buffoons like Malvolio or Congreve's Lady Wishfort; it surely originates at a deeper level, in the sense that comedy by its nature exploits and victimizes all its subjects, treating even their most deeply heartfelt experience as part of a mere game. A full theory of the comic would need to dwell on this effect. Here, however,

I need to stress not the severe liabilities of comic characters' existence, but rather the abundant compensations that they receive.

For one thing, by setting aside the constricted, disordered, perilous world of natural probabilities, comedy is peculiarly able to value and reward such qualities as vitality, audacity, and the love of pleasure—things that in a world of more stringent causality become loaded with danger. In tragedy the overreacher and unbridled egoist are led to bitter knowledge of their limitations, but comedy makes daring overreachers like Horner often flourish with impunity: they seem to lead charmed lives, even though they may sometimes be abruptly chastised in the last act by playwrights anxious to restore to their works a semblance of moral propriety. The patterned, ritualized artifice of the comic world (which, I have suggested, we are made to recognize as analogous to that of civilized life itself) forms a kind of sanctuary within which personality is wonderfully free to deploy and to advertise itself with a minimum of rigid defensive posturing. The argument about freedom is central. Play, says Huizinga, "is free, is in fact freedom" (p. 8). The same point is central to Freud's analysis of joking, which "begins as play," he says, "in order to derive pleasure from the free use of words and thoughts" (*Jokes*, 137). Comedies, taking their impetus from just this equation of play, freedom, and pleasure, are perpetually marked by the euphoria of discovering how supple, resilient, agile, effortlessly fluent and adaptable human character can be, unlike tragedies, which center on fatal rigidity.

"I could skip / Out of my skin now, like a subtle snake, / I am so limber," crows Jonson's roguish parasite Mosca, voicing the exhilarating sense of freedom from natural contingencies that comic artifice bestows (*Volpone*, 3.1.5–7). The same freedom is exemplified in the amazing verbal fluency and the ingenious disguises of Malevole, the protagonist of Marston's *Malcontent*, who "with most tumbler-like nimbleness" (1.3.79) confounds his enemies—though the modal ambiguity of this tragicomedy is signaled in Malevole's own affirmation of "phlegm and heavy steadiness" as a moral norm superior to that of the "nimble bloods, / Light-jointed" (2.5.61–62) who practice vice and treachery. The fundamentally protean, improvisational quality of the comic manifests itself more unconditionally in Mirabell's and Millamant's hyperwitty duets, in Mr. Pecksniff's infinitely inventive and resourceful hypocrisy, in Don Giovanni's endlessly renewed gift of seduction, in the chameleonlike disguises of the rogue hero in *The Blind Beggar of Alexandria*, or, in ultimate form, in Shakespeare's Puck and Ariel, where comic limberness goes so far as to skip out of its skin altogether into virtual disembodiment. These examples illustrate a main principle in comic poetics: that in comedy, "limberness" and "charm" are more or less synonymous terms, each having to do with a genius for improvisational self-production. The comic paradigm stands out clearly, for example, in Rosalind's ravishing performance in *As You Like It*, where at one point we witness the fantastically convoluted spectacle of a boy (actor) playing the role of a woman (Rosalind) impersonating a man (Ganymede) pretending to be a woman (Rosalind)—limberness that makes the head spin and that primarily expresses, along with some potentially disturbing intimations about sex, the kind of comic euphoria that I have described. Charm is such a potent force for the comic imagination that the straitjacket of selfhood seems to dissolve in its presence—or, rather, we can think of charm as a kind of radioactive energy released by just this process of dissolution (which often, as we have noted, is a dissolute process indeed).

The mercurial limberness that comedy evokes images and reinforces that euphoric sensation on the spectator's part of shedding his or her own everyday self for the duration of the comedy; at the same time, the image of the comic hero or heroine as a "subtle snake" works to undercut the sense of natural personality and thus to dissolve strong empathetic feeling, insinuating deep into the weave of comedy its well-remarked tendency toward a cool, judicious, detached view of human affairs. Comedy is the natural medium of a writer strongly susceptible to charm but skeptical as to the wholesomeness of extravagant states of feeling—such a writer as Trollope, to whom comedy's tendency to chasten habits of emotionalism seemed (as it did to Thackeray also) one of its vital attributes in an age of such disturbed and hyperventilated emotional life as the nineteenth century.

The Indecency of Laughter

As noted already, the attempt of modern commentators to free comedy from the stigma of unseriousness has led them frequently to try to break down, either by overt argument or only implicitly, the commonsense equation of comedy and laughter. Given the perpetual conflict in Western life between unruly instinctual impulse and cultural repression, laughter, as an explosive eruption of pleasure (one closely analogous in some ways with sexual climax), has been suspect from classical antiquity onward, and often denounced as lewd and harmful.[10] As one might expect, the aversion to laughter took particularly extreme forms in Victorian times, as suggested by the two editions in the 1870s of George Vasey's *Philosophy of Laughter and Smiling*, which argues at length that laughter is not only morally objectionable, but medically dangerous as well. Vasey's grisly account of how health is undermined by promiscuous laughter is unmistakably analogous to the accounts of the dire bodily effects of sexual activity found in such a work as Dr. William Acton's notorious *Functions and Disorders of the Reproductive Organs* (1857).[11] At more than one point, indeed, Vasey directly compares laughter to the vice with which Victorians were supremely obsessed, masturbation (pp. 150, 169–71). The association of laughter and lubricity is by no means fortuitous, and sheds light on the persistent condemnations of comedy itself, where the pleasures of laughter and of sex are closely identified, not just metaphorically but in the most direct ways.[12] One thinks, for example, of the hilarious "china" scene in *The Country Wife* (4.3), where Horner and Lady Fidget copulate just offstage, virtually under the nose of her husband, then, returning to view, entertain themselves and us with a string of lewdly witty *double entendres*. For these libertines, sophisticated wit and carnality are inseparable; the one would lose all its zest without the other; and the laughter that breaks out in the theater sounds in turn very much like cries of erotic pleasure, signaling the spectators' vicarious participation in comic adultery. In a covert metaphor that lies, after all, not far beneath the surface, the expert pleasure-arousing manipulation of language performed in a scene like this takes on powerful erogenous connotations.

The subliminal awareness that laughter is allied with indecent pleasures, particularly erotic ones, helps perhaps to explain why many theorists are so determined to banish laughter from comedy as something, in the words of one, "erratic and unreliable," essentially disreputable, incompatible with maximum seriousness (Potts, 19).[13] Laughter is degraded (and our view of comedy thus obstructed) similarly by the standard view that comic laughter expresses contempt for the ugly and the ignoble, and that the only pleasure it affords is a derivative of this contempt. Few theoreticians go so far on this point as Baudelaire, who interprets laughter as "one of the clearest tokens of the Satanic in man" (p. 453), but it is not surprising that a literary mode supposedly devoted to the constant punishment of "pettiness and vanity and folly" should be found by one fairly typical commentator to have at its core "always a strain of melancholy" (Kronenberger, 3, 4). The punitive model of comic laughter is indeed a melancholy one, if only because of the drastic devaluation of comedy, the limitation of its expressive range and its isolation from the body of literature at large, that this model implies. Bergson, in particular, makes this implication plain. Beginning with the assumption (disavowed by Freud [*Jokes*, 196] and intuitively contradicted, as we saw, by William Prynne) that the basis of comic laughter is always a feeling of superiority and "an unavowed intention to humiliate" (p. 148), Bergson asserts, echoing the long antilaughter tradition, that laughter springs from a "self-assertive and conceited" attitude, indeed from mere "spitefulness"; its aftertaste is "bitter" and expresses, says Bergson, "a curious pessimism" (pp. 188–90). What follows from this set of assumptions is, among other things, the most pervasive fallacy of modern comic theory: the tacit (or sometimes explicit) divorcing of comedy from imagination. Bergson, Meredith, Albert Cook, and others tend to assign comedy wholly to the sphere of the rational intellect: "Its appeal is to intelligence, pure and simple," says Bergson (p. 64), who with unsparing frankness confesses his final belief that comedy is after all something less than art (pp. 170–71).[14] In reconceiving comedy as grounded in pleasure and in the central metaphor of "limberness," and thus as allowing for laughter that glorifies its subjects rather than repudiating them, we can perhaps set Bergson's melancholy verdict convincingly aside.

CONCLUSION: THE PLAIN AND THE EXOTIC

The fairly widespread tendency to blur the distinction between comedy (based on the pleasure principle) and realism (based on the joint principles of seriousness and verisimilitude) is summed up in the familiar view that comic language is by its nature plainspun and direct, and that comedies convey a peculiarly commonsensical, down-to-earth view of life, a view informed, as one writer puts it, by "a mediocre kind of sanity" (Watts, 197). The same point is put less invidiously in the claim that comedy "has its feet on the ground" (Feibelman, 272). However it may be phrased, this is one form of the argument that comedy is poor in imaginative values. The truth is that comedy is strongly addicted to strangeness and to gaudy extravagance. Consider, for example, the image of Sir Epicure Mammon, the would-be voluptuary of Ben Jonson's *The Alchemist*. Believing that alchemy is about to enrich him, Sir Epicure, thrusting the ethic of unbridled pleasure once again into the comic foreground, dreams of future debaucheries:

> I will have all my beds blown up; not stuffed:
> Down is too hard. And then, my oval room,
> Filled with such pictures, as Tiberius took
> From Elephantis, and dull Aretine
> But coldly imitated. Then, my glasses,
> Cut in more subtle angles, to disperse
> And multiply the figures, as I walk
> Naked between my *succubae*. . . .
>
> (2.2.41–48)

This grotesque character, far from reflecting an imagination bounded by "a mediocre kind of sanity," embodies and glorifies a sense of humor of the most hyperbolic kind. Trollope reveals his own sensitivity to this effect (as well as his collusion in comedy's scandalous overriding of moral restraints) by noting admiringly that "Mammon rises to poetry in the descriptions he gives of the pleasures of lewdness and greediness." [15] It is the almost demented extravagance of Sir Epicure's narcissism and lasciviousness that seizes Jonson's fancy; we *laugh* at his outcry "Down is too hard" not because a joke has been told but because he literally takes our breath away with the outlandishness of his fantasy life. It is a deeply characteristic comic image. Again there is the telltale coincidence of laughter and sensual pleasure, such sensual pleasure at least as is suggested in lunatic visions of beds becoming tumescent and naked women teeming on the walls; and again we see in Sir Epicure's erotic daydreams a pattern of just that protean limberness and genius for self-magnification that I have argued is a sign of comedy—a pattern strikingly caught in the imagery of Sir Epicure refracted and multiplied, along with his gallery of pornographic pictures, into a myriad of shimmering reflections. The exhilaration that humor like this provokes is that of our ability to share in conjuring forth a grotesque of such a wildly exotic species. It could be argued that this points to complicity of a deeper kind—to the delight of finding ourselves able harmlessly to indulge (thanks to the diplomatic immunity of comedy) our own repressed hankerings for "the pleasures of lewdness and greediness." However we interpret the comic charm of Sir Epicure, it clearly originates in his essential exoticism, and this strain of imagination is primary in much comedy.

Purely verbal exoticism has always been a principal component of comic literature. *Love's Labour's Lost*, like many another comedy, is little more than a festival of what is called at one point "Taffeta phrases, silken terms precise, / Three-pil'd hyperboles, spruce affectation, / Figures pedantical" (5.2.406–8); the impulse to hyperrich virtuoso language in Congreve can render *The Way of the World* almost unintelligible on the stage; Mrs. Malaprop's singular turns of phrase—her evocation, for example, of allegories on the banks of the Nile—fills *The Rivals* with exotic wordplay of another kind. Far from being bound in plain and simple language, there is thus a long tradition of comic writing, culminating perhaps (outside the limits of comedy proper) in Joyce, in which an important theme is precisely comedy's tendency almost to swallow itself up in linguistic extravagance, as the voluptuous excitement of playing with language verges upon anarchy.

By the same token, comedy consistently uses its presumed setting in plain reality only as a kind of staging area for excursions into strange realms where things prove to possess a vividness and energy and other qualities unheard of in prosaic ordinary life. In fact, in comedy the exotic continually opens the way to the plainly fantastic, as it does in *A Midsummer-Night's Dream*. Comedy deals initially with prosaic materials like rude mechanicals, ordinary merchants and their wives, and common fools, and yet it thrives on make-believe and on devices like love philters, magic spells, and (especially) impossible disguises and seemingly magical shape-changing. In this complex of materials we again see what may be vestiges, of course in radically attenuated form, of the magical ceremonies and costumings from which ancient comedy supposedly arose. In any case, if there is a fundamental joke in comedy it is that involving some event or character that is wildly improbable but presented with a poker face as simple reality. "Those things do best please me," says Puck in *A Midsummer-Night's Dream*, speaking as the voice of comedy itself, "That befall preposterously" (3.2.120–21).[16] One example of such things would be the superbly comic scene in Ingmar Bergman's film comedy *Smiles of a Summer Night* when the ascetic theology student, driven to attempt suicide as the only escape from his guilty, typically comic temptation toward love and pleasure, accidentally triggers the secret mechanism that brings the wonderful bed and its voluptuous sleeping beauty (his young virginal stepmother) serendipitously through the solid bedroom wall. Again, our pulsation of delighted laughter simulates the pulsation of erotic pleasure about to ensue. In effect if not in fact this saving event is a stroke of sheer magic; it epitomizes the way comedy causes exotic charm unexpectedly to irradiate scenes deceptively like those of ordinary life.

The key to comic style, as I have suggested already, is its always *double* effect in which the exotic and the prosaic, which want to fly apart and set up two separate kingdoms (those, say, of romance and realist fiction) are yoked by violence together, laughter being the the most immediate by-product of this friction-rich coupling. Both elements are essential; the moment one defaults the aura of comedy evaporates, transformed into some monistic mode: Romantic reverie, rationalist polemic, naturalism, melodrama (which Frye identifies in a brilliant aside [p. 40] as comedy devoid of humor). The determining factor in comedy is that the comic poet fall into some kind of strong imaginative sympathy with the absurd, aberrant, grotesque, extravagant, or fantastic materials that he or she evokes. The essential comic effect, the one that stands out so clearly in the figure of Sir Epicure Mammon, is thus always a process of magnification rather than what it seems to be, reduction.[17] From this principle comes the insidious sense of slippage between ostensible didactic motives and felt imaginative ones that informs so much comedy, the tendency of purely comic values (energy, vividness, freedom, wit, charm—all the values that center on pleasure) to detach themselves from and brazenly to take precedence over civic ones.

Comedy functions in this way as an imaginative response to the secular equivalent of the prospect of barren fields in primitive fertility ceremonies: the prospect of the deadening banality of life. Its paramount function is not to suppress (or, for that matter, to foment) disorder but to show the exotic, the extravagant, the antic, taking vivid shape in the midst of common existence. Thus it is that comedy seems necessarily (though much more overtly at some times than at others) to reassert its sacred origins by giving off suggestions of epiphany. For all his commitment to what a reviewer already cited called "almost perversely prosaic" realism (Smalley, 523), Trollope, as we shall see, is keenly attuned to this suggestion, and when he introduces in *Ayala's Angel* his supreme comic hero, he pictures him as shooting merry flames from his eyes and as shimmering all over with a magical radiance, like a god. Ordinarily this dimension of a comedy will be stressed by explicit thematic attention to the drabness and constriction—the "unutterable tedium," in a phrase from *Ayala's Angel* (chap. 3)—of normal existence. "O, how full of briers is this working-day world!" exclaims Shakespeare's Rosalind (*As You Like It*, 1.3.12). The original gesture of comedy, the one on which all its other gestures depend, is to recreate this world as a field of exotic, always delightful, always more or less scandalous, surprises, and one in which life is (or ought to be) identical with pleasure.

With this as our guiding premise, we can now begin to explore the world of Trollope's comic fiction.

2

Trollope and "The Good Things of This World"

Dost thou think, because thou art virtuous, there shall be no more cakes and ale?

Twelfth Night

TROLLOPE AND HIS CONTEMPORARIES

On the next to last page of his *Autobiography*, Trollope declares that one chief goal of his life has been "to enjoy the excitement of pleasure," while being careful at the same time to avoid "its vices and ill effects." "The preachers tell us that this is impossible," he says, claiming nevertheless to have succeeded fairly well, though he alludes interestingly to certain unspecified mishaps along the way. In this passage he specifies gambling, women, and tobacco as among his potentially dangerous pleasures—it is apparent from reading his fiction that he had a very keen susceptibility to female beauty especially— and elsewhere in the *Autobiography* he almost lyrically confesses his addiction to foxhunting, an amusement that he indulged in, he says, in a notable turn of phrase, as a lifelong "duty" (p. 64). Coming from a Victorian gentleman as proud of his rectitude as Trollope was, these avowals of a strong taste for frivolity and pleasant dissipations and this presentation of himself as something of a renegade from current moral prejudices should not be blown out of proportion. Nor should they be overlooked, for they define an important motive of his fiction, which steadily, as we shall see, identifies the suppression of pleasure as the most malign (and most complex) feature of Victorian life, and no less steadily plots a course for the revitalization of the pleasure principle. But the *Autobiography* passage is a study in conflicting impulses. Trollope shows himself a man of his age in his anxious sense of having to negotiate a perilous course, after all, in order to embrace pleasure without falling victim to "its vices and ill effects." This uncomfortable-seeming ambivalence, full of tension, proves to be an immensely fruitful one for Trollope's career as a novelist, dictating, in particular, his elaborate operations in the sphere of comedy.

The significance of the issue of pleasure for nineteenth-century culture can be glimpsed by placing Trollope's autobiography alongside such other characteristic Victorian autobiographies as Mill's and Newman's. "[My father] had . . . scarcely any belief in pleasure," says Mill in a key passage. "The greatest number of miscarriages in life, he considered to be attributable to the overvaluing of pleasures. Accordingly, temperance . . . was with him . . . almost the central point of educational precept" (p. 30). Under the influence of this secularized puritanism, Mill devotes his life to the cause of social reform and of intellectual truth, and discovers almost too late the extent of the inner damage done to him by the denial of pleasure. In his account of his restoration by Wordsworth's poetry the word "pleasure" occurs again and again. In these poems, he says, "I seemed to draw from a source of . . . sympathetic and imaginative pleasure" (p. 89). Newman in his *Apologia Pro Vita Sua* shows a deep responsiveness to the imaginative and aesthetic pleasures of Roman Catholic ritual, but mainly his story is a quintessentially Victorian fable of self-denial in obedience to high moral duty. The poignantly remembered image of the snapdragon on the wall opposite his freshman's rooms at Trinity is an emblem of all the cherished Oxford pleasures that he sacrifices, not without a pang, to follow the true faith (p. 225). Both these books and lives depict that disavowal of pleasure that forms such a prominent strain in Victorian culture and personality, and that one needs to focus upon to understand the genesis, the rhetoric, and the importance of Trollope's comedy.

The proscription of pleasure and the corresponding glorification of duty, work, self-control, and self-denial is writ still larger in Victorian fiction. George Eliot offers an especially vivid case in point, having early in life gone through a phase of extreme Evangelical asceticism that left permanent marks upon her imagination. Her attitude during this period is summed up in a letter of 1838 in which she attempts to justify her instinctive enjoyment of music on the grounds that musical art is a noble attainment that deserves to be honored. She decides, however, that this argument is a dangerous casuistical snare. "By once admitting such reasoning," she declares, reciting the lethally descending series of pleasures that is a key rhetorical trope of comic and anticomic writing, "we disarm ourselves of every weapon against opera dancing, horse racing, nay even against intemperance, which I have heard justified on the plea that since Providence has sent luxuries we are condemning them by abstinence" (*Letters* 1:9–10). Her eventual rejection of supernatural religion did little to allay her deep anxiety about the baneful consequences of pleasure, if we are to judge by her novels. In *Adam Bede* (1859) it is a treacherously short, easy step from wearing gilded earrings to fornication and infanticide, and the moral ideal is represented by a fanatical puritan who condemns "simple natural pleasure" (p. 139) as spiritual peril; in *The Mill on the Floss* (1860) Maggie Tulliver vindicates her character by sternly repressing her temptation by erotic pleasure; in *Middlemarch* (1871–72) the representative devotee of pleasure is Rosamond Vincy, selfish, vain, and cruel. A full study of such novels would of course call for many qualifications, for George Eliot is far from being a doctrinaire puritan; but the main outlook embodied in her fiction is clear enough. Her imaginative world is a scene of strenuous moral struggle where impulses "to enjoy the excitement of pleasure" lead infallibly to disaster and where the ethic of renunciation, therefore, is the measure both of prudence and of virtue.

In some ways Dickens offers an even more telling case in point, for he was by nature a buoyant, pleasure-loving man who hated and steadily attacked the repressive neo-puritanism of his day. And yet Dickens's fiction betrays a steady evolution in the direction of orthodox earnestness and its dour judgment of pleasure. *Pickwick Papers* (1837), Dickens's first novel, is a paean to frivolous freedom in which excessive indulgence in milk punch is not only regarded tolerantly but is associated with Mr. Pickwick's almost saintly innocence and sweetness of spirit. Already in *The Old Curiosity Shop* (1841) the moral ambience has markedly changed: Dick Swiveller's initial frivolity is seen as a weakness of character (however beguiling) that he must finally conquer, and his love of "the rosy" is associated with sordidness and stumbling drunkenly through the streets; and in the sybaritic Quilp, another lover of strong drink, ordinary pleasure becomes demonic. Quilp's deranged carnal appetites (for swilling scalding hot potions, devouring gigantic prawns with the heads and tails on, lusting after little girls) are part and parcel of his moral depravity. In later novels Dickens's pleasure-lovers like "Gentleman" Turveydrop, Harold Skimpole, or Henry Gowan emerge as among his most despicable characters (Mr. Micawber briefly flourishes as a throwback to an earlier spirit), while all moral approval is channeled to such figures of self-denying stoicism as Agnes Wickfield, Esther Summerson, and Amy Dorrit. The deepening puritanical cast of Dickens's writing is unquestionably the medium of his greatest works of imagination, but all the magnificence and imaginative exuberance of novels like *Bleak House* and *Little Dorrit* come surrounded with a melancholy moral ethos that condemns pleasure and lightness of heart, that renders these works half repellent and their heroines notoriously unpalatable. In setting out his radical vision of the social and spiritual crisis of modern Britain, Dickens, like all prophets, sacrifices certain dimensions of his own humanity—and, for all his inspired use of farce, grotesque humor, and satire, estranges himself altogether from the unifying vision of comedy.

These and other less eminent writers of the day exemplify, then, the Victorians' insistence on drawing a sharp line between frivolity and seriousness (a line that the comic imagination defines itself by forever striving to efface), and their perception of ordinary pleasure as laden with moral danger. Max Weber's thesis that Puritan asceticism, "the most urgent task [of which was] the destruction of spontaneous, impulsive enjoyment" (p. 119), became in the capitalist period the basis of culture in England and elsewhere thus finds much support in the evidence of the Victorian novel. Puritanical attitudes came into particularly sharp focus, of course, in the area most pertinent to comedy, that of erotic relations, which for the Victorians, as Steven Marcus and others have reminded us, was charged with often hysterical anxieties. Peter Gay and other revisionist historians have argued that Victorian sexual repression was less extensive and less damaging psychologically than the traditional picture would suggest, but there is no gainsaying the evidence of Victorian proneness to, in Gay's own words, "a neurotic incapacity to tap the sources of erotic pleasure" (p. 161). Victorian prose fiction registers this neurosis with such obsessive insistence and in such vividly highlighted imagery—registers it both in explicitly thematized forms, as, say, in *Jane Eyre* or *Jude the Obscure*, and in networks of unconscious imaginative distortions— that to seek to deny its decisive influence upon this culture would surely be futile. We need, however, to see the troubled sexual life of the Victorians as just one component of a broadly pervasive disavowing of pleasure itself. Such a strain of feeling can of course be fundamental, as this one evidently was, without being uniform or universal. In a complex society, any significant trend is bound to generate countertrends, so it is fully to be expected that the ascetic puritan mentality in Victorian England would always have coexisted (often within a single personality) with other mentalities, ones more open to spontaneity and pleasure, that it could never subdue. Indeed, it is precisely the continuing tension between repressive ideology and unrepressed impulses that causes nineteenth-century puritanism to manifest itself as distinctly as it does in the records of Victorian life. Contemporary cultural analysts bear clear witness to the overwhelming significance of this pattern of thought that I am rather loosely (as an analysis like Weber's entitles one to do) calling "puritanism." Matthew Arnold, prefiguring Weber, defines "Hebraism" in terms of its stress on "strictness of conscience" and its obsession with sin, and asserts in 1868 the "long exclusive predominance" of this factor in English culture. "Any glance at the world around us, shows that with us, . . . the ruling force is now, and long has been, a Puritan force" (pp. 132, 156, 149). Arnold disagrees with Mill in many ways, but here he echoes Mill's assessment in *On Liberty* (1859) of the modern-day prevalence of the "Calvinistic" will to suppress all "strong wishes and native pleasures" (p. 61). Victorian imaginative literature qualifies but also amplifies and steadily confirms Arnold's and Mill's authoritative testimony.

In these cultural circumstances true comedy, with its primordial attachment to pleasure as the animating spirit and the vindication of moral values, had a potentially vital role to play, but was, as we have already seen, almost entirely in abeyance. Trollope's comedies as a result show a keen sense of performing a specific cultural function. They continually dramatize the problematical status of pleasure in Victorian life, and thus reflect upon themselves, making us aware that in choosing to practice the art of comedy in fiction and in carrying on, as we shall see that he does, a concerted advocacy of pleasure, Trollope deliberately sets himself in a tense, uneasy relationship to his reading public, and courts the risk of being misunderstood and undervalued. We shall see examples of how he attempts to make artistic capital of his self-imposed liabilities at the end of this chapter, in discussions of *Miss Mackenzie* and *The Belton Estate*, two comic fables of the libidinal awakenings of repressed, pleasure-starved women, a category he sees as epitomizing fundamental issues in the life of the culture as a whole. In the meantime, we can survey the main outlines of Trollope's theme and get a preliminary idea of how central it is to his fictive world. For clarity of exposition I shall present this ramifying theme as though it were a linear and logical argument, but this design, it should be realized, is an artificial one that gives little sense of the perplexed configurations that the theme of pleasure takes on in many Trollope novels.

Riding to Hounds and Other Worldly Ceremonies

At one point in *The American Senator*, a novel that systematically studies the network of social institutions built upon the pleasure principle, Trollope states explicitly the comic thesis that underlies much of his life's work—that underlies, indeed, the very vocation of novel writing. "Recreation," declares the hero of this story, "is as necessary to the world as clothes or food" (chap. 73). As we shall see in the course of this chapter, Trollope's novels persistently work to restore to the word "recreation" some of its deep etymological meaning, arguing that pleasurable release from the constraints of ordinary life can bring about the renewal of damaged personalities. We need to begin, however, by briefly glossing the other operative word in the above sentence, "the world," which figures as the central term in one of the most interesting recent discussions of comedy, Robert Bechtold Heilman's *The Ways of the World: Comedy and Society*. Heilman's argument, abundantly confirmed by Trollope's fiction, is that "the acceptance of the world" is the governing moral principle of comedy. But it is important to note that "the world" to which comic characters normally reconcile themselves is not the community of mankind or even the whole social order of their day but specifically the worldly world, *le monde* of sophisticated upper-class society. This sphere is rarely idealized in comedy, but is shown instead as riddled with foolish affectation, malice, and manifold other shortcomings. Why does comedy persist in not rejecting so imperfect and so narrowly circumscribed a world? Heilman, desiring like some other recent scholars to see comedy as thoroughly imbued with humanitarian values, claims that it conveys in its code of accepting the world "an acknowledgment of the rights and claims of others, erring and flawed though the others may be, and our kinship with them" (p. 126). Few if any comedies, however, are so softhearted or so morally inspirational, though Steele's *Conscious Lovers*, as we saw, is an example of an attempt to revise comedy along such lines. Comedies urge accommodation with the imperfect world, first, for the excellent reason that no other practical alternative is available—comedy being the reverse of quixotic. (Elizabeth Bennet, for instance, cordially accepts the despicable and dangerous Wickham as her brother-in-law not to acknowledge his rights or her kinship with him, but simply because the alternative would be a destructive scandal.) But "the world" in comedy has a more active, more positive claim on our allegiance than mere expediency. It may not foster an ideal moral climate, but, having nothing better to do, it does foster *pleasure*: of witty sophisticated conversation, of sexual dalliance, of gossip, of sports, of amused observation of the vagaries of human nature. Comedy celebrates "the world"—idle upper-class society—in brashly pagan terms, as an incomparable resource of this complex of interrelated "recreations."[1]

Trollope principally lays his fiction in or on the outskirts of this same symbolic or mythic scene, where worldly life and the life of pleasure are ideally one and the same: a privileged sphere of ladies and gentlemen who spend the lion's share of their time and energy in simply amusing themselves. He invests this scene with such vivid verisimilitude and such density of social texture that readers have always mistaken it for a sheer report of reality, one that historians can study for reliable information on just how life was lived in the nineteenth century. Already in his own day he was celebrated for what a reviewer called his "singularly valuable and faithful pictures of some portions of the age they delineate" (Smalley, 481). Richard Holt Hutton declared, in fact, that Trollope's fiction "will picture the society of our day [for future ages] with a fidelity with which society has never been pictured before in the history of the world" (ibid., 508). The assumption that the upper classes of Trollope's fiction are identical to those of historical actuality has impelled readers both to praise his "realism" and to attack him for his supposed political alignment with these despicable social elements.[2] The fidelity of his "pictures" to nineteenth-century actuality, however, is only of an oblique, tendentious, deeply compromised kind—every particle of them, after all, is imaginary—whereas their fidelity to the mythic realm of comedy and, in particular, to the comic image of "the world" as the scene of the traditional drama of the supremacy of pleasure, is everywhere manifest.

Nothing better illustrates the glorification of worldly pleasure in Trollope than his most notorious eccentricity as a novelist, his perpetual foxhunting episodes. It is tempting to dismiss these passages as nothing more significant than self-indulgence on the part of a writer who confesses to having "dragged [hunting] into many novels" simply because he was addicted to the sport and wrote "on no subject with such delight as that of hunting" (*Autobiography*, 64). The notion of fiction as an outlet for delight is worth noticing. But Trollope's hunting scenes also have the important textual function of dramatizing the pleasure principle in a form so emphatic, so undiluted, that it will reverberate throughout a large fictional structure. Hunting stands, in James R. Kincaid's precise phrase, as Trollope's premier "symbol for community and for joy" (p. 59). All the imagery of hunting—the galloping over hill and dale, the breathless leaping of fences and streams and ditches, the fluidly shifting groups of riders—expresses that limberness and buoyancy that I have stressed in comedy, and gives these qualities their full charge of euphoric delight. At the same time, riding to hounds is nothing if not an elaborately formalized worldly ritual, an aspect of it that Trollope dwells upon with constant disquisitions on all the etiquette of costume, procedures, and social precedence, all the legal technicalities, and all the institutional structure, that govern hunting at every moment. Euphoric release and obedience to social formalities turn out, in the central paradox of comedy and the one that gives the hunt all its significance for Trollope, to be identical.[3]

Hunting in Trollope's stories can yield pleasure vertiginous in its intensity, pleasure capable of making people alter the directions of their lives. The histrionic Lizzie Eustace makes a career of simulating exaltation and nearly all other feelings, to the extent that she seems to become a wholly unreal person living a life of sheer masquerade (*The Eustace Diamonds* thus gives a strong twist of existential anxiety to the theme of "the dear pleasure of dissembling" that is so venerable a subject of comedy); but the exhilaration of Lizzie's first day of hunting gives her a moment of genuine, unfeigned, pungent experience for the first and only time in the novel. It is a moment that vividly exemplifies Trollope's preoccupation with the theme of the effect of pleasure upon repressed or depleted personalities. "This was to live," she thinks to herself, in a strongly charged phrase. "Surely in all the world there was nothing equal to this." "On they went, and Lizzie was in heaven. She could not quite understand her feelings. . . . The leaping was delightful, and her horse galloped with her as though his pleasure was as great as her own" (chap. 38). The strong erotic overtones of Lizzie's pleasure here highlight the central irony that this professional temptress and sexual desperado has in fact led a long life utterly barren of sexual pleasure. In comedy, masquerading and pleasure usually go hand in hand; in *The Eustace Diamonds* the two have split apart, a fracturing of the paradigm of comedy that serves as Trollope's primary figure for the personal decay that the novel explores. Lizzie's pang of pleasure in the hunting field is seen as potentially showing her the way to a renewal of her vitiated humanity—a quintessentially comic moral that she is finally incapable of acting on.

A passage less fraught with innuendo is the hunting episode in *Ayala's Angel*, one of the high points in one of Trollope's most lambent comedies. Hunting forms a perfect opportunity for comic action since it so vividly combines imagery of euphoric limberness with the idea of a movement from common reality into the "green world," the realm of holiday, celebration of nature, and unstinting pleasure, and in *Ayala's Angel* Trollope invokes this mythic pattern strongly. Ayala leaves the poverty-stricken home of the Dosetts in Kingsbury Crescent for a visit to Sir Harry Albury's country house at Stalham, and it seems to her that in doing so she has set foot in "a world of joy": "Oh, what a difference was there between Stalham and Kingsbury Crescent!" Ayala exemplifies the patented Trollopian heroine in whom excellence of character coexists nicely—quite unlike the usual image of a Victorian heroine—with an energetic appreciation of worldly "recreation," and so she finds herself supremely happy amid "the luxurious comfort of Stalham, where everybody was at his ease, where everybody was good-natured, where everybody seemed to acknowledge that pleasure was the one object of life!" This object is attained most fully on the day of the hunt, when Ayala and her friend Nina are led for a glorious run by Larry Twentyman (chap. 24). What with riding to hounds and other such amusements, Ayala spends at Stalham a week "filled full with ecstatic pleasures!" (chap. 25), and the novel, imbued as it is with the comic mentality, leaves no doubt that holiday-making of this kind is the best thing in the world for young ladies. Ayala's dour guardians the Dosetts raise protests against her exposure to so much worldly amusement, which they declare to be full of moral dangers, but their protests are gaily overridden and are seen before long, even by themselves, to be unfounded. *Ayala's Angel* thus acts out in explicit form that fable of the disarming of the anxious Victorian conscience by pleasure that Trollope, at the risk of incensing his public, or that at least of making his work seem trivial to serious-minded readers, inscribes at the center of his career as a novelist.

The kind of joyous physical pleasure that Lizzie and Ayala experience on horseback is usually only a secondary aspect of Trollope's hunting scenes, however. These are mainly social, worldly occasions in which there is less of galloping over fields, after all, than of the hunting chatter that clearly was music to the author's ears: swapping horse stories and local lore, arguing over tactics, boisterously joking. The dramatic line of the novel recedes as Trollope pauses to report generous samplings of this talk, making us feel in the shift of narrative rhythm the mood of exquisite pleasure that these episodes are meant to convey.

> "I call that a pretty little run, Sir Harry," said Larry Twentyman.
> "Pretty well," said Sir Harry; "the pace wasn't very great, or that pony of mine which Miss Dormer is riding could not have lived with it."
> "Horses, Sir Harry, don't want so much pace, if they are allowed to go straight. It's when a man doesn't get well away, or has made a mess with his fences, that he needs an extra allowance of pace to catch the hounds. If you're once with them and can go straight you may keep your place without such a deal of legs." To this Sir Harry replied only by a grunt, as on the present occasion he had "made a mess with his fences," as Larry Twentyman had called it.
>
> (*Ayala*, chap. 24)

The kind of free social interplay that this deliberately nondescript prose evokes is an image of comic limberness in a new, subtler form, and an image that for Trollope goes far to define the joy of hunting. When first introduced to the sport as a young man in Ireland, he soon came to love it, he tells us, "with an affection which I cannot myself fathom or understand" (*Autobiography*, 64)—an affection assuredly rooted in the personal "re-creation" that hunting offered him by allowing him for the first time since the days of his childhood disgrace to mingle with members of what he felt to be his proper social class. To hunt was almost to become himself again. Inevitably, the hunt became in his fiction a main symbol of his most comprehensive fictional theme, the way social institutions foster individuality by providing the vital sense of communal identity.[4] The foxhunting ritual is especially well suited to expressing this theme, first, because it embodies (in an era of disorienting change) customs and social patterns sanctified by ancient traditions, but mainly, as I have already suggested, because it makes such a graphic image of a conjunction between the pleasure principle and social order. It has been argued that pleasure is inherently subversive,[5] but Trollope, making the fundamental argument of comedy, refutes this view, suggesting everywhere that just as pleasure is profoundly beneficial to individuals, so it is both the chief reward and the binding, sustaining force of social order. The community of hunters functions as well as it does, incessantly making readjustments to alleviate conflicts and allow for fractious personalities, instructing individuals in the need to submit to shared rules of conduct in order to enjoy personal freedom, for one (so to speak) overriding reason: because it furnishes such rich pleasure to its members. The hunt, in other words, is conceived by Trollope as a holiday, a charmed space set aside from normal life for indulgence in play—but is closely tied all the while, in his view, to the principles that govern civilized life in general. Holiday itself, we are constantly reminded by these episodes, is merely a social conventionality like any other.

The argument about the interlocking relations of pleasure, individuality, and social order embedded in Trollope's hunting theme is serious, but unmistakably "comic": that is, it comes to us enveloped in laughter. Personal and collective absurdities are almost always highlighted in these episodes, where laughter seems like a reverberation from the physical exhilaration of hunting as it seems on so many occasions in comedy to be a reverberation of sexual pleasure. Trollope's humorous view of the hunt epitomizes Freud's notion of the comic as centered in the image of adults behaving like children (*Jokes*, 224–28): in this case, becoming so absorbed in a preposterous form of play that they take it as earnest life-and-death reality. This is what we see, for example, in the episode of the great encounter in *Mr. Scarborough's Family* between two rival hunts under their respective masters Mr. Harkaway and Mr. Fairlawn, who quarreled thirty years before about some small hunting matter and have cherished the quarrel ever since. "No one in these modern days," the narrator informs us, "knew aught of the quarrel, or cared. The men of the two hunts were very good friends, unless they met under the joint eyes of the two masters, and then they were supposed to be bound to hate each other." Reading this sentence, and then watching the two groups of grown men almost come to blows respecting the right of Mr. Fairlawn's hunt to enter a certain wood, we feel ourselves suddenly hoisted by the helium balloon of comedy out of the generally harsh and bitter world of this novel into a realm of dizzying silliness. The feeling is the quintessentially comic one of holiday, of delightful disengagement from the rigidities and pressures of ordinary adult life. Not just incidentally, the scene hints at the same time that an institution allowing for indulgence in a playful, pleasurable *semblance* of hatred can work to dissipate forces of potentially real hatred like the ones that break out so often and with such destructive effect elsewhere in *Mr. Scarborough's Family*: an implication that sheds light on the socially therapeutic role of the institution of comedy itself, focused as it steadily is on the playful representation of potentially anarchic impulses.

As I have emphasized, the pleasures of the hunt in Trollope are largely those of sociability in general, which he devotes what may seem a disproportionate space in his fiction to evoking. The mark of his comic affiliation is the great value that he attaches to all the skills of refined worldly intercourse that go by the name of urbanity: lightness of touch, zest for conversation, stylistic elegance, a sense of humor. So important are these qualities to him that he is almost always ready— it is one of the signatures of his novelistic style—to suspend the progress of his story to put them on display, in episodes where little occurs besides the give and take of conversation. Often we can make out in a given novel contrasting images of sociability in which genuine urbanity is set off against some false or debased imitation of it.

In *The Eustace Diamonds*, for example, an important structural pattern lies in the contrast between Lizzie's crowd at Portray Castle, a group of disreputable pseudo-aristocrats whose conversation is necessarily as coarse as themselves, and the Palliser circle at Matching Priory centered on Lady Glencora, Madame Max Goesler, and Lady Chiltern, where vivacious urbanity flourishes and where, in the book's final chapter, we witness a classic ritual of comedy, the witty punishment of a pompous, boorish killjoy (Mr. Bonteen) who intrudes his heavy presence in the midst of a group bent on "recreation." In passages like these we feel ourselves very distinctly on the classic terrain of comedy, in the presence of latter-day versions of Beatrice, Millamant, and Elizabeth Bennet. But the pleasures of urbane conviviality are not always of this ironic and aristocratic cast, for Trollope often focuses upon a more bourgeois and domestic society where the wit is less brilliant but more richly imbued with affection. A good case in point would be the long scene of unexceptional dinner-table conversation, full of good-natured teasing upon this and that trivial topic, that occurs in *The Claverings* when Harry dines for the first time with his prospective brother- and sister-in-law the Burtons, along with Mrs. Burton's brother (chap. 8). There could hardly be a better passage to illustrate why Trollope has been disparaged as bland and pedestrian, but this passage (that would need to be quoted at length to convey its effect) and many similar ones in Trollope's novels have a significant role to play. "I cannot hold with those," says the narrator in *Framley Parsonage* (chap. 10), "who wish to put down the insignificant chatter of the world." Artistically, what gives this passage its character—and its audacity—is its complete absence of plot value: as a transcript of "insignificant chatter," it functions purely as an exhibit of a certain texture of social relations. And the basis of this exhibit, again, is the abundance of common pleasure, mainly of lively, frivolous conversation and persiflage, that this society finds room for. One may note in passing that such a passage from so close an observer of contemporary manners goes far to qualify the assumption that the Victorian middle classes led only a "dismal and illiberal life" (Arnold, 102), and that a "national deficiency in liveliness and sociability," dooming "the cultivation of the art of talking agreeably on trifles," caused society of the period to be "kept up for any reason rather than the pleasure it [afforded]" (Mill, *Autobiography*, 135). Wherever historical truth may lie, the relaxed give and take of the Burtons' talk, like the more emphatic metaphors of Trollope's foxhunting scenes, projects again an image of that fluent ease of movement that is comedy's ideal of charm and of pleasure.

REPRESSION

English comedy in the seventeenth century, said Thackeray, had the mission of opposing "the new, hard, ascetic, pleasure-hating doctrine" of the Puritans (*English Humourists*, 199), and in fact, it is one of the principal occupations of comedy to wage war on puritans, who are its natural enemies and natural prey. A puritan in a comedy is generally an ugly spectacle, for his very presence is the specter of the annihilation of comedy: he would shut up the theater if he could, and burn the playwright at the stake. So he is not shown much mercy.

The heirs of the seventeenth-century Puritans, the Evangelicals, established their deep influence upon the English mentality and English culture from the time of their upsurge in the Methodist movement at the end of the eighteenth century. When Trollope turned to novel-writing in the late 1840s, the force of the original movement had only begun to wane, and a second Evangelical revival took place in Britain in the years after 1858 (Kitson Clark, 21, 178). Trollope, more impervious to this resurgent influence than any other major Victorian writer, repeatedly declared his aversion to satire, which he found intellectually dishonest, but throughout his career he made many wicked exceptions to this rule on behalf of Evangelicals; the steady malice that he shows toward them is one of the plainest signs of his devotion to the cause of comedy. Thus the perennial issue in comedy is at once joined in *Barchester Towers* when the newcomers, Obadiah

Slope and the Proudies, proclaim their campaign against "the iniquity of Sabbath amusements" and "so grievous a sin" as Sunday traveling (chap. 5), not to mention overindulgence in "the meretricious charms of melody" in cathedral services (chap. 6). The whole action of the novel is oriented toward defending the legitimate rights of pleasure (which Trollope sees to be tied ultimately to proper observance of Christianity itself) against this assault of dour oppressiveness. The champion of the pleasure-party in Barchester is the Archdeacon, who "enjoyed the good things of this world, and liked to let it be known that he did so" (Ch. 4). Indeed, the Archdeacon is a lover of Rabelais, although this is one vice that he only dares pursue in secret (*The Warden*, Ch. 8). As the spirit of comedy dictates, the Archdeacon's frank devotion to worldliness and pleasure is the surest sign of his essential wholeness of character; his antagonist Slope, by contrast, has done permanent violence to himself, has become crafty, devious, and ambitious, by willfully depriving himself of pleasure. "He had early in life," we are told, "devoted himself to works which were not compatible with the ordinary pleasures of youth, and he had abandoned such pleasures not without a struggle" (chap. 15). Trollope suggests that we have here the whole cause of Slope's degeneracy.

The same fundamental myth of the struggle of pleasure against agencies of repression is played out in *Rachel Ray* (1863), where the latter again take the form of a cabal of dour Evangelicals preaching a code of "the utmost rigour of self-denying propriety" (chap. 3). Mrs. Prime, the heroine's widowed sister, who has fallen under the baleful puritan influence and has "taught herself to believe that cheerfulness was a sin" (chap. 1), sees in the young brewer Luke Rowan, Rachel's jolly lover, only the peril of perdition. "Why, if he were not wicked and abandoned, did he wear that jaunty look, —that look which was so worldly? And moreover, he went to balls, and tempted others to do the like!" (chap. 12). She is staunchly "of opinion that young people shouldn't be allowed to please themselves" (chap. 23), and frets bitterly when she thinks that Rachel and her mother are conspiring to undo her grim influence, talking behind her back "about love and pleasure" (chap. 29). In the sunny comic world of *Rachel Ray* these railings have scant influence; even the supposedly subjugated Mrs. Ray is likely at any moment "to doubt whether, after all, the world was so very bad a place, and whether the wickedness of tea and toast, and of other creature comforts, could be so very great" (chap. 2). A better rhetorical strategy than Mrs. Prime's has been developed by Mr. Comfort the clergyman, who pronounces from the pulpit, as befits his position, "somewhat melancholy discourses against this world's pleasures and vanities" (chap. 8), but who in private life is thoroughly profane in his taste for—the ever-recurring Trollopian phrase—"the good things of this world" (chap. 5), and who freely gives wise worldly counsel to his parishioners, even when, as here with Rachel's mother, they are perplexed by his doctrinal inconsistencies. Luke Rowan, he says, is a rich young man, and Rachel would do well to take him:

> "Take him!"
> "Yes, —why not? Between you and me, Rachel is growing into a very handsome girl, —a very handsome girl indeed. I'd no idea she'd be so tall, and carry herself so well."
> "Oh, Mr. Comfort, good looks are very dangerous for a young woman."
> "Well, yes; indeed they are. But still, you know, handsome girls very often do very well. . . ."
>
> (Chap. 5)

In another kind of novel Mr. Comfort, with his keen eye for beautiful girls and his mercenary view of marriage, would figure as a mere hypocrite; in this comic one he is distinctly sympathetic, endowed above all with tolerance, good sense, and kindness. His hypocrisy, in fact, emerges finally as a signal virtue, his means of preserving his humane character without forfeiting his influence over his flock. In this feeling of customary moral reflexes being provocatively short-circuited, we have the essence of the comic effect, an effect, we can see, that Trollope throws into high relief wherever he can.

The adversaries of the Evangelicals in *Rachel Ray* are, above all, strong devotees of pleasure. Rachel herself "had never said out boldly that she liked the world and its wickedness," but such is plainly the case, and it is again a sign of the comic logic underlying the novel that this irrepressible taste for pleasure amounts to a guarantee of her soundness of character. "She walked . . . as though the very act of walking were a pleasure" (chap. 1), says the narrator (hinting pretty strongly at the sensual invitation that she unconsciously projects). As for Luke Rowan, his mythic role as the bestower of comic pleasure is nicely defined in his main mission in the town of Baslehurst (besides his mission of marrying Rachel): that of taking over the local brewery so as to produce good beer in place of bad. "It was a sour and muddy stream that flowed from [the brewery's] vats; a beverage disagreeable to the palate, and very cold and uncomfortable to the stomach" (chap. 3). One glimpses despite Trollope's prosaic manner the outline of a myth of a dying, poisoned kingdom waiting to be ceremonially restored to fertility—the comic analogue of which, as we have said, is pleasure.

The irony underlying Trollope's comic treatment of puritan repressiveness in these and other novels, and underlying the mythic structure of comic literature at large, is of course that puritans in comedies, far from impeding theatrical pleasure, find themselves forced to collaborate energetically in it: their ritual denunciations of pleasure serve no other purpose than to heighten the triumph of the pleasure-lovers who invariably confound them in the end. What comic author could fail to recognize puritanism as an invaluable resource—as almost the precondition—for the writing of comedy? By the same token, George Meredith remarks that the word *theatre* "prod[s] the Puritan nervous system like a satanic instrument" (p. 6), but what real-life puritan could fail to recognize that the existence of the scandalous institution of comedy is a wonderful spur to puritanical proselytizing? The relations of puritans and comedians, in other words, need to be described as a complex reciprocity in which each antagonist covertly serves the vital interests of the other. "It was with many misgivings that I killed my old friend Mrs. Proudie," Trollope remarks in the *Autobiography* (p. 275), hinting at his awareness of her, and of the tyrannical mentality that she represents, as his necessary allies in the production of a certain kind of fiction. This deep structure in comic myth contains comedy's fundamental insight into the operation of puritan repressiveness in human society: the insight that puritan hostility to pleasure may function ultimately to reinforce and energize rather than to suppress the pleasure principle. Freud, referring specifically to erotic pleasures, makes just this speculation. "An obstacle is required in order to heighten libido," he declares; "and where natural resistances to satisfaction have not been sufficient men have at all times created conventional ones so as to be able to enjoy love." He appears to think that "the ascetic current in Christianity," while masquerading Tartuffe-like as an implacable adversary of the pleasure principle, is in actuality an extension of it and its secret accomplice, charged with the mission of providing a stimulus without which the life of pleasure would necessarily deteriorate ("Debasement," 187–88). Freud's model of the drama of psychic repression, in other words, is essentially a comic one, save for its emphasis on the pain and damage entailed by this process and for the implication that ascetic impulses may at given periods acquire enough force truly to abrogate pleasure. The Freudian model, at all events, comments suggestively on the structure of comic novels like *Barchester Towers* and *Rachel Ray*, where the puritans' attack on pleasure leads with such delightful certainty to the triumph of their well-organized adversaries. It is less relevant to some darker versions of comedy that we shall consider.

As the case of Obadiah Slope suggests, Trollope's formulations of the comic argument tend to complicate the entertainment function of comedy by taking on a strongly psychologized character: by locating the origins of the action in psychic disorders and obliging the reader to try to understand the genetic patterns of these disorders. Cases like Rachel Ray's, where the fable is essentially that of the eager pleasure-seeker victimized by external repression, hold far less significance for Trollope, and occupy far less space in his fiction, consequently, than stories of characters who have in some fashion internalized the puritan mentality and thus become self-divided, perversely recalcitrant, as Mr. Slope manifestly is, to their own instinctive longings for pleasure. Trollope develops this powerful proto-Freudian theme in scores of variations, ever more plainly identifying the neurotic estrangement from pleasure as a hallmark of modern life and as the central theme of serious modern comedy. This pathological syndrome takes its deep significance for Trollope in being intimately linked to many of what he sees as the worthiest elements of his culture: its moral idealism, its cult of altruism, its romantic and chivalrous concept of love, among other things. His stories turn endlessly on this paradox—that is, on the extreme difficulty of making reliable discriminations between morbidity and authentic virtue. To do so, he realizes, calls for perfecting the most precise moral science and gathering the most extensive collection of data, and even then—unfortunately for moral certitude but fortunately for novelistic interest—particular cases are likely to seem baffling.

Trollope's characters do not passively absorb like sponges the puritanical phobia toward pleasure that pervades their environment, nor is it thrust upon them by unavoidable circumstances: their psyches seize upon it actively, for reasons that the stories subtly invite us to unravel. Almost invariably what we find or surmise at the core of such characters is some form of the self-hatred that Evangelical culture both foments and legitimizes. A couple of eloquent examples of this condition would be two of Trollope's most famous creations, Josiah Crawley and Lily Dale. Crawley, especially, sheds light on our theme. From the moment he appears on Trollope's horizon in *Framley Parsonage*, his role is that of an implacable enemy of pleasure. An inveterate opponent of hunting, which in his view "is in itself cruel, and leads to idleness and profligacy" (chap. 15), he eagerly takes on the role of Touchstone, rebuking his foxhunting fellow clergyman Mark Robarts for consorting with what Crawley brands "the vainest of worldly pleasure-seekers" (chap. 15). Applying the same standards to himself, he fiercely rejects any thought of worldly luxury for himself and even for his family, doing his best, for example, to prevent Lucy Robarts from giving his children her gift package of gingerbread-nuts, guava jelly, oranges, and sugarplums (chap. 22). Trollope sees authentic nobility in Crawley's almost apostolic virtue, but sees him at the same time, and no less clearly, as a deeply neurotic personality whose denial of pleasure is the symptom of nothing more elevated than a "feeling of disgrace that he was poor" (chap. 22). He wars against pleasure (as we come to understand) because he feels that he himself does not deserve any, and he boasts of his privations, with a neurotic illogic that renders him an irresistibly comic figure as well as a nearly tragic one, as signs of moral superiority. What emerges most clearly from Trollope's elaborate, always paradoxical analysis of Crawley, in which the traditional comic schema is absorbed altogether into psychological diagnostic work, is the principle that in order to accept pleasure one needs first to be able to accept oneself.

Much the same thesis underlies the fable of Lily Dale's slide into masochistic old-maidism in *The Small House at Allington* and *The Last Chronicle of Barset* following her jilting by Adolphus Crosbie: having suffered this debasing trauma, she thinks too little of herself ever after to feel entitled to pleasure, and thus gravitates toward a life of neurotic self-denial. That critics have praised her for her high-minded fidelity to Crosbie's memory (Terry, p. 84; Harvey, p. 61) is the sign of the persistent and insidious resemblance between certain moral ideals and the syndrome of morbid refusal of pleasure—a resemblance especially likely to perplex Victorian readers. The result, in any case, is a viciously circular predicament, since pleasure cannot simply be taken by characters like this as a kind of medicine for their illness: they must be willing to accept pleasure ahead of time, but this acceptance can only be induced, it seems, by some liberating influx of pleasure. Just how lethal this paradox is, is the lesson of the deepening morbidity of the latter phase of Lily Dale's story, and it is the central theme, as we shall see, in *Miss Mackenzie* and *The Belton Estate*.

As the two examples of Crawley and Lily bear witness, then, in Trollope's fiction pleasure ultimately is conceived in nothing less than salvational terms, as the remedy for despair. To be estranged from pleasure is both the sign and the cause of losing hope in one's life, of being deprived, that is, of a sense of personal value. The outcome of this state in Trollope's world is isolation, for the breakdown of the ego necessarily implies—is almost identical with—the breakdown of bonds with others; personal inhibitions of the kind that we are discussing always have, therefore, a strong social reverberation (in fact, Trollope's usual method is to portray in detail the social consequences and to let us infer from them their psychic origins). The affirmation of pleasure, by the same token, always signifies for Trollope some form of social reintegration. In this, his fiction steadily expresses comedy's fundamental Malinowskian insight into the bonding powers of pleasure.

From Trollope's image of morbid self-deniers and pleasure-refusers arises the complementary image of the active pleasure-seeker who finds pleasure to be, after all, maddeningly elusive, and suffers as a result all the same painful consequences. Trollope returns constantly to this second type, keeping the theme of the complexities of the pleasure urge in the foreground of his fiction. Various novels pose the problem in terms that potentially jeopardize the whole program of comedy, hinting that a self-contradiction may lie at the heart of the pleasure principle itself, such that to long for pleasure is to be prevented from attaining it, and that to attain it is to empty it of value. "Perhaps the only pleasure left to the very rich is that of thinking of the deprivations of the poor," he remarks in passing in *Ayala's Angel* (chap. 5). Much the same idea is formulated in the scene of Harry Clavering's dinner at the Burtons'. Mr. Burton has just voiced a wistful longing for a life all of after-dinner enjoyment:

> "And all old port?" said Jones.
> "Yes, and all old port. You are not such an ass as to suppose that a man in suggesting to himself a continuance of pleasure suggests to himself also the evils which are supposed to accompany such pleasure. If I took too much of the stuff I should get cross and sick, and make a beast of myself; but then what a pity it is that it should be so."
> "You wouldn't like much of it, I think," said his wife.
> "That is it," said he. "We are driven to work because work never palls on us, whereas pleasure always does. What a wonderful scheme it is when one looks at it all. No man can follow pleasure long continually. When a man strives to do so, he turns his pleasure at once into a business, and works at that." [6]

Burton's disenchanted view, with its stress on the inevitable unsatisfaction of pleasure and its degrading effect if indulged in too freely, and then on the restorative virtue of hard work, clearly poses a threat to the comic ethic that Trollope elsewhere endorses more unconditionally. If one doubted that Trollope's strong focus on the issue of pleasure is partly a sign of his own deep-running ambivalence on this subject, the above passage should make the point clear. Usually, though, his frustrated pleasure-seekers are of a different kind from Burton, and testify not to a necessary revulsion from pleasure but to forms of personal disablement that bring upon them the most terrible and macabre doom that this novelist can conceive: the state of ardently craving pleasure but being incapable of attaining it.

Mr. Scarborough's Family, for example, is a kind of parodic anti-comedy, and as such is continuously concerned with the darker implications of the pleasure principle. There is a Mr. Baskerville, an idle gentleman of pleasure who is an image of stark ennui. Before the opening of the hunting season "Mr. Baskerville amused himself as well as he could by lying in bed or playing lawn-tennis. He sometimes dined at the hotel in order that the club might think that he was entertained at friends' houses; but the two places were nearly the same to him. . . . A more empty existence, or, one would be inclined to say, less pleasurable, no one could pass" (chap. 6). Recreation evidently needs a more sharply stimulating character than this, needs to be impelled by a sharper desire, if it is not to lead to lethal boredom and deterioration—though the problem is inescapably circular. Another kind of deprivation of pleasure is seen in the same novel in Peter Prosper, the reluctant and abstemious lover in the buffo subplot, who is horrified by his prospective bride's taste for such "unchequered delights" as a pony carriage, champagne, and despatched crabs (chap. 27). But these and other probings of the problematics of pleasure in this novel are merely framing elements for the study of Mountjoy Scarborough, whose self-destructive addiction to the excitement of gambling forms one of Trollope's grimmest images of the taste for pleasure and stimulation gone haywire and turned into a curse. When he is in the grip of his "irrepressible desire for gambling," it is "as though his throat were parched with an implacable thirst" (chap. 41). Mountjoy is that horrifying negation of comic man, the man incapable of tasting pleasure.

The pursuit of pleasure has gone more subtly awry in the case of Mr. Maurice Maule, an aging, idle man-about-town in *Phineas Redux*. The curious thing about Trollope's half-scandalous devotion to pleasure is that it had to coexist in him with a positively Carlylean regard for the virtues of hard work; and in Mr. Maule we have a classic Victorian image—one evidently modeled, in fact, directly upon Dickens's villainous Sir John Chester in *Barnaby Rudge*[7]—of the corrupting effect of idleness. Except for being stricken with "the curse of misusing his time," Mr. Maule has the look of a comic devotee of pleasure and "the good things of this world." "He became an idler, a man of luxury, and then a spendthrift. He was now hardly beyond middle life, and he assumed for himself the character of a man of taste. He loved music, and pictures, and books, and pretty women. He loved also good eating and drinking; but conceived of himself that in his love for them he was an artist, and not a glutton" (chap. 21). The scalpel-sharp irony of this passage hints that the man is a glutton for pleasure because his love of it is really feigned or "assumed," not genuine—and that he is thus at bottom just an elaborately disguised variant of that morbid antipathy to pleasure that we have discussed. He pursues pleasure so fiercely, and on so many fronts, for the same reason that Josiah Crawley so fiercely condemns it: because they both are incapable of experiencing it. Thus he is condemned to Trollope's comic version of the torments of Tantalus, in which comic limberness, deprived of its vital principle, becomes a state of inanition and helpless drift.

> He had not been near his property for the last ten years,
> and as he was addicted to no country sport there were ten
> weeks in the year which were terrible to him. From the
> middle of August to the end of October for him there was
> no whist, no society, —it may almost be said no dinner.
> He had tried going to the seaside; he had tried going to
> Paris; he had endeavoured to enjoy Switzerland and the
> Italian lakes; —but all had failed, and he had acknowledged
> to himself that this sad period of the year must always be
> endured without relaxation, and without comfort.
>
> (Chap. 21)

His one overriding and authentic sensation is torment. He is, in particular, "tormented with the ambition of a splendid marriage," but at a deeper level Mr. Maule is tormented by an awareness of the perishability of his putative pleasures, and of himself. So the guiding scheme of life of this would-be voluptuary is in fact to deprive himself of the slightest self-indulgence, for fear of hastening the onset of old age.

> After dinner he would occasionally play another rubber;
> but twelve o'clock always saw him back into his own
> rooms. No one knew better than Mr. Maule that the
> continual bloom of lasting summer which he affected
> requires great accuracy in living. Late hours, nocturnal
> cigars, and midnight drinkings, pleasurable though they
> may be, consume too quickly the free-flowing lamps of
> youth, and are fatal at once to the husbanded candle-ends
> of age.
>
> (Chap. 21)

Like Lizzie Eustace's, Mr. Maule's indolent pleasure-loving existence is a grotesque illusion. Similarly blighted characters whose single-minded devotion to pleasure hints at its agonizing elusiveness for them would include, for example, the Marquis of Brotherton in *Is He Popenjoy?*, a querulous, malignant, broken-down Italianate debauchee who has finished, as A. O. J. Cockshut nicely observes (p. 25), in a state of anesthesia, unable to feel anything except a surprising touch of spiritual despair, or the sybaritic Count Pateroff in *The Claverings*.

"Slowly the count ate his dinner, enjoying every morsel that he took with that thoughtful, conscious pleasure which young men never attain in eating and drinking, and which men as they grow older so often forget to acquire. But the count never forgot any of his own capacities for pleasure, and in all things made the most of his own resources" (chap. 14). The undertone of repressed anxiety in such intense absorption in his own "capacities for pleasure" comes to the surface in Count Pateroff's fantastical discourse on what he declares to be the most pathetic of all men, "the man who cannot digest," the pleasure-lover whose own system forever denies him his pleasure—clearly the doom that this voluptuary lives in perpetual dread of. "The angel with the flaming sword which turned two ways," he cries, "was indigestion!" (chap. 19). Pateroff is another witness to the truth of the proposition that "no man can follow pleasure long continually."

In almost obsessively exploring through such characters the psychic and spiritual dilemmas of pleasure, focusing on subtle dysfunctions of personality, Trollope is projecting traditional elements of comedy into a new mode, exposing them to a modern analysis. His persistent note of disenchantment with pleasure and dissolute pleasure-seekers reflects, too, an incurable moral ambivalence, for at heart he is a severe Victorian moralist determined to uphold a stringent code of what one of his young ne'er-do-wells nonchalantly calls "wisdom and prudence and virtue and self-denial" (*Popenjoy*, chap. 33). Too much has sometimes been made by Trollope's critics of his tolerance and flexibility, his affection even for disreputable characters, his willingness to see all sides of moral issues, his hesitancy to pass judgment. It is true that he believes less in flagrant evil (which usually, as in the cases of Brotherton, Augustus Melmotte, or Lopez in *The Prime Minister*, he associates with near insanity) than in mere laxness, in subtle unravelings of moral fiber that are not inconsistent with good intentions or with personal charm. Trollope's studies of such processes yield characters like Adolphus Crosbie, the philanderer Colonel Osborne of *He Knew He Was Right*, Nathaniel Sowerby of *Framley Parsonage*, or George Hotspur of *Sir Harry Hotspur of Humblethwaite*. Such characters may bear little resemblance to the melodramatic villains of other Victorian novelists, but they are genuinely despicable nonetheless, and one trait they have in common is their self-indulgent love of pleasure. By the same token, Trollope perplexingly insists that authentic nobility of character will most likely be found, after all, not among the worldly or those who think that "pleasure [is] the one object of life" but among crabbed, intolerant, sometimes narrow-minded ascetics like the austere curate Mr. Saul in *The Claverings*, Josiah Crawley, Sir Peregrine Orme in *Orley Farm*, or Plantagenet Palliser—the last three, we should

material cares, "always thinking of his money" (chap. 6). The prospects for comedy seem dim indeed in this gray realistic world that appears to be ruled implacably by the laws of cause and effect, which in comedy exist only to be gaily flouted. The subversive intent of Trollope's design for this novel is signaled by the chorus of protests that it provoked from reviewers, who condemned its "monstrously prosaic" realism (Smalley, 221), repeatedly exclaiming, as I have noticed above, that "nobody but Mr. Trollope would have dared" to attempt a novel in which the usual formulas of entertainment are so grossly violated.

The novel does not begin as a comedy, then; rather, it progressively becomes one. How does this movement reveal itself? For one thing, in the unfolding structure of the plot, which, in accordance with the patterned choreography proper to comedy, involves the heroine's being caught up in a merry *ronde* of marriage proposals from no fewer than four suitors (the joke taking some of its spice, of course, from her being supposedly so unsuited to the role of romantic heroine). Also we observe Trollope slowly assembling onstage an array of subtly hyperbolic characters whose chief function, in effect, is precisely to assert the claims of a literary mode seemingly disavowed from the start. The subtlety needs to be stressed, for the "humor" characters of *Miss Mackenzie* are so close to realistic character studies that it requires a fairly sharp eye to detect them for what they really are. Mr. Rubb the oilcloth manufacturer, for example, is the real Mr. Collins of this novel, and the scene in which he makes a spectacle of himself by wearing yellow kid gloves to a tea party (chap. 11) ought to remind one of the scene in *Pride and Prejudice* where Collins displays his own vulgarity at the Netherfield ball (chap. 18), not to mention the ludicrous apparition of Malvolio in yellow stockings cross-gartered (*Twelfth Night*, 3.4). Yet Rubb is not a mere buffoon but a complex, nuanced character with a significant inner life: he challenges the oft-asserted rule that comic characters are necessarily two-dimensional abstractions. More elemental comic types are found, however, among the Evangelicals of this novel, notably Mr. Stumfold, the urbanely jocular clergyman, Mrs. Stumfold, his tyrannical wife, and especially the unctuous, squint-eyed curate Mr. Maguire, one of Trollope's funniest and most scurrilous libels on the Low Church. This gathering of increasingly outrageous "humor" figures tells us that we are escaping the gravitational field of ordinary reality and entering into the world of stylized gamelike inventions where comic values prevail and where laughter is the breath of life. And as these effigies of comedy glide complacently into view, the story, in obedience to the essential thematics of comedy, comes to focus ever more intently upon the central issue of the legitimacy of pleasure.

At first the issue seems to take perfectly straightforward form. The pathos of Margaret Mackenzie's life prior to the opening of the story is that her self-devotion to duty and self-abnegation have left her life utterly destitute of enjoyment; she daydreams about fashionable and exciting new worlds open to her as a result of her inheritance (chap. 1), and the prospects of comic action seem plain. Trollope's device for bringing out his theme in high relief is to move his unlikely heroine to Jane-Austen-land, to "Littlebath," a move from solitude to society that itself is emblematic of the comic pattern. Littlebath society, it turns out, is sharply divided along the lines of the classic polarity of comedy into two irreconcilable factions: the strait-laced Evangelicals and their antagonists, the worldly pleasure-seekers, given to all the innocent amusements of such a place: cards, balls, flirtations. That we are in the very sphere of the comic and its animating myth of worlds devoted solely to pleasure should be apparent to any reader—though it is noteworthy that the reviewers, whose whole critical apparatus for describing fiction centered on the idea of verisimilitude, gave no sign of being aware that *Miss Mackenzie* was anything other than an exercise in (rather unsavory) realism.

Conventional as it undoubtedly is, Trollope's study of the Littlebath Evangelicals carries a shrewd analysis of the sabotaging of pleasure in Victorian society. Mr. Maguire is a familiar bogey, the stridently hypocritical warrior against worldly pleasure whose own heart seethes with ill-disguised lust and cupidity. His appalling squint in one eye is the emblem of his moral crookedness, and by its flagrant obviousness it serves to make us aware of how perversely willing his admirers must be to acquiesce in his aggression upon them. Mr. Stumfold, on the other hand, represents a far cannier style of manipulation. "He was always fighting the devil by opposing those pursuits which are the life and mainstay of such places as Littlebath. His chief enemies were card-playing and dancing as regarded the weaker sex, and hunting and horse-racing . . . as regarded the stronger. . . . But not on this account should it be supposed that Mr. Stumfold was a dreary, dark, sardonic man. Such was by no means the case" (chap. 2). Knowing his reputation for hostility to Littlebath worldliness, Miss Mackenzie is taken aback by his vivacious manner and gentlemanly ways. He gives pleasant entertainments for his (mostly female) followers, and in his speech is almost irreverent and playful: "he spoke of St. Paul as Paul, declaring the saint to have been a good fellow" (chap. 4). In the words of Trollope's narrator, it is this "aptitude for feminine rakishness" that is the secret of Stumfold's popularity and influence, and the point of this finely calibrated satire is to suggest just how insidious the subversion of pleasure may be in skillful hands, especially when taboo erotic life can be displaced onto some other more respectable form of stimulation. Stumfold has grasped Freud's insight that "the ascetic current of Christianity" actually inflames the libido, so he cunningly defuses the libido by allowing a bit of titillation to the members of his flock—but only on the condition of their enslavement to him (and to his brutally tyrannical wife) and of their wholly repudiating the realer, more robust pleasures of freedom and the assembly rooms. Trollope here devises comedy of an altogether Blakean insight into the "soft deceitful wiles" by which puritan repression does its sinister work. It is also a classic insight of comedy, which has always recognized puritans, as Quicksilver says in *Eastward Ho*, to be "the smoothest and slickest knaves in a country" (2.2.184–85).

In fullblown comedy, pleasure is euphoric because it carries no conditions; it is the pleasure of holiday. But *Miss Mackenzie* alters comic formulas and shows Trollope at his usual work, injecting modern awareness into old-fashioned patterns, by finding that her impulse to pleasure is harder to realize than she had thought. In spite of her own strong temptation toward "the pleasures of iniquity" (chap. 4), she doesn't dare to put her name down at the assembly rooms, "where they dance and play cards, and where the girls flirt and the young men make fools of themselves" (chap. 3), and she determines to turn a cold shoulder to an interesting suitor "because," as the narrator says, succinctly defining the theme, "she preferred the proprieties of life to its pleasures" (chap. 5). There is a discovery made here that is foreign to the usual design of comedy: the discovery that something within Miss Mackenzie herself, the legacy (as we are left to infer for ourselves) of her early deprivations and her education in self-repression, is inimical to the very pleasure that she seeks in order to leave her past behind. By this displacement of the dramatic crux from external "blocking" characters to the heroine's own inhibitions, Trollope seems to be turning his embryonic comedy into psychological drama before our eyes. Hence the intensity of feeling that arises, for example, in one remarkable scene where the heroine studies herself in a mirror and glimpses a possibility of rejuvenation and a reawakening to pleasure, erotic pleasure in particular. She finds that her hair, despite a few grey strands, is soft and silky still, that her eyes are bright and her cheeks still have a bloom of youth. "She pulled her scarf tighter across her bosom, feeling her own form, and then she leaned forward and kissed herself in the glass" (chap. 9). In its depth and complexity of feeling, this image shows how far the usual playful ambience of comedy has been contaminated in this novel. For Elizabeth Bennet, for Falstaff, for Mosca, pleasure is as natural and effortless as breathing; for Miss Mackenzie, who is being astutely used by her creator to define the precise fault line between comedy and the world of realistic drama, pleasure is deeply problematic, fraught with anxieties, snarled in psychosomatic disabilities. "I wish I dared to do what I pleased!" she exclaims (chap. 9).

Strongly psychologized as it thus is, we recognize the comic pattern of *Miss Mackenzie* in the persistence with which Trollope identifies pleasure as a *social* function. This is the principle implicitly holding together various apparently extraneous materials in the novel. For example, the absurd dinner party given by Mrs. Tom Mackenzie in chapter 8 may seem like nothing but a humorous digression, but its image of pleasure spoiled by snobbish pretension and rigid, chafing protocol is meant to suggest the possibility of that species of pleasure produced by social arrangements in tune, as they ought to be, with naturalness and refinement. The book stresses this implication in a series of parallel episodes of social occasions transformed, generally by aggressive egoism, into moments of strain and mortification: the elaborately orchestrated soirées at the Stumfolds', the ghastly charity bazaar at the end (chap. 27), or the ill-starred party at Miss Todd's, made excruciating (and hilarious) by the pushy, uncouth presences of Mr. Maguire and Mr. Rubb. In one passage that crystallizes the comic argument, Mr. Rubb compliments his hostess on having done away with "stiffness and formality, and all that kind of thing"; it is a relief, he declares, to have dispensed with "that horrid decorum."

> "There's nothing I hate like decorum. It prevents people knowing each other, and being jolly and happy together. Now, the French know more about society than any people, and I'm told they have none of it. . . . It's given up to them that they've got rid of it altogether," said Mr. Rubb.
>
> "Who have got rid of what?" asked Miss Todd, who saw that her friend [Miss Baker] was rather dismayed by the tenor of Mr. Rubb's conversation.
>
> "The French have got rid of decorum," said Mr. Rubb.
>
> "Altogether, I believe," said Miss Todd.
>
> "Of course they have. It's given up to them that they have. They're the people that know how to live!"
>
> (Chap. 11)

The funny exchange brings out Rubb's buffoonery (one recalls Mr. Bennet asking malicious leading questions to Mr. Collins) but also is linked to the idea running through the novel, and throughout Trollope, of ideal, delightful society in which decorum and spontaneity, formalized order and individual "limberness," are perfectly harmonized, not adversaries as Rubb supposes, but functions of one another.

Thus, pleasure is strongly identified in *Miss Mackenzie* with possibilities of decorous society, even though such society is not much in evidence. But this theme is ever more clearly subordinated to the theme of Margaret Mackenzie's painful quest for self-discovery; and as the novel thus becomes more and more inward, its aura of comedy markedly recedes. As in the cases of Josiah Crawley and Lily Dale, Trollope stresses that it is his heroine's self-dislike that cuts her off from real pleasure, especially erotic pleasure: at heart, says the narrator, "she despised herself, thinking herself to be too mean for a man's love" (chap. 11). Like Esther Summerson, Amy Dorrit, and other important mid-Victorian heroines, Miss Mackenzie becomes an essay in the insidious linkage between self-sacrificing goodness and deep damage to the ego. This linkage is highlighted, for example, as Miss Mackenzie arrives at the bedside of her mortally ill brother. "There are women," says the narrator, "who seem to have an absolute pleasure in fixing themselves for business by the bed-side of a sick man" (chap. 14). The hint of something vampirish lying hungrily concealed within the figure of the ministering Victorian angel is not developed here by Trollope, but the point about the grim perversion of the pleasure principle by a mood of self-sacrifice is as emphatic as possible. It helps us better understand the deep psychological dynamic of the story, and why Miss Mackenzie, turning down younger, more ardent suitors, gravitates ever more strongly to the "ruined, wretched, moody" (chap. 17) John Ball.

What Trollope attempts in this novel, in other words, is the risky literary exercise of discovering how far Jane Austen's mode of comedy can be stretched to accommodate the distinctive materials of modern fiction, its melancholy view of character and its atmosphere of what Matthew Arnold called "spiritual discomfort." The focus falls ever more steadily upon the dismaying realization that the heroine has become permanently incapacitated for any full experience of enjoyment. The novel thus emerges as something considerably more problematic, I would say, than the "comedy of rebirth" that it is rather hyperbolically styled by James R. Kincaid (p. 86), though he is clearly on the right track. Whatever "magical regaining of youth" that Miss Mackenzie experiences in the course of her story is in fact very sharply limited by Trollope. Her morose and reluctant fifty-year-old suitor, having long neglected her despite their engagement, is finally nudged by her aristocratic protectress into proposing anew and she accepts "thankfully, quietly, and with an enduring satisfaction, as it became such a woman to do" (chap. 30); but the tone is muted and all suggestions of a magic transformation are carefully avoided by Trollope. As we shall discuss in chapter 5, transformations of character are hardly to be looked for in the world of Trollope's fiction. What *is* reborn in this comedy, albeit in only a qualified form, is comedy itelf.

The agent of this process is Margaret Mackenzie's cousin, Mrs. Walter Mackenzie of Cavendish Square, who surges into our heroine's story at the lowest point of her fortunes with the epiphanic suddenness and the concentrated benignity of a fairy godmother—or rather, of the Comic Spirit in flesh and blood. (She fills exactly the same role in this respect as do such other vivacious emanations of comedy as Mrs. Patty Cornbury in *Rachel Ray* or Lady Harriet in Elizabeth Gaskell's *Wives and Daughters*.) "The Mackenzies," as Margaret finds when she goes to stay with them, "were people who went much into society, and received company frequently at their own house" (chap. 26). In a novel that emphasizes so strongly the pernicious effects of solitude and self-suppression, Mrs. Mackenzie's witty, sophisticated, unashamed devotion to worldly pleasure amounts to a message of salvation. In what she calls Margaret's "dowdiness and gloom" she sees not the trappings of self-denying virtue but only a morbid avoidance of enjoyment. "Do you know," she says to Margaret's reluctant suitor Sir John Ball,

> "I fancy she has a liking for pretty things at heart as well as another woman."
> "I hope she has," said he.
> "Of course you do. What is a woman worth without it? Don't be angry, Margaret, but I say a woman is worth nothing without it, and Sir John will agree with me if he knows anything about the matter."
>
> (Chap. 27)

Mrs. Mackenzie thus gives voice, with a clear awareness of setting forth an important doctrine, to that strong endorsement of ordinary vanity and other petty vices that is the hallmark of one strain of comedy and the key to its deep humanity. We can guess that the impression of sordidness so troubling to the novel's reviewers came ultimately from the book's articulate contradicting of that ethic of self-sacrifice and angelic high-mindedness that Victorians were so accustomed to equate with virtue, and that Trollope presents here as saturated with neurosis. Mrs. Mackenzie, who understands the effectiveness of pleasure as an antibiotic against fanaticism and morbidity, fits Margaret, against her wishes, with "the gayest, lightest, jauntiest, falsest, most make-believe mourning bonnet that ever sprang from the art of a designer in bonnets" (chap. 27) and gives her shrewd instruction in the wiles of mating strategy: "No man wishes to marry a dowdy, you know," she says (chap. 29). Her intervention having once brought about the union of the unlikely couple, Mrs. Mackenzie superintends the scene, done with elaborate comic choreography, in which the rascally Maguire is finally driven in confusion from the stage, to vollies of laughter from his former victims (chap. 29). The servant who carries notes back and forth, we are told, "enjoyed the play" immensely. "Such a game as we've had up!" he says to the coachman that afternoon in the kitchen (chap. 29).

Thus Margaret is transported at the end of her novel rather abruptly, thanks to her determined protectress, back into the domain of comedy, where life is a game and the gratification of pleasure the prevailing fact of existence. Trollope's bold novelistic scheme is not perhaps a complete success: the novel's shiftings of mode are a distraction, even though they signal the author's willingness to explore and to experiment with the structures of comedy in provocative ways, and even though, in a sense, they are what *Miss Mackenzie* is about. Trollope is endeavoring to treat comedy not as a static, monolithic design, but as a flexible form that registers in its various distortions the force of cultural pressures being exerted upon it—particularly that of the insidious assault upon pleasure that for Trollope is central to the damaging of personality in his era. What he shows most clearly in this novel is that modern personalities like Margaret's and John Ball's are so deeply estranged from pleasure that they cannot through their own energies bring comic action about; this can only happen through the intervention of outside agencies like Mrs. Mackenzie, and can only be felt as a violation of the central logic of the story. It is perfectly clear that John Ball, who never evinces the slightest sexual interest in Margaret, would never have married her if he had been left to his own devices, and that the novel in that case would have turned at last into a kind of tragedy. This, we feel, is the way the story really ended.

Cold and Warmth: "The Belton Estate"

Especially at the beginning, Trollope fills *The Belton Estate* with such amounts of "realistic" chill and gloom that comic pleasure seems again almost to be out of the question. The tale begins with the suicide of Clara Amedroz's older brother and then dwells deeply on the grief, remorse, and bitter anxieties of Clara's querulous widower father (a more poignant version of Jane Austen's Mr. Woodhouse in *Emma*, it seems). Two of the main episodes in the subsequent plot are the deaths and funerals of Mrs. Winterfield, Clara's aunt, and of Mr. Amedroz himself. We hear along the way of the death in delerium tremens of the alcoholic first husband of Clara's friend Mrs. Askerton (chap. 14) and of the ceaseless physical pain endured by Will Belton's humpbacked sister Mary (chap. 13). In her lack of vivaciousness, Clara—like Margaret Mackenzie, past the prime of youth—is the opposite of the kind of lightfooted heroine who traditionally presides over the world of comedy. "It seemed to her that she was used to be in the house with death, and that the sadness and solemn ceremonies of woe were becoming things familiar to her. There grew upon her a feeling that it must be so with her always" (chap. 22). Giving imaginative resonance to this feeling, one of the prevailing images in this (for Trollope) unusually visual novel is that of the heroine brooding in darkened, cold rooms in empty houses. Everything in *The Belton Estate* thus seems to deny the possibility of the spirit symbolized in Margaret Mackenzie's jaunty, perfidious mourning bonnet. As in the case of *Miss Mackenzie*, contemporary reviewers exclaimed in chorus about the pungency of Trollope's realism, some even claiming again—the reproach that Trollope constantly incurred—that he had carried it so far as to be shockingly indecorous ("it is worth considering," intoned a writer in the *Saturday Review*, "whether there is not such a thing as a realism that is sordid and pitiful": Smalley, 263). What is this, in short, if not a novel constructed systematically on principles adverse to comedy?

An observant reader is likely to be surprised, then, by the pattern of sly allusions that Trollope develops once again to his great model, the North Star of his navigation in comedy, *Pride and Prejudice*. Lady Catherine de Bourgh comes to life again as Lady Aylmer, Clara's tyrannical prospective mother-in-law, and Mary Belton is recognizable as a version of Miss Darcy. But the central analogy with Jane Austen's novel has to do with the entail hovering over both the Amedroz and the Bennet households. As in *Pride and Prejudice*, *The Belton Estate* begins with the unknown heir writing to invite himself to visit the house he is due to inherit, and then, once on the scene, deciding to make up for the harshness of the entail by marrying the daughter. It will be recalled that Mr. Collins is only momentarily blocked by finding that Jane Bennet, the eldest, is to all intents and purposes engaged. Faced with this annoying inconvenience, he displays comic limberness to a high degree. "Mr. Collins had only to change from Jane to Elizabeth— and it was soon done—done while Mrs. Bennet was stirring the fire" (chap. 15). Will Belton is scarcely less impulsive in deciding to propose to Clara. "After much consideration—very much consideration, a consideration which took him the whole time that he was brushing his hair and washing his teeth, —he resolved that he would . . . speak to Mr. Amedroz" (chap. 4). These and other reminiscences of *Pride and Prejudice* carry a promise of fidelity to comic form and underline the repetitiousness that is integral to it. Comedies eternally repeat one another—and then make us laugh at the spectacle of characters repeating themselves. But the repetition here, needless to say, is accompanied by a sharp twist, for in place of the pompous egotistical fool that is Mr. Collins, ruddy-faced, convivial Will Belton, with his radi-

ant aura of good humor, is the Comic Spirit (or one form of it) personified, and his arrival at the Amedrozes' decaying house (like Collins's
arrival at the Bennets', for that matter) has again that unmistakably
epiphanic quality that comic action tends to generate. His name contains a significant pun, for he single-handedly overturns all the por-
tents of tragic realism and recreates the novel as a comedy by sheer
force of will, against all odds.

At the same time, Trollope stresses the *effortlessness* of everything
that the omnipotent Will accomplishes. "His will [is] so masterful, his
strength so great" (chap. 22) that problems dissolve in his presence.
He restores order to the mismanaged Belton estate with almost magical ease on the first morning of his visit, before Mr. Amedroz is out of
bed (chap. 3), and then sets out at once on his longer-term project of
redeeming Clara from her barren, isolated life by the magic of love
and sex. The eventual success of this project, too, is a foregone conclusion, signaled as it is by the narrator's frequent hints and repeatedly predicted by Clara's perceptive friend Mrs. Askerton. In disarming suspense in this way Trollope breaks recklessly with the usual
formula of success in popular fiction, especially in the "sensational-
istic" 1860s, when novelists were taxing their ingenuity to devise ways
of keeping readers wrought up to the highest possible pitch of anxious excitement (Tillotson, "The Lighter Reading"). Reviewers accordingly complained of the lack of dramatic excitement in this novel that
leaves readers, as Henry James declares in a malicious review, not
"thrilled . . . or deeply moved in any way" (Smalley, 255). Another reviewer, objecting that Clara chooses the right man and rejects the
wrong one far too easily, goes so far as to suggest for the author's
benefit little scenarios of how he might have filled out his story so as
to generate "real mental struggle in the mind of his heroine" (ibid.,
260). For better or for worse, Trollope chooses to forego this kind of
interest in *The Belton Estate* in order to make the outlines and the underlying structure of a certain comic myth stand out with pristine
clarity, and to stress in particular the role played in it by Will Belton.
Considered as a revision of its immediate predecessor *Miss Mackenzie*,
the present novel centers upon the restoration of the comic hero, seen
in so drastically attenuated a form in John Ball, to all his ancient
potency.

The state of affairs that Will encounters when he arrives in Somer-
setshire is that of the comic paradigm turned inside-out: instead of a
pleasure-world, the novel evokes the image of a world suffering a
nearly total eclipse of pleasure. One source of this condition in *The
Belton Estate* is a strain of puritanical seriousness and austerity that
Trollope again represents as deeply woven into the fabric of Victorian
social life and thus of individual experience. Clara's Perivale aunt,

Mrs. Winterfield, a figure of severe Low Church piety, devotes her whole life to opposing pleasure. "Life at Perivale," we are told, "was a very serious thing. As regards amusement, ordinarily so called, the need of any such institution was not acknowledged" (chap. 1). Clara's aunt, an inveterate enemy of "cards and supper parties" (chap. 10), derives her sole enjoyment, of a strongly masochistic kind, attending church three times a day, where she suffers "from cold in winter, from cough in spring, from heat in summer, and from rheumatism in autumn" (chap. 7). The atmosphere of self-punishment is much the same at Aylmer Park (an ironically perverted version of Jane Austen's Pemberley), "a country house in which people neither read, nor flirt, nor gamble, nor smoke, nor have resort to the excitement of any special amusement" (chap. 26). Here the problem is the lethal combination of aristocratic pretentiousness and restricted means rather than Evangelical piety, but the result, the deliberate, systematic suppression of enjoyment, is just the same—hinting that the barrenness of pleasure in this society is an endemic condition almost independent of particular causes. Thus "Lady Aylmer contented herself with receiving little or no company, and with stingy breakfasts and bad dinners for herself and her husband and daughter" (chap. 17). Miss Aylmer, who drops a life's correspondence with a friend in Italy to spare the cost of postage, has "no pleasures" (chap. 17) and seems indeed, like a number of others in this story, to embrace this condition with a perverse gratification. Her father, the henpecked Sir Anthony Aylmer, whose life is "not very attractive," presents an even more grotesquely humorous picture of the effects on personality of a deprivation of all pleasure. "He had been fond of good dinners and good wine," says the narrator, focusing with his usual keenness on signs of deranged libido, "and still, on occasions, would make attempts at enjoyment in that line; but the gout and Lady Aylmer together were too many for him, and he had but small opportunity for filling up the blanks of his existence out of the kitchen or cellar. . . . He took some pleasure in standing, with two sticks on the top of the steps before his own front door, and railing at any one who came in his way" (chap. 17). In such an ambience as this, the search for pleasure necessarily takes on a desperate, self-destructive cast, as we see in the case of Mrs. Askerton's first husband, the one who drinks himself to death, and especially in the tragic story of Clara's older brother, who sinks into hopeless dissoluteness—largely gambling and, apparently, womanizing—before killing himself. In *Miss Mackenzie* libido has pathetically decayed; here it seems impacted, dangerously bottled up, thus prone to violent outbreaks.

As I have suggested, *The Belton Estate* seems intent on tracing the deep foundations of comedy; in accordance with this impulse,

Trollope is led in this novel to express comedy's fundamental advocacy of pleasure in the clearest possible, indeed in militant, terms. In one noteworthy passage, for instance, the narrator intervenes to contradict directly, and in sweeping terms, Mrs. Winterfield's puritanical scorn of the world. Significantly, "the world" refers here to another sphere than that of high society. "But if she was right, . . . then why has the world been made so pleasant? Why is the fruit of the earth so sweet; and the trees,—why are they so green . . . ? Why are women so lovely?" (chap. 7). Seen with unperverse vision, this novel asserts, proclaiming the doctrine of comedy, the world before us is a sheer invitation to pleasure, and not to respond to it is akin to mental illness. What is striking in the above passage, however, is the way it absorbs the idea of pleasure into an invocation of natural fruitfulness and beauty, and this is exactly what occurs, in a fashion not at all characteristic of Trollope, throughout the novel. The love story and the comedy of contemporary manners in *The Belton Estate* are everywhere attached to metaphors of nature, and we are constantly reminded that the essential drama of this novel is the mythic drama of sterility versus fertility. We are thus reminded of comedy's presumed ancient origins in fertility ceremonies, the deep structure of which, Trollope suggests, is latent even in worldly comedies like *Miss Mackenzie*. It is to throw this structure into the highest possible relief that Trollope does everything he can to deemphasize the overt, dramatic content of this strange novel, reducing plot and characterization to a near minimum, and almost perversely undercutting the dramatic interest of the scanty story line that he does provide.

The terms of the novel's dominant symbolism, then, are cold, barrenness, and death, and their opposites: warmth, fertility, and life. Hence, for one thing, the strong correlation of the love story with the seasonal cycle, the happy union occurring, it is hardly necessary to say, "about the middle of the pleasant month of May" (chap. 30)—another device stressing the natural inevitability of the story's happy ending. Hence too Trollope's pattern of suggestions of the myth of the Waste Land, of a poisoned, dying, fractured, wintry world. At the opening of the story only "remnants" remain of the Amedroz family, and Clara's father is sinking into hypochondria and decrepitude; the estate is burdened with debt and rapidly being laid waste by brutal haycutting and mismanagement. The town of Perivale is likewise in the grip of advanced decay—a spectacle that Mrs. Winterfield's Evangelical temperament finds deeply edifying, unlike Trollope's narrator (chap. 7). The book's comedy of manners is tied to this pattern by Trollope's deepening suggestions of a metaphoric identity between priggish respectability, the special satirical target of this novel, and the seasonal cold that is stressed obsessively throughout.[8] The cold season makes us think of the coldness of egoism and of "cold propriety" (chap. 29). Captain Aylmer especially is called "chilly hearted," or words to that effect, over and over by both the narrator and Will Belton ("a cold-blooded fish of a man, who thinks of nothing in the world but being respectable," says Will: chap. 20). "Coldness and formality" (chap. 27) thus become intimately associated with the novel's ubiquitous motifs of death and decay, and serve Trollope to create subtly macabre effects in which cold-heartedness is seen as amounting to actual death-in-life. Clara very strongly senses just this implication, for example, at funereal Aylmer Park. "Clara knew that the Aylmers were cold people. . . . But she had not expected to be so frozen by them as was the case with her now" (chap. 25); small wonder that she feels herself "cold and uncomfortable" (chap. 25) in such surroundings. By this point the ever-recurring adjective has acquired a sinister aura, and suggests that what the Aylmer connection signifies for Clara is death itself, in moral and psychological, and of course sexual, senses at least.

Will Belton appears on the scene, therefore, not just as a jolly fellow and bringer of pleasure but as a restorer of life itself: indeed, the word "life," with an ever-expanding range of connotations, is insistently associated with him. "There's so much life about him!" exclaims Clara (chap. 4), wondering at "the life which he had contrived in so short a time to throw into the old place" (chap. 6). Will is an expert farmer—fertility is his whole life's work—and his gift of a cow to Clara is exactly symbolic of the nourishing and fructifying function that he has been brought into the tale to perform. Ultimately he has been brought in to impregnate the heroine, a truth that most modern comedies, veiling their ancestral ties to fertility ceremonies, obscure, but that this one keeps alluding to slyly. "When he threw his seed corn into the earth," says the narrator, transcribing Will's thoughts, he would await the arrival of the crops without anxiety; "and he was now prepared to follow the same plan, with the same hopes, in this matter of his love-making" (chap. 4). The scene of his final acceptance by Clara reinforces a broad pattern of implications, then, by being explicitly treated as the enactment of a pagan rite of fertility, somewhat disrupted by Will's impatience to embrace his new fiancée: "She had anticipated that the high rock was to be the altar at which the victim was to be sacrificed; but now he would not wait till he had taken her to the sacred spot" (chap. 31). The ceremonial "sacrifice" that drives away sterility is almost too plain a figure for the imminent sexual consummation of this union. In conformity with this pattern of motifs and with the original logic of comedy, Clara, the sacrificial victim, by the end of the novel has immersed herself in the study of farming—and has given birth. Coldness and sterility have been routed, in other words, by the forces of fertility.

Pervasive as they are, however, these symbolic motifs never obscure the story's psychological immediacy or its focus on the cultural dynamics of the problem of pleasure. As in *Miss Mackenzie*, the heroine of this novel is first and foremost a perverse denier of her own libido. She at first falls in love with the cold, priggish Captain Aylmer, and only with difficulty comes at last to transfer her affections to Will Belton. The weird attractiveness that Captain Aylmer has for Clara was declared by one reviewer, mentioned above, to be entirely implausible, but this is hardly so, even though it sharply violates the decorous erotic patterns of most Victorian fiction. The point from the start—like all of Trollope's key points, it is never expressly stated—is that Clara's harsh, narrow life has given her, too, an active though wholly unconscious aversion to pleasure. "She did not dress young, or live much with young people, or correspond with other girls by means of crossed letters; nor expect that, for her, young pleasures should be provided. Life had always been serious with her" (chap. 1). When she refuses Will's first impulsive proposal of marriage it is, we are able to surmise, largely in obedience to her ingrained predisposition to make herself "serious, grave, and old" (chap. 11). The novel with wicked subtlety shows quite precisely that Clara's tendency to morbid self-denial and Sir Anthony Aylmer's grotesque disintegration of personality are after all closely coordinate phenomena, symptoms of a widespread famine of pleasure.

In several passages it suggests, too, that the perverseness of Clara's sex life is not just an isolated aberration but is to a large degree characteristic of modern women in general. This is taken for granted, for example, by Clara's friend Mrs. Askerton, an astute analyst of love, who comments trenchantly:

> Women are so cross-grained that it is a wonder to me that
> men should ever have anything to do with them. They
> have about them some madness of a phantasy which they
> dignify with the name of feminine pride, and under the
> cloak of this they believe themselves to be justified in
> tormenting their lovers' lives out. The only consolation is
> that they torment themselves as much.
>
> (Chap. 31)

Where, the novel incites us to ask, does this neurotic repression of the pleasure instinct, particularly in the sexual realm, come from? *The Belton Estate* abstains from the kind of deep analysis of such problems that we get in other Trollope novels, and yet it implies that the answer lies in a fundamental disorder in relations between the sexes in Victorian society. This apparently is the logic behind the outbreak in this novel of a strong strain of feminist polemics. Clara very articulately complains to the Captain, who pooh-poohs her arguments, about the subservience of contemporary women. "Women," she says, "—women, that is, of my age—are such slaves! We are forced to give an obedience for which we can see no cause, and for which we can understand no necessity." The truth of women's lot "is that we are dependent."

> "Dependence is a disagreeable word," he said; "and one never quite knows what it means."
> "If you were a woman you'd know."

> (Chap. 7)

She shocks her aunt—"one of those women who have always believed that their own sex is in every respect inferior to the other" (chap. 7)—by declaring "I think it would be well if all single women were strangled by the time they are thirty" (chap. 8), so debased is their lot in life.

Trollope's sympathy with this feminist militancy is evidently unqualified (as a long passage in chapter 11 confirms), and he clearly sees the mixture of sadism and masochism in Clara's sex life to be a perverse outgrowth of just the social disabilities that she complains of. To improve women's standing in the world, he implies, would be to rejuvenate erotic pleasure. It is within this context of implications that one needs to view the hinted allusions in *The Belton Estate* to *The Taming of the Shrew*. Clara is no "irksome brawling scold" like Katherina (1.2.184), whose name her own echoes, but she is, as the scorched Captain ruefully declares, "manifestly a hot-tempered woman,—a very hot-tempered woman indeed!" (chap. 28). The plot, as in Shakespeare's comedy, is that of the tremendously resourceful outsider who comes a-wooing and tries to subdue this resistant woman by love. Clara sees her story in just these terms: she is finally "mastered" by Will, obliged to "confess her own submission" to a "rough," imperious lover. "She knew that she would have to yield" (chap. 31). The scene of Will's final triumph quotes *The Taming of the Shrew*, act 5, scene 1, nearly verbatim:

> "Oh, Clara, I am such a happy fellow. Do give me a kiss. You have never given me one kiss yet."
> "What nonsense! I didn't think you were such a baby."
> "By George, but you shall; —or you shall never get home to tea to-night."

> (Chap. 31)

Clara's final need to "yield" to Will's "tyranny" (chap. 3) should not be taken as a dismissal by Trollope of her complaints about the subservience of Victorian women; what it does signify is his insistence that the conflict between the sexes must in some fashion be defused in order for women like Clara to overcome the perverseness that seems inherent in modern sexual relations.

She is drawn to Captain Aylmer precisely because the prospect of life with him is so unappetizing. He is not, to say the least, a lovable man, for he is lacking in charm, self-seeking, hypocritical, and nasty; he is, in fact, the classic pompous killjoy of comic drama. What Trollope focuses upon in the treatment of his relations with Clara, however, is the sexual frigidity of this "cold-blooded fish of a man," who acquires as the novel goes on an increasingly menacing aura. One notices especially the macabre suggestions surrounding his courtship, inseparably bound up as it is with the mortal illness of Clara's aunt, who, as death approaches, tries to bring about the union of her niece and nephew. Clara is shocked afterwards to think of having engaged in wooing while in the same house, "in the terrible solemnity of lifeless humanity, was still lying the body of her aunt!" (chap. 9). Beyond her suggestion that they have failed to show due respect for the corpse, there is a hint that she is horrified to think that her lovemaking has in fact been scripted by the corpse—and even more, that there is something obscenely corpselike about her lover himself. Captain Aylmer, when his proposal of marriage has been accepted, bestows on Clara "a cold, chilling kiss" (chap. 11) that suggests both his own libidinal failure and his ghoulish inappropriateness as the sexual partner of a beautiful young woman like Clara, whose own libido is not dead, only temporarily paralyzed. The necromantic quality of all this strain of imagery, the note of sexual horror that it finely introduces into the story, is hard to mistake.

Clara is sufficiently morbid that she is partly magnetized by Captain Aylmer's fishy coldness. And she has a certain personal affinity for this obnoxious lover, for she is herself more than a little touched with priggishness, even though Trollope leaves no doubt about her ultimate curability. This he artfully does by joining her with her young neighbor Mrs. Askerton, whose main function in the novel is to serve as Clara's comic tormentor, referring plainly to aspects of her courtship situation that good manners forbid mentioning and poking fun at her strong tendency toward strait-lacedness. Mrs. Askerton is Bergson's ideal of free, supple comic energy—a freedom that she has carried to the openly scandalous extent (Trollope makes a point here of underlining the moral danger lying latent even in a relatively innocuous

comedy like this one) of living with her husband as his mistress before their marriage. In her colloquies with this lady, Clara reveals, almost in equal measure, both her stiffness and her willingness to tolerate her friend's teasing, which always has a pungent edge of comic
truth-telling, as in their typically edgy discussion of Clara's final expulsion of Captain Aylmer:

> "I hope you had him on his knees before he left you."
> "Why should you hope that? How can you talk such
> nonsense?"
> "Because I wish that he should recognize what he has
> lost; —that he should know that he has been a fool; —a
> mean fool."
> "Mrs. Askerton, I will not have him spoken of like that.
> He is a man very estimable, —of estimable qualities."
> "Fiddle-de-dee. He is an ape, —a monkey to be carried
> on his mother's organ. His only good quality was that you
> could have carried him on yours."
>
> (Chap. 29)

Could there be a very wicked play on words here? It is no wonder that
at first the impeccably prim Clara finds that "there was something in
the lady's modes of speech, and something also in her modes of thinking, which did not quite satisfy the aspirations of Miss Amedroz as to
a friend" (chap. 2). It is a sign of the fundamental argument of comedy, and of its necessarily equivocal standing in the nineteenth century, that this "fast-going lady" (chap. 3) who, as Captain Aylmer
says, "is, —is, —is, —not at all what she ought to be" (chap. 26)
emerges surprisingly as the novel's touchstone for clear vision and
good feeling.

Clara's salvation is achieved in the simplest comic terms: she simply
decides at last to accept the pleasure offered her, or rather forced upon
her, by Will. The Captain does contribute materially to his own defeat,
driven as he is by the same comic fatality that impels others of comedy's champions of priggish rigidity—Morose, Malvolio, Pinchwife—
compulsively to expose their ridiculousness to public view and thus
to nullify their own power; but to describe this process, central though
it is to the novel's effect, would take us off the immediate point. Will,
with whom we are concerned for the moment, has none of that lively
wit or that taste for playful fun that comic heroes usually possess. His
overriding claim to the rank of hero lies, in fact, simply in the vivacity
of his sexual interest in the heroine, which contrasts so markedly with
the Captain's libidinal coldness. Will does not wrap Clara in the idealized angelic imagery common in Victorian love stories; instead, he
daydreams about her body: "he portrayed to himself, in his mind,
Clara's head and face and figure and feet; —and he resolved that she

should be his wife" (chap. 4). In the interest of propriety he tells himself to wait a decent interval after Clara's separation from Captain Aylmer before assailing her again. "Wait! He could not wait. How are you to bid a starving man to wait when you put him down at a well-covered board?" (chap. 31). The image of the heroine as a mouth-watering meal stretches the limits of literary decorum almost to breaking, but this is Will's main calling: to override rules of politeness. He scandalizes Clara at one point by seizing her unexpectedly and kissing "her forehead and her cheeks, and her lips, and her eyes" (chap. 22), and the scene of her eventual acceptance of his offer of marriage is marked again by his insistent kissing of her, which she struggles to fend off (chap. 31). Will instinctively knows that the most energetic and direct measures are called for to arouse Clara from the perverse spell of self-denial that has been cast upon her.

The issue within the story is an altogether serious one: in leading Clara to accept pleasure, this impetuous hero is leading her to accept life itself and saving her from some form of the suicidal fate that her brother has suffered. Since this is a comedy, however, the grave implications, so to speak, of Will's role are coupled closely to humor, reminding us again, as it is one of comedy's missions to do, of the bonding powers of laughter. The main humorous device in this case is a ludicrous inversion of youth and age, a device that pervades comedy and is based ultimately, as this novel makes clear, on comedy's intuition that real pleasure is the prerogative of children. Freud, as I noted, illuminatingly identifies the motif of adults acting like children as a major aspect of humor, but in analyzing it as a "degradation" (*Jokes*, 227) fails to see the strongly positive cast that this kind of regression often possesses in comedy, where adults giving vent to childish natures exemplify in a new and especially significant form that gift of fluent shape-changing that comic drama glorifies. Real grownups, on the other hand, are set in their ways and cut off from playful pleasure. Thus it is consonant with the traditional argument of comedy that Trollope stresses the broad streak of childishness in Will Belton's character. We can only laugh, for example, at Will's uncontrollable childish spite toward Captain Aylmer, but it is a laughter that, rather than degrading him, affirms his place as the hero of the comedy, for it shows how free he is of the strait-laced, repressed priggishness that is such a blight in this world. Will denounces the Captain as an "accursed beast" (chap. 23), has a great temper tantrum and spills glasses on the table when he meets his unoffending rival at the hotel (chap. 24), then ever after gives out a patently inaccurate account of his own misbehavior, calling Captain Aylmer "a quarrelsome fellow" and accusing him of starting the spat about hunting in Norfolk in which Will himself was in fact the sole aggressor (chap. 31). A very earnest reader not

in sympathy with comedy could well misconstrue the function of
these jokes at Will's expense. One such reader, in fact, was the *Athe-
naeum* reviewer who complained at length, just as Captain Aylmer
does, about the disgusting spectacle of Will's unmannerly behavior at
the hotel (Smalley, 262). This is a trivial literary scandal to be sure, but
one that reminds us again of the liberating dynamic of the comic
mode, and of the risks that Trollope ran in practicing it for a public in
which the Captain's sensibility was all too deeply instilled. But Will's
misbehavior at this point, as at other points, ought to count wholly in
his favor, reflecting as it does the unimpaired childlike vivacity that
enables him to be Clara's deliverer from a life devoid of pleasure. "I
didn't think you were such a baby," she says lovingly at the moment of
accepting him (chap. 31).

By the end of the novel, thanks to the combined ministrations
of Will and Mrs. Askerton and to the negative example of Captain
Aylmer, she has not only come to accept pleasure by uniting herself to
Will, but has begun to drop her prim regard for respectability—which
by now we recognize as a kind of armor against pleasure—and to
speak with the mischievous voice of Mrs. Askerton herself. In the last
scene, she gives the comic sign of her rejuvenation: she allows herself
for once to act playfully, thus reflecting the freeing-up of her previously impacted emotional life. In this scene, Clara, now a bride of two
years, discusses with Will Captain Aylmer's new bride Lady Emily
Tagmaggert, and with comic (not harsh or even genuine) malice merrily makes fun of the lady's red nose and advanced age. The scene assures us that the last bit of priggishness has been cleansed from
Clara's character; it also shows the mood of affectionate, joking intimacy that prevails in this marriage (Will's only contributions to the
discussion being little compliments on Clara's own beauty). One recent critic quotes with approval the opinions of a Victorian reviewer
who found this scene shockingly undignified, actually "sordid," and
argues that the two lovers, previously seen as "idealizations," are suddenly shown here in harshly unattractive terms and that our expectation that they would "live together passionately forever" is shattered
by realistic irony (Cohen, 44–46). In fact, as we have seen, neither of
the two lovers, and especially not Clara, has been much idealized, the
idea of a life of eternal passion has no place at all in Trollope's comedy
(or in any comedy), and to take so grimly censorious a view of playfulness is to contradict all the delicately nuanced rhetoric of the novel.
One can only remark yet again on the perils of writing comedy for
readers so disabled by "over-seriousness" that the language of comedy, which is the language of pleasure, has become unintelligible to
them.

3
Charm and Desire

Charm is the great English blight. . . . It spots and kills anything it touches.

Evelyn Waugh, *Brideshead Revisited*

Comedy, as we have seen, revolves around images of vivacious charm, identifying this quality with playful, buoyant limberness and freedom of movement, and thus with the love of pleasure; it gives such prestige to charm, indeed, that more reputable values are often eclipsed altogether. Trollope does not go quite so far, but his own fixation upon personal charm as a motive for fiction is one of the plainest signs of his affiliation with comedy. He came to this subject via the natural bent of his imagination, for few novelists have ever possessed a gift like his for portraying charm in fictional characters—a gift closely associated with the capacity for intimate imaginative sympathy. A nineteenth-century reviewer observed that Trollope "has an unrivalled knack of drawing attractive young ladies, well-mannered young gentlemen, and extremely agreeable persons of more mature age of either sex" (Smalley, 216). The condescending tone of this remark is testimony that such a "knack" is likely to seem a trivial or even a disreputable trait in a novelist, especially from the point of view of a Victorian public imbued with a moral code of duty, seriousness, and self-abnegation, and especially when the novelist bases much of his fiction on the very dubious asumption (but the one inherent in comedy) that charm is a nearly infallible sign of worth. To inquire into this subject, therefore, not only enables one to study the role that the idea of charm plays in the thematic and stylistic program of comedy, but also highlights another aspect of Trollope's uneasy relationship with contemporary taste.

His many figures of charm play more than the ornamental role that Waugh's sneer implies. Charm in Trollope's fiction is essentially a synecdoche for an ideal of richly and soundly developed personality, free of the inhibitions, repressions, and morbid introversion that he saw as widely prevalent factors in nineteenth-century life. The idea of charm is inseparable in Trollope, in other words, from interpretation of society; indeed, charm by its very nature is purely a social phenomenon, as his novels never let us forget. Unlike moral or psychological qualities, charm is nonexistent outside the particular social occasions when it makes itself felt. However we may sometimes speak of it for the sake of convenience, charm is not an absolute property that an individual can simply possess, but a wholly relative one; it refers to an *interaction* that, first, expresses the personality of the person being charmed fully as much as that of the charmer (though the latter always appears to dominate the scene), and that can only be analyzed, furthermore, as a function of the patterns of taste and manners and other conventional norms that determine social intercourse in a given milieu. Thus Trollope's paragons of charm—Lily Dale, Madame Max Goesler, Jonathan Stubbs, and many others—do not emerge from thin air; they are the emanations of a vision of ideal society, an ideal society that he imagined actually to be realized, at least in fragmentary, intermittent form, in the real world of his day. But Trollope understands charm in political terms too, as *force*, as is suggested in the dictionary definition: "compelling attractiveness." In its root sense, the word refers to the casting of a bewitching spell, and for Trollope, shrewd analyst that he is of intricate power relations among men and women, charm turns out to be a potent element in nearly all personal transactions. His fiction persistently reminds us that the charm of vivacity and "limberness" can imply its opposite image, the paralysis of the mesmerized, subjugated spectator. In describing his characters as "pleasant" or "unpleasant" (a frequent turn of phrase in Trollope), he highlights no trivial factor, therefore, but a main aspect of their power to impinge on the destinies of others. For one thing, charm is the specific medium of sexual power, and its patterns are those of fundamental social structures governing relations between the sexes; in this guise its troubling implications often lie close to the surface in Trollope. To follow some of them, we shall need to be much concerned in this chapter with a distinctive mode of Trollope's fiction that can be called *noncomedy*, works that originate in but are not comedy, and that seem designed among other things to make thoughtful readers wonder what the determining elements of true comedy *are*.

TRUE CHARM AND FALSE

Nothing makes us feel the logic of comedy more pervasively in Trollope than his way not only of building dramatic action around the careers of gay, appealing characters whose main attribute is that charismatic power he calls "charm," but of depicting the social scene as first and foremost a hierarchy of this factor, the varieties and gradations of which he registers with almost scientific precision. It is a sign of how deeply his fiction is anchored in comedy, indeed, that even primarily tragic books like *Orley Farm* follow the same principle. At one end of this novel's spectrum are found characters like the hobbledehoy Perry Orme or Judge and Lady Staveley, characters defined by their abundance of spontaneous, captivating charm; at some ambiguous middle position falls Lady Mason, whose expertly cultivated sexual magnetism is the source of her power in a strongly male-supremacist environment ("Lady Mason was rich with female charms, and she used them partly with the innocence of the dove, but partly also with the wisdom of the serpent" [chap. 35]); then there is Sophia Furnival, who exerts all her own skill to acquire the same power but somehow never quite succeeds ("Nevertheless she was not altogether charming" [chap. 10]); young Lucius Mason is the figure, familiar in comedy, of strenuous, austere, tactless virtue, who as a matter of principle scorns to be charming; and at the far opposite end of the spectrum is the coarse and repellent Mrs. Mason of Groby Park. Trollope in *Orley Farm* thus constantly situates his characters in terms of their relative richness or poverty of social appeal, persistently challenging the reader to discover some equivalency between this issue of personal charm and the tragic problems of justice and honor upon which the main plot turns.

He is fascinated in particular with women and with the secrets of specifically feminine charm, as witnessed by the reviewer who dubbed him "the ladies' man of our time" (Smalley, 190), the leading and most sympathetic student of women in contemporary fiction. To some extent, this strong bent of his imagination simply reflects the traditional supremacy of women in comedy. Meredith contends that the prosperity of comedy in a given society can be directly correlated with the freedom enjoyed by women in it: the freer women are and the richer their individuality, he argues, the stronger will be the impulse to write comedy (pp. 31–32).[1] R. B. Martin declares this notion incomprehensible (pp. 95–97), but comedy has always celebrated the wit, good sense, quickness, and sexual charm of women, and has employed female voices to expose the congenital foolishness of men. Beyond a doubt, the maintenance of a certain ideal feminine image has been one of comedy's paramount offices in our culture; by the same token, one central cause of the paucity of true comedy in Victorian literature was the oppressive sanctification of women as angelic beings elevated above common life, a conception that renders them quite unfit for comic purposes. The vigor of Trollope's comedy, its power to shed light on contemporary social and literary structures, and his infatuation with women, in any case, are closely connected.

The mythology of femininity that comedy projects is a powerfully eroticized one. To understand the implications of this fact for Trollope's fiction, the best explanatory text may be an essay of Freud's that continually throws light on various aspects of comedy, "On the Universal Tendency to Debasement in the Sphere of Love." In this piece Freud moves from a specific analysis of male impotence to the revelation of a profound disorder endemic, he claims, to sexual relations in civilized society. The cause of this disorder is a disjunction of love (that is, affection and admiration) and desire; its symptom is a pervasive, pathological loss of sexual pleasure, whether in the specific form of impotence or, more generally, in that variety of this condition that Freud calls "psychanaesthesia," the condition of those men able technically to engage in sex but "without getting any particular pleasure from it" (p. 184). He portrays this condition as virtually universal in modern life. "The whole sphere of love in such people," he says in a well-known formula, "remains divided in the two directions personified in art as sacred and profane (or animal) love. Where they love they do not desire and where they desire they cannot love" (p. 183).

Whether or not we wish to follow Freud in attributing the dissociation of love from desire to the "family romance" and to the taboo on incest, he diagnoses in this essay a manifest pattern in Victorian culture, a pattern enshrined in popular fiction in particular, where it forms almost the basic narrative convention. Love in Victorian fiction is strongly identified with reverence; nothing is more crucial to the maintenance of literary decorum, therefore, than that images of loved women be purified of erotic overtones, rendered dignified rather than seductive, while images of seductive women are necessarily "debased," seen as deficient in moral character, seriousness, social status, or in some other important quality. The supposedly lovable Agnes Wickfield, a solemn monitress of duty, is a classic instance of the former (it is a sign only of Uriah Heep's despicable perverseness that Agnes inflames his lust); the intoxicatingly sexy but hopelessly infantile Dora Spenlow illustrates the latter. The cornerstone of this area of *David Copperfield* is the premise that these are two radically separate and irreconcilable images of women, and that to choose one is necessarily to exclude the other. This unequivocal choice between sacred and profane ("or animal") love is rehearsed over and over in Victorian fiction, approval always going to the same term of the dialectic, needless to say.

Trollope's preoccupation with images of charming ladies derives from and constantly reinforces the conventions of comic literature, but needs finally to be understood as an attempt to address this pathological state of affairs by constructing an image of love in which the two fragmented components, the "affectionate" and the "sensual," are reunited. The determination to desexualize female virtue, he remarks with striking prescience in *The Vicar of Bullhampton* (chap. 37), "is but a remnant of the tawdry sentimentality of an age in which the mawkish insipidity of the women was the reaction from the vice of that preceding it." The comment suggests that in the area of sex, Trollope's gravitation to an anachronistic fictional mode ought again to be seen as a strategy for giving fiction leverage upon the cultural predicament of his day. He carries out this operation, like all his operations, in the most unobtrusive fashion, in the guise of simply producing lending-library entertainment; but his aim, to use Freud's terminology again, is to educate the instincts of love, and thus to arrest the decline of pleasure in modern civilized life. He seeks in particular to rehabilitate the female image by overturning the ghastly idealizations of "tawdry sentimentality" that people of his day loved to contemplate; and the result is the liberation of a new stream of sensibility in Victorian fiction.

One signal of Trollope's effectiveness in this project was the controversy that his "daring" work sometimes aroused. As we have seen, he commonly was accused in his day of having an immoral or immodest tone, a charge he was quick to deny. "I will not allow that I am indecent," he wrote to Thackeray concerning a story rejected for publication in the *Cornhill* on the grounds that its portrayal of a liberated young woman of apparently free sexual principles was offensive to moral sensibilities (*Letters*, 128). He denounced the "squeamishness" of the Victorian public (ibid.) and energetically defended writers like Rhoda Broughton and Lady Wood who had offended the squeamish in similar ways (*Letters*, 434, 450–52). We shall miss an important dimension in Trollope, I shall make bold to say, if we fail to see him as a conscious agent in the modernist campaign to overturn Victorian prudery waged more militantly by the likes of Flaubert, Hardy, Lawrence, and Joyce. Trollope's role in the campaign was obviously a more equivocal one than theirs. His annotations of old comedies throw intriguing light on this issue in his novels, for they are full of exclamations of disgust for the "lewdness," "vulgarity," "beastliness," "obscenity," "coarse ribaldry," and "most libidinous language" that run throughout these plays. Of all the early dramatists, it was probably Fletcher that he found lewdest and most objectionable. The main plot of Fletcher's comedy *The Coxcomb*, for example, "is so offensive," says Trollope, "as to make the reader wonder that it should not have of-

fended even the taste of the age of James I."[2] What seemed most offensive to him in Fletcher as in other playwrights was the licentious
speech of female characters. "In these days we can hardly understand
the delight which was taken in the obscene language of women who
were, after all, supposed to be patterns of virtue." He concludes (correctly enough, no doubt) that the essential motive of this feature of
old comedy was pornographic, and that it was closely tied to the ex-
clusion of women from the stage. "We should remember that the
actors of these parts were men, and that the audience had to be stirred
to lust by words,—and not by dress and female gestures of indecency
as in our days."[3] Instinctively he assumes that the degradation (and
implicitly the impoverishment) of erotic pleasures can be traced to
basic disorders in current sexual institutions, just as modern sexual
life seems caught in an oscillation between phases of "vice" and of
"tawdry sentimentality."

It is easy to extract from Trollope's annotations a typical Victorian
condemnation of the vein of sexual scandal that runs through comedy; Jeremy Collier himself was hardly more indignant than Trollope
at the pervading immorality of the comic stage. Yet major qualifications must at once be made to such a comparison. For one thing, Trollope constantly declares that even the smuttiest and most "disgusting" comedies, such as Beaumont's and Fletcher's *The Knight of Malta*
or Fletcher's *A Wife for a Month*, are in fact highly entertaining in spite of
themselves. He condemns the bawdy-tongued heroines of Fletcher's
The Wild-Goose-Chase, then praises this superlative comedy as "as excellent play, full of wit, with much language almost worthy of Shakespeare." The various characters, he says, "are kept up with such infinite life that the piece is charming to read, and must have charmed
when acted"[4]—an equation of "charm" with "life," incidentally, that
goes to the heart of our theme. Divided judgments like these highlight
the obvious paradox in the spectacle of a prudish Victorian moralist
who endlessly describes himself as disgusted and repelled by Jacobean comedy, yet who reads it almost insatiably for decades, and
shows, indeed, a special fascination for the very playwright he condemns most strongly for his lewdness (for Trollope read Fletcher's
huge body of work twice, first in the early 1850s—this being the only
reading project recorded for these dates—then again from 1869 to
1874). One need not be a Freudian analyst to draw the conclusion that
Trollope was keenly attracted to the "indecency" of comedy and to the
enfranchisement it offered from the straitjacket of the Victorian cult of
sexual purity, particularly with reference to women. His fulminations
against it, we may assume, are in direct proportion to his instinctive
attraction toward it.

The plainest evidence of this is the fact that female charm in Trollope almost always connotes distinct, unmistakable (though sometimes only latent) sexual appeal; and by the same token, most remarkably perhaps, what it specifically excludes is "debasement" of the love object, even though the sway of the pathology described by Freud is such that readers may automatically interpret any evidence of "animal" desire as debasing. Especially in his physical descriptions of women, it is the frank erotic susceptibility of Trollope's narrator that takes one by surprise, breaking as it does with the spiritualized tone that prevailed in descriptions of good women in Victorian fiction. Some pretty girls, he says in introducing the "so charming" Mary Flood Jones in *Phineas Finn*, are so "cold-looking" that one's courage fails at the idea of "attacking" them. "But, again, there are other girls to abstain from attacking whom is, to a man of any warmth of temperament, quite impossible. They are like water when one is athirst, like plovers' eggs in March, like cigars when one is out in the autumn. No one ever dreams of denying himself when such temptation comes in the way" (chap. 2). The note of erotic delectation in such a passage, given the usual decorums of Victorian fiction, is positively glaring, and it does not abate in Trollope's voluptuous descriptions of the girl's hair, "the softest hair in the world, of a colour varying between brown and auburn,—for sometimes you would swear it was the one and sometimes the other." His novels are full of similar descriptions of young women in which their beauty, and the relation of physical beauty to what is more significant, charm, is analyzed detail by detail, by an observer who is manifestly a connoisseur of the tints of ladies' skin and hair, the modeling of their faces and their bodies, the way they move their limbs.[5] As with the elusive, mercurial color of Mary Flood Jones's hair, Trollope in these passages constantly invokes that imagery of fluent mobility that is the keynote of comic charm in all its varieties. His description of the "soft, graceful, and fawnlike" Madeline Staveley in *Orley Farm* is another typical passage, beginning with a long, minute study of her enchanting mouth and of the way her smile irradiates her whole countenance.

> I never saw the face of a woman whose mouth was equal
> in pure beauty, in beauty that was expressive of feeling, to
> that of Madeline Staveley. Many have I seen with a richer
> lip, with a more luxurious curve, much more tempting as
> baits to the villainy and rudeness of man; but never one
> that told so much by its own mute eloquence of a woman's
> happy heart and a woman's happy beauty. It was lovely as
> I have said in its mirth, but if possible it was still more
> lovely in its woe; for then the lips would separate, and the

breath would come, and in the emotion of her suffering
the life of her beauty would be unrestrained.

(Chap. 19)

Trollope in this passage carefully inscribes the typical line between
carnality (which he does not pretend to be a stranger to) and respectful admiration of "pure beauty," but only to show this line being oblit-
erated by the almost shockingly eroticized image of Madeline in what
he euphemistically calls her "woe." Stylistically, such a passage calls
to mind many similar ones from Jacobean comedies in which the note
of indecency is not veiled but flagrant: for instance, in Shirley's *The
Grateful Servant*, Grimundo's evocation of a certain lascivious young
beauty possessing, he says, "such a charming brow, speaking eye,
springing cheek, tempting lip, swelling bosom" (3.4), or the more
richly lubricious description that Jonson's Mosca gives to his master
Volpone of Corvino's wife Celia:

> O, sir, the wonder,
> The blazing star of Italy! A wench
> O' the first year! A beauty, ripe, as harvest!
> Whose skin is whiter than a swan, all over!
> Than silver, snow, or lilies! A soft lip,
> Would tempt you to eternity of kissing!
> And flesh that melteth in the touch to blood!
> Bright as your gold! And lovely as your gold!
> (1.5.107–14)

No doubt unconsciously, Trollope adapts this scandalous comic imagery to serve in his own more respectable context, but much of its
disturbing energy survives the adaptation. What we see in the portrayal of Madeline Staveley, therefore, is the fusing of the two principles that the Victorians generally saw as antithetical, that of refined
femininity and that of intense sexual attraction—based here on an
awareness of the woman's own responsiveness to sex. As this passage
suggests, it does not disqualify a Trollope heroine to be an object of
desire; on the contrary, it is almost a prerequisite.[6]

Physical descriptions of attractive women, however, are finally only
ancillary to Trollope's vocation as a student of charm in its specifically
comic inflections. He knows well that a woman need not be beautiful
to be charming and that sex is just one aspect (though a major one) of
the question of charm; nor is charm by any means monopolized by
women in his novels. Some of his leading incarnations of charm are
men: Brooke Burgess in *He Knew He Was Right* or Colonel Stubbs in
Ayala's Angel, for instance, witty, vivacious men whose manner is so
full of "infinite life," and thus of "compelling attractiveness," that re-

sistance to them melts magically when they sweep into view. For men and women both, possibly the fundamental point in this argument is that the theme of personal charm in Trollope is inseparably bound up with the portrayal and critical analysis of a whole social milieu. On the one hand, his figures of comic charm pointedly expose broad patterns of rigidity, repression, and melancholia in contemporary life; yet they do the reverse, too, testifying by their very plausibility as social beings to unrepressed strains of liveliness and ease, wit and urbanity, in the Victorian bourgeoisie and upper class. Trollope's central contribution to social history may be just this documentation of the capacity of the livelier side of human nature to survive, even, within limits, to flourish, in the often inhospitable atmosphere of nineteenth-century society. Comedy for Trollope is a vehicle for insisting to posterity that the Victorians were not simply a vast assemblage of Dombeys, Murdstones, Tulkinghorns, Miss Wades, Podsnaps, and Veneerings.

To illustrate some of these points and to anatomize Trollopian charm in more detail, let us look at *Doctor Thorne*, a novel in which Trollope expounds the comic philosophy of personal charm in a methodical way. Elizabeth Bowen in her discussion of this novel has emphasized this dimension of it. Trollope, she says,

> is a great conveyor of that to which he greatly reacted:
> charm—whether of face, person or manner, landscape,
> the visage or environment of a house. Aesthetically and
> fondly he loved girls, bevy-in-muslins, swinging their
> bonnets by the ribbons, dispersing over lawns liquid with
> sunset—he depicts floating pleasures, whose spell is in
> their evanescence, their slipping by. Had he been a
> painter, he would have been an inland Boudin.
>
> (P. xxv)

This is a valuable comment for the latently erotic, proto-Proustian sensibility that it discovers beneath Trollope's determinedly prosaic idiom; still, Bowen's imagery is far too deliquescent for Trollope and for *Doctor Thorne* in particular, a novel that demonstrates with special clarity that Trollope's standard of charm is nothing if not a robustly comic one. In an important *Autobiography* passage, he speaks of certain Americans he has known "who have in all respects come up to my ideas of what men and women should be: energetic, having opinions of their own, quick in speech, with some dash of sarcasm at their command, always intelligent, sweet to look at (I speak of the women), fond of pleasure, and each with a personality of his or her own" (p. 315). It would be hard to frame a more concise or more comprehensive statement of the specifically comic ideal, one in which moral qualities are conspicuous by their absence, where vividness of charm and distinctness of personality are primary, and where fondness for pleasure is the animating force. (Nothing could be further from the "humility and passivity" that Frank O'Connor says that Trollope glorifies [p. 172].) The exemplars of comic charm in *Doctor Thorne* embody just this ideal and have nothing of the langorous transparency of a Boudin shore scene, where one never sees a closeup view of a human face. They do not vaporize or float anonymously into the sunset swinging their bonnets, but energetically dramatize their presence by asserting themselves against the multifarious constrictions of a social environment, constrictions that (in a fundamental paradox of comedy) nurture and invigorate rather than suppress individual personality. For example, there is the beautiful Patience Oriel, whose favorite amusement is snaring Frank Gresham in the toils of her witty, flirtatious teasing, a social ritual with a vital role to play, the novel implies, in both stimulating and chastening erotic development (and thus draining off the malignant sexual energy witnessed at first in Henry Thorne's seduction of Mary Scatcherd). But the delightful Patience only plays a supporting role to Mary Thorne, whose great charm lies in her "vehemence" (chap. 3). She is full of prickly pride and pungent wit, as she lets Lady Alexandrina de Courcy know when that pompous young lady ventures to snub her:

> "Rank . . . has its drawbacks, Miss Thorne, as well as
> its privileges."
> "I should not object to the drawbacks," said the doctor's
> niece, "presuming them to be of some use; but I fear I
> might fail in getting on so well with the privileges."
> The Lady Alexandrina looked at her as though not fully
> aware whether she intended to be pert. In truth, the Lady
> Alexandrina was rather in the dark on the subject. It was
> almost impossible, it was incredible, that a fatherless,
> motherless, doctor's niece should be pert to an earl's
> daughter at Greshamsbury. . . .
>
> (Chap. 4)

This formidable girl is one of Trollope's many young ladies whose outward beauty is imperfect ("she had no brilliancy of complexion" [chap. 41]) but is amply compensated for by what matters most to Trollope, "expressiveness," individuality, and witty intelligence. Squire Gresham belatedly comes to recognize in her face, we are told, "an expression of mental faculty which the squire now for the first time perceived to be charming" (chap. 41). This stress on "mental faculty" as the very basis of female charm—as comic agility or "limberness" in its highest form—applies to all of Trollope's fiction and marks one of its most significant divergences from contemporary taste, schooled as it was to admire quite different qualities in women.[7] No less striking in mental faculty and "vehemence" is another prominent embodiment of charm in *Doctor Thorne*, the heiress Miss Dunstable, who figures in Trollope's great taxonomy of charm as an example of how far authentic charm can coexist with want of beauty, even with brash vulgarity of manner, when these qualities are joined to wit, an "aptitude for mirth" (chap. 5), and fundamental good feeling.

Among Miss Dunstable's favorite targets for wit are her insincere suitors like Mr. Moffatt and Frank Gresham. Frank, though, belongs in his own right to the ranks of charm in this novel, and represents a type of character especially dear to Trollope's imagination, precisely because it embodies such a subtle flavor of charm: the awkward, immature young man. In dealing with the likes of Patience, Mary, and Miss Dunstable, Frank, perpetually made a fool of, is hopelessly boyish and inarticulate. "Mental faculty," evidently, is not the crucial element in male charm that it is in female. And although he is by no means without good feeling, Frank's character leaves much to be desired. For all his supposed devotion to Mary, he is led half astray by Patience and almost proposes out of sheer vanity to Miss Dunstable. "He was certainly an arrant puppy, and an egregious ass into the bargain" (chap. 20). Yet Frank possesses, for all the thinness of his character, a mysterious, all-exonerating aura of irresistible charm, "a joyous, genial lustre" (chap. 24) potent enough to captivate even the discriminating Mary Thorne. To the extent that this elusive property can be analyzed, it seems to amount to little but a rich, spontaneous responsiveness to the pleasures of living—pleasures, like hunting and flirting with pretty young women, that the son and heir of a country squire (even an impecunious one) has ample access to. Trollope does everything he can to emphasize the outrageous point that Frank's paramount and redeeming virtue is simply his uninhibited capacity for enjoying himself. The split second after he has proposed to Mary and been accepted by her, his thoughts revert to his usual amusements, dogs and horses. "He was very much in love, no doubt; but that did not interfere with his interest in other pursuits" (chap. 36). The charm that Frank epiphanically radiates—"Did not the sun shine down upon him with a halo, so that he was bright as an angel?" (chap. 29)—is in effect the "compelling attractiveness" of pleasure itself, and in comedy all other values are subordinate to this one.

Much of the comic structure of *Doctor Thorne* recurs in *The Small House at Allington*, another novel that can be schematized not too misleadingly as a pattern of intricate variations on the theme of charm.

Again this faculty of personal charm everywhere turns out to be laden with weighty consequences. The chief standard-bearer of the ideal of charm in this story is of course Lily Dale, who, like Mary Thorne, makes a striking comic departure from the style of dignified, morally inspirational heroines ubiquitous in Victorian fiction. But there is no doubt of how fervently Trollope glorifies her. He evokes her beauty with his customary rapt attention to detail, noting, for example, that there runs through her ambiguously colored hair, which is otherwise almost indistinguishable from her sister Bell's, "a golden tint that gave it a distinct brightness of its own" (chap. 6). At another point she drops a low curtsey, "gently swelling down upon the ground with her light muslin dress," as the narrator lyrically puts it, "till she looked like some wondrous flower that had bloomed upon the carpet" (chap. 9). Lily's beauty makes such a captivating image because it is so "expressive" (chap. 6), a word that continually recurs in Trollope in this context, and that everywhere serves as his touchstone of true charm. It signifies, first of all, that air of a spontaneous overflowing of personality, of the absence of inhibition or of any calculated effect, that is the precondition of charm—though comedy always makes evident that charm is not the product of personality in any raw natural state, but only of personalities so finely attuned to the nuances of civilized style and decorum as to be able to play upon them with effortless, unconscious expertness. (Lily's ravishing curtsey, for example, is both spontaneously expressive and an exquisitely stylized gesture at the same time.) The word "expressive" also signifies what Adolphus Crosbie is so struck by in Lily: her "quick intelligence" (chap. 6) and her "pretty wit" (chap. 7). Only when one has taken the measure of Victorian literary sensibility by reading many novels of the period can one fully appreciate the bravery of Trollope's overturning of the convention, anchored of course in deeply inculturated ideals of femininity, of gravely demure and proper, even lugubrious, heroines, whose excellence lies in saintly moral goodness and in vast reservoirs of benevolent feeling rather than in anything like an agile intellect. Trollope deplored the racy, immodest heroines of Jacobean comedy—but then he betrayed the hold they had on his imagination by creating a series of racy heroines of his own who bear the unmistakable stamp of their seventeenth-century ancestors. Lily, one of the raciest, is a revelation because she is "pert and saucy" (chap. 42), full of impudent banter and often, indeed, mildly scandalizes her mother and sister with her free talk. Like Lady Glencora Palliser, she is addicted to slangy language, for which she is repeatedly criticized as being unladylike. "Lily, how can you say such shocking things?" exclaims her sister at one of Lily's bursts of ribaldry (chap. 42). She is not lewd like Fletcher's heroines, of course, but she is irrepressibly playful:

> "Mamma, Mr. Crosbie wants to play croquet by moonlight."
> "I don't think there is light enough for that," said Mrs. Dale.
> "There is light enough for him," said Lily, "for he plays quite independently of the hoops; don't you, Mr. Crosbie?"
>
> (Chap. 3)

The artistic economy of *The Small House at Allington* is largely determined by the generous samplings that it provides of this kind of inconsequential banter—except that it is not inconsequential at all, but vital to Trollope's representation of the delectable charm in Lily that captivates Crosbie very much against his will and thus sets the stage for the calamity that eventually overtakes them both. The erotic dimension of this effect is only thinly veiled. It would be going much too far to call Lily a flirt, but her teasing humor, her trespassing of decorous maidenly reserve, carries unmistakable overtones of sexual freedom and makes sufficiently clear that she, too, is an object not just of moral admiration but also of desire.

Joined to Lily's "pretty wit" is a quality that Trollope calls by one of the cardinal words in his lexicon as a novelist: "sweetness." The word recurs often throughout *The Small House* and all Trollope's fiction, and wherever it occurs it stands for what he prizes most highly. Even Crosbie, the jaded man about town, is "fascinated by [Lily's] sweetness" (chap. 15), that is, by her lovingly tender nature and her uncorrupted wholesomeness. Crosbie's sensibility is of too coarse a grain really to understand Lily. He rhapsodizes conventionally to himself about "her innocence, her purity" (chap. 6), even as he finds her free manners exciting, but the essence of her charm in fact is that she is able to be deliciously sweet without being "innocent" at all. The first time she meets Crosbie, she recognizes him for just what he is, a conceited coxcomb, and gives him the slang label that Bell and Mrs. Dale find so ungenteel: "Mr. Crosbie," she declares, "is a swell" (chap. 2). Lily in her way is a shrewd, discerning young lady of the world, despite having passed her life in the rural isolation of Allington.

This union of sweetness and saucy, witty intelligence produces in Lily, then, that "expressiveness" that is the central quality of Trollopian charm. What it connotes, again, is a gift of seemingly spontaneous freedom of movement, a fluency or limberness of personality that makes all the many kinds of personal rigidity, constraint, and repression stand out in high relief: the repression of a bitter, melancholy, misanthropic nature like Squire Dale's, who despite his good heart is incurably "hard, dry, unpleasant" (chap. 1), the rigidity of the likes of the famous society beauty Lady Dumbello or Lady Alexandrina de Courcy, automatons always gauging every movement and word for effect, and thus capable only of "a certain cold, inexpressive beauty" (chap. 17), or the constraint exhibited by a man like Crosbie, too locked into his ambitions of worldly advancement to allow his feelings free play. This polarity between the supple and the rigid is exactly the one implied throughout the field of comedy. With all its rich comic materials, however, *The Small House* turns at last into a kind of tragedy, and the crucial influence is precisely the factor of charm, for Crosbie possesses a simulacrum of wit and true charm deceptive enough to fool even the keen-eyed Lily, and thus to destroy her happiness for ever. I shall return to *The Small House* presently to study in more detail that hazardous interlocking of charm and desire that perverts comedy disastrously in this novel.

Crosbie is just one of Trollope's many exercises in false charm. *Ralph the Heir* furnishes a noteworthy example in the form of a walk-on character called Mr. Poojean, a would-be wit who bombards Clary Underwood with his insufferably tedious humor at an inopportune moment (chap. 12). A more significant figure is that of Lizzie Eustace, one of Trollope's supreme exemplars of false charm. One central joke of *The Eustace Diamonds* is that Lizzie, who devotes all her energy and her highly developed histrionic skills to simulating charm, is wholly devoid of it and incapable of deceiving anyone, at least for long. Trollope defines charm, we may say, as that quality that can never be successfully counterfeited. It must be wholly spontaneous and unconscious, and is instantly dispelled by premeditation. Lizzie imagines, for example, that her great secret of beauty is her eyes. "But, in truth, the charm of her face did not lie in her eyes. This was felt by many even who could not read the book fluently. They were too expressive, too loud in their demands for attention, and they lacked tenderness" (chap. 2). She is *too* expressive, too glaring: that is, all is for effect, and all is imitation for Lizzie. So she invariably betrays herself: "Her voice as she thus spoke was perfect. Her manner was almost perfect. Perhaps there was a little too much of gesture, too much gliding motion, too violent an appeal with the eyes, too close a pressure of the hand" (chap. 9). At another moment it is all too apparent that "her whole body had been so arranged as to combine the charm of her beauty with the charm of proffered intimacy" (chap. 23). No amount of expert arrangement can conceal the absence of that spontaneous fluency of movement that expresses pleasure and conveys true charm.

The Lizzie Eustace fable thus stresses the proximity of this quality to personal authenticity and naturalness, and underlines the point to which all the above discussion tends: that Trollope's fictional cult of charm derives its force from the moral argument embedded in it, an argument whose central principle is the affirmation of richly consti-tuted, harmoniously integrated individual personality deploying it-self with maximum vividness. This is the ideal that Trollope makes it his task to defend, through the instrument of comedy, against the ten-dencies in contemporary culture that seem to contradict it. For all his admiration of Thackeray, he objected strongly to what he saw as Thackeray's ingrained tendency to cynicism (*Thackeray*, 203–4); and when in *The Eustace Diamonds*—one of his own closest approaches to cynicism—he speaks of Mr. Dove's idealism in the study of the law as helping to preserve his colleague Mr. Camperdown "from that worst of all diseases, a low idea of humanity" (chap. 28), he gives voice to a fundamental principle of his own as a novelist. The kind of radiant charm with which he endows characters like Lily, Glencora, Violet Effingham, Will Belton, Brooke Burgess, Colonel Stubbs, and scores of others is an affirmation of humanity itself amid a culture increas-ingly inclined to morbidity in its glorification of self-sacrifice, work, and duty, its fixation upon ideas of heroic and saintly virtue, its op-pressive seriousness, its repression of the libido—tendencies that ul-timately spring from and reinforce, as this fiction lets us see, the dis-ease of our time, a low idea of humanity.

Charm Devalued

Yet the cult of charm is not without its severe inner contradictions, of which the chief one lies simply in the fact that no values asserted in a work of fiction can possess any but the most equivocal significance, since they are so deeply implicated in the conventions of the literary mode used to express them. Trollope cannot solve this fundamental predicament of art, but he shows his acute consciousness of it by carrying out the most detailed investigations of the interconnections between particular moral assumptions and particular literary forms. He analyzes literary modes by cunningly destabilizing them in one way after another, so as to throw their determinant features into ab-normally high relief. Seen from another angle, this process looks like a systematic presenting of certain values in one modal context after another, as though to test by this device the stability and permanence of those values.

The novel that follows *Doctor Thorne* in the Barset series and in many respects rehearses its story all over again, *Framley Parsonage*, offers a striking instance of this tactic. If we looked only at the central love story between Lord Lufton and Lucy Robarts, *Framley Parsonage* would seem a perfect Trollopian comedy; it shows in any case the familiar preoccupation with charm. In Lucy's case the idea of charm as opposed to mere beauty is carried even further than usual. Over and over she strikes people as "plain" and "insignificant," even as a "dumpy little black thing" with "no personal attractions whatever" (chap. 25), but this impression just as regularly evaporates as her witty intelligence comes into play and as her "genial, good-humoured, racy smile" (chap. 16) takes effect. Throughout the novel, Lord Lufton debates with his mother, Lady Lufton, the comparative attractiveness of Lucy and of Lady Lufton's candidate for her son's hand, the statuesque beauty Griselda Grantley, whose profound stupidity Lord Lufton has had the wit to discover (sharp-tongued Lucy says her rival is "a mere automaton, cold, lifeless, spiritless, and even vapid" [chap. 21]). "You like silent beauty, whereas I like talking beauty," Lord Lufton says pithily to his mother. "You want me to marry some bouncing amazon, some pink and white giantess of fashion" (chap. 43). But Lord Lufton prefers charm, which is to say, expressive intelligence and a lively capacity for enjoyment. "[Lucy's] ready wit and speaking lip, not her beauty, had brought him to her side" (chap. 16).

We may not realize that this now-familiar myth of the omnipotence of charm is intimately connected to a certain philosophy of pleasure—until Trollope performs the experiment of breaking the vital bond between charm and pleasure before our eyes. This is the function of the rest of *Framley Parsonage*, where pleasure is powerfully devalued. The novel's party of worldly sophisticates, where the comic impulse should normally originate, includes, among others, the Duke of Omnium, Sowerby, and the latter's sister Mrs. Harold Smith, a lady with "a keen sense of the value of all worldly things, and a keen relish for all the world's pleasures" (chap. 2). On the other side of the great divide of comedy, which Trollope inscribes in this novel with special deliberateness, stand such crypto-puritanical figures as Lady Lufton and Josiah Crawley. Both these enemies of worldly enjoyments are treated with a good spice of humor. Lady Lufton, for example, "probably thought that they ate babies in pies during their midnight orgies at Gatherum Castle; and that widows were kept in cells, and occasionally put on racks for the amusement of the duke's guests" (chap. 11). And Crawley, the walking antithesis of charm—he is "a strict, stern, unpleasant man" (chap. 14), in contrast to Sowerby's "easy, comfortable, gay manner" (chap. 24) or that of the worldly Mark Robarts, who always "made himself pleasant" (chap. 15)—is scarcely less fanatical than Lady Lufton in his denunciations of the corrupting influence of the vice he most despises, foxhunting, and of "worldly pleasure-seekers" in general (chap. 15). But Trollope surprises us, and deflects the comic impulse, by siding after all with these dour antagonists of pleasure. The entertaining banter exchanged among the fashionable set in this novel turns out to be only a mask for hollowness and cruelty, as shown, for example, by the duke's brutal foreclosure on his supposed friend Sowerby. The central plot of Mark Robarts's involvement with Sowerby and his crowd expresses very clearly the moral that one frequents worldly pleasure-seekers at one's grave peril: that "acceptance of the world" that R. B. Heilman calls the defining note of comedy, in other words, is just what is explicitly repudiated here. Thus Mark at one point reads himself a little sermon on the possibility of reconciling pleasure and virtue. He determines not to be known "as a denouncer of dancing or of card-tables, of theatres or of novel-reading; he would take the world around him as he found it" and seek to teach by his own example "that men may be gay and yet not profligate, that women may be devout and yet not dead to the world" (chap. 14). Such principles are the very basis of morally respectable comedy—and are indicted in *Framley Parsonage* as nothing but dangerous self-delusions, as Mark discovers to his pain. "He had been fond of pleasure and had given way to temptation" (chap. 42): this is the moral to be drawn from his near ruin at the hands of Sowerby. In *Framley Parsonage*, pleasure is fraught with moral ambiguity, and comedy is surprisingly nullified. The plainest sign of this, no doubt, is the injection into the story of a recurrent strain of anguish and grief, as, for example, in the depiction of the horrible, maddening poverty of the Crawleys, or in the episode of Sowerby's tormented revisitation of the family estate that he has lost (chap. 37): it is hard to see how the novel could be described as "a perfect English idyl" (Kincaid, 121). A subtler effect is the way this insistent deglorification of pleasure makes Lucy's charm seem almost trivial and irrelevant. The dramatic interest of the book flows powerfully toward Sowerby, Crawley, Mark Robarts, and Lady Lufton, leaving the charming girl, the nominal heroine, to recede into a somewhat marginal figure. This fragmentation of structure may seem a flaw in *Framley Parsonage*, but it is one very deliberately effected by Trollope.

In other novels, Trollope deglorifies charm still more drastically by disrupting the near-perfect fit between charm and worth that comedy typically takes for granted. This is the central principle, for example, of *The Claverings*, one of Trollope's most subtly constructed exercises in noncomedy. His angle of thought in this novel (based, as noted

above, on Vanbrugh's *Provoked Wife*) is signaled by the presence in it of
one of the few characters in his fiction in whom something like authentic charm is joined to real malignancy: the debonair, genuinely
witty and entertaining, but finally sinister Count Pateroff, who makes
a close parallel to Vanbrugh's Constant. Trollope is so immersed in the
comic ethos and in its nearly unconditional celebration of charm that a
character like this is bound to be a rarity in his fiction. Yet the example
of Pateroff points to the main line of development in this novel, which
centers on an anatomization, or one might better say a vivisection, of
the charming hero Harry Clavering, whose outward charm is gradually peeled away to reveal the hopeless mediocrity underneath. His
personal attractiveness is attested to by his Phineas-Finn-like ability to
charm Florence Burton (the acquiescent Lucy Morris of this story),
the glamorous Lady Ongar, and his prospective sister-in-law Cecilia
Burton as well. (Harry, like Phineas, arouses suspicion from the
first—among male readers at least—by being far more attractive to
women than to men.) But as he vacillates ever more hopelessly between
Florence and Lady Ongar, in a pitiful parody of comic limberness, finally reaching a state of virtual paralysis as (in a quintessentially
comic perplexity) he becomes engaged to both of them at once, his
mediocrity becomes unmistakable. Trollope highlights this discovery
at every moment, stressing, for example, Harry's permanent incapacity ever to work for a living, his snobbery, his self-satisfaction and
proneness to self-flattery. His insignificance is all too plain when he is
cruelly juxtaposed with the brilliant, forceful Pateroff, who makes a
fool of him on every occasion. No wonder that Mrs. Oliphant found
that Trollope's "humiliating" treatment of Harry "goes against the very
character of a hero" (Smalley, 285). The nadir of Harry's dignity comes
when, overwhelmed by his predicament, he takes hypochondriacally
to his bed, in which helpless state he is bullied by his mother into
fulfilling his promise to Florence even though, as he has confessed to
himself, he loves her less than Lady Ongar (chap. 41). Mrs. Clavering
then explains to Florence the desirability of solemnizing the marriage
without delay. "You see Harry is a young man of that sort—so impetuous I mean, you know, and so eager—and so—you know what I
mean—that the sooner he is married the better" (chap. 47). This shop-
worn, disgraced lover is treated at the end with considerable toleration compared, say, to Adolphus Crosbie, partly because he is made to
do the right thing in the end, and largely because he is found to be,
after all, beneath contempt. Thus Trollope in *The Claverings* goes about
as far as he ever does in suggesting the possible triviality of charm.

A related work, to cite just one more, is the very interesting *Ralph
the Heir*, a novel that, like *The Claverings*, abounds in humor and comic

situations, but that finally dismantles its own comic premise. Like Frank Gresham with his "joyous, genial lustre," the novel's nominal hero Ralph Newton has that magic natural attractiveness that in comedy generally sweeps all before it: "there was a kind of sunshine about the young man" (chap. 5) that even disarms greedy creditors (of which he has many). He is "so good-humoured, and so gay, and so pleasant" (chap. 50) that he seems, in Trollope's comic universe, bound to succeed. But again in *Ralph the Heir* Trollope introduces a strain of puritan melancholy and fatalism that plays havoc with comedy. In his blithe flirtations with one girl after another (a proceeding here severely reprimanded) and especially in his spendthrift devotion to pleasure, which has saddled him with ruinous debt, Ralph becomes ever more clearly an image not of comic suppleness and charm but simply of impoverished character.[8] Frivolity and pleasure are harshly judged throughout the novel, and at one point Squire Newton, whose own life is tragically shadowed because of a youthful dalliance that produced an illegitimate child, (mis)quotes from *King Lear* (5.3.170–71) the ultimate anticomic utterance: "The gods are just, and of our pleasant vices make instruments to scourge us" (chap. 23). Polly Neefit, the breeches-maker's vivacious daughter, does her best to keep the potential of comic charm alive in this novel, but for the most part charm in *Ralph the Heir* is severely devalued. Hence the blunt judgment finally passed on Ralph. "There was an ease and grace always present in his intercourse with women," remarks the narrator, "which perhaps arose from the slightness of his purposes and the want of reality in his character" (chap. 47). It is a radical revision of comic principles indeed to treat "ease and grace" as almost necessarily meretricious, as badges of personal deficiency. Once again in this novel, then, we see Trollope sharply qualifying that sponsorship of charm that is one of his strongest artistic motives and one of his essential links to comedy.

ROMANTIC PASSION

This qualifying process leads necessarily to deep disturbances in the field of sex and love. As Northrop Frye says, Eros is the presiding genius of comedy (p. 181). Given comedy's basis in the pleasure principle, it could hardly have been otherwise, for the reason declared in a startling speech from Shirley's comedy *The Grateful Servant*. "Wenching!" exclaims the pseudo-pandar Grimundo, "why, 'tis the topbranch, the heart, the very soul of pleasure . . . lechery is the monarch of delight, whose throne is in the blood, to which all other sins do homage, and bow like serviceable vassals, petty subjects in the dominion of flesh" (3.4). Comedy need not have the baldly libidinous tone of a passage like this, but it does see love as chiefly an avenue to pleasure, and tends to give short shrift to the impulse to view erotic relations in moralized terms of any kind—especially when chaste adoration is held up as a model of love. Comedy, which glorifies sexual gratification, is the persistent antagonist of sentimental romance, which sublimates carnality as much as possible, idealizing passion and emotional transport. Comic lovers mate like birds in spring, impulsively and unreflectively, for the delicious pleasure of it and because they can't help themselves; and comedy, fundamentally unsentimental and even amoral in its attachment to the pleasure principle, aligning itself with nature rather than aspiring to transcend it, voices approval. Trollope exactly affirms comic doctrine in *The Belton Estate*, therefore, when he pretends to wonder at the odd reticence of English maidens in the matter of love-making, "—as though love-making were in itself a thing injurious and antagonistic to happiness, instead of being, as it is, the very salt of life" (chap. 4). The same attitude underlies his advice that in selecting a mate the best method, after all, is an impulsive "leap in the dark" (*Ralph the Heir*, chap. 56): immediate pleasure, says the comic side of Trollope's sensibility, is a good guide.

The comic image of love as sheer pleasure is exhilarating, but it is subversive to the idealization of sentiment—and to put it this way is to understand from another point of view why the nineteenth century had so little tolerance for true (that is, traditional) comedy. Comedy has an ingrained tendency toward cool, ironic, unsentimental treatments of love, as it does toward other forms of pleasure. We can infer that the essential reason for its antipathy to emotion is that emotion inhibits the forms of carnal and worldly pleasure that comedy glorifies. Extreme feeling fixates, binds the person under its influence to some object; experiencing pleasure, on the other hand, requires a certain *disponibilité*, a cultivated responsiveness to stimuli, a self-possessed state in which absorption in experience and detachment are held in fine balance. Since passionate feeling is anathema to this privileged state, unbridled passion can scarcely fail in comedy to appear aberrant, ridiculous, or at least foolish. Rosalind's teasing of Orlando in *As You Like It* administers the classic comic reproof to passion in a tenderly affectionate mode, as does the witty ridicule lavished upon the morbidly sentimental and idealistic lover Faulkland in *The Rivals*. Often this reproof is given in considerably harsher terms, as it is in the many comedies like *The Country Wife* where love is depicted as mere lust and any belief in sentimentalized passion is treated as a preposterous delusion. *Pride and Prejudice* is far from being so cynical, yet it is a reflection of the comic perspective on passion that the long-awaited scene of Elizabeth's acceptance of Darcy's proposal, the scene occupying the emotional apex of the novel, is virtually skipped over.

Jane Austen devotes exactly three sentences to this event and merely summarizes the lovers' words, rather than quoting them directly (pp. 273–74). Readers anticipating the pleasures of emotional stimulation get a bracing cold shower, in other words, in this brief, stiff, perfunctory scene, which functions as a satire upon excesses of erotic emotionalism and as an exercise in the reserve and detachment that comedy prizes.

Trollope's affiliation with comedy has much to do with his own antipathy to the emotionalism that pervaded the literature and the domestic culture of his age, a tendency originating, no doubt, in a spreading impression of a peculiar emotional barrenness in middle-class life in the age of industrial capitalism and of its characteristic form of religion, cold, repressive puritanism. "I believe there is less personal affection in England than in any other country of which I know anything," says Mill in a canceled passage of his *Autobiography* (p. 33), explaining that his father's policy of "starving the feelings" (p. 32) was representative of the nation at large, not an individual aberration. Just as Mill, reacting against his nightmarish fear of a total loss of feeling, indulged in the most extravagant emotionalism with regard to Harriet Taylor, so the whole culture that he indicted for feelinglessness became addicted to almost pathological intensities of feeling. (We are returning from another angle, it will be seen, to the "psychanesthesia" diagnosed by Freud.) Trollope's insight into this state of affairs comes to him directly from Thackeray, who carries out in *Vanity Fair* a sustained, vitriolic analysis of the excesses of nineteenth-century emotionalism, which leads in that novel, among other things, to a devastating collapse of pleasure. The story of Amelia Sedley's self-neutering (and her emasculation of her faithful lover Dobbin) by her lugubrious worship of George's Osborne's memory— prefiguring, for example, Mill's extravagant worship of Harriet's memory, or Queen Victoria's of Prince Albert's, or Carlyle's of Jane Welsh's, or Ruskin's of Rose La Touche's—is designed as a fable of the disordered emotional dynamics of the culture at large; and we notice again, as in *Pride and Prejudice*, the telltale comic irony that cools off the grand scene of Dobbin's long-awaited acceptance by Amelia, whom by now we realize to be quite unworthy of the cult that Dobbin has built around her. "Kiss, kiss, kiss, and so forth," gibes the narrator (chap. 67).

Running throughout Trollope's fiction is this same skepticism of romantic emotionalism and of maudlin sentiment. He brings his skepticism to bear by seeming at times to align himself with conventional sentimentalities, sometimes fervently declaring his belief in the beauty of young love, the sacred value of faithfulness, the bliss of matrimony. A recent critic tells us accordingly that "love in all its purity and permanence is the moral centre of Trollope's work," that "fidelity unto death is one of the conventions Trollope constantly upholds . . . as a holy grail," and that his touchstone is "the ecstatic, transfiguring excitement of love" (Terry, 102, 98, 74). J. Hillis Miller proposes much the same view. "Falling in love is for Trollope an absolute," he declares (p. 124). "One person can, for Trollope, stand in the place of God to another" (p. 133). Walter M. Kendrick offers the same picture, which of course anchors Trollope squarely, perhaps without intending to, in the most bathetic Victorian sentimentality. According to Kendrick, all of Trollope's fictional psychologizing goes to sanctify "the wordless love of the silently speaking heart" (p. 134). But this hyperbolic language is drastically out of key with the complex realities of much of Trollope's fiction, which among other things incorporates a steady critique of the sentimentalized religion of love these critics foist upon him.

The desentimentalization of love takes many forms in Trollope's work, and over and over again administers that jolt to our sensibilities that constitutes one of the chief functions of comedy. The story of Lily Dale's sentimental self-immolation after her jilting by Crosbie, for example, is Trollope's own version of the Amelia Sedley fable: although critics have misread this plot, we are meant to recognize the self-lacerating excess of Lily's behavior, and to draw the evident moral that passion of such intensity is deeply malignant. *The Small House at Allington* contains also the coolly ironic cautionary tale of Colonel Orlando Dale, who in his youth made a reckless, wildly romantic elopement with a penniless girl (not, however, named Rosalind), and who has since declined with his wife into "an effete, invalid, listless couple, pretty well dead to all the world beyond the region of the Torquay card-tables" (chap. 2)—an astringent verdict indeed on the results of romantic passion. In *The Eustace Diamonds*, Lizzie longs for a Corsair or a Giaour to fulfill her erotic fantasies, parodies the Amelia Sedley myth with her pretense of a posthumous cult for her husband Sir Florian, and attempts to immerse herself in Shelley's poetry, which Trollope treats as ludicrously ungrammatical rubbish (chap. 21). High-flown romantic passion in this novel is a joke. As for Lucy Morris, the nominal heroine, she settles for much less than "ecstatic, transfiguring love" in her union with Frank Greystock, who flutters like a moth around Lizzie's candle throughout the novel. Passion is similarly punctured in *The Claverings* when Florence Burton, seconded by her wise sister-in-law and evidently by Trollope himself, does the sensible thing and simply overlooks the faithlessness of her weak-willed suitor Harry Clavering and takes him back, despite his painfully obvious mediocrity. Lofty notions of "purity and permanence" in love are explicitly tossed overboard in stories like these, which argue that those who are not willing to settle for impurities in this life will have to do without altogether. In the last chapter of this book we shall look at *Ayala's Angel*, an extended comic study of the concept of a grand erotic passion, in which the heroine, thanks to her liberating discovery of worldly pleasure, learns the foolishness of romance and the need of accommodating herself happily to ordinary imperfect reality.

In other novels, Trollope carries the comic celebration of love as sheer pleasure so far as more or less to eliminate any strong sense of intimate affection between the lovers. In *Rachel Ray*, for example, the love story is central, but the comic sensibility here is too sure of its functions to involve us in a tale of devoted sentiment and "the silently speaking heart." In fact Trollope is at pains to stress the light-hearted impulsiveness of this courtship, the freedom from deep feeling. He barely troubles to introduce the young brewer Luke Rowan to the reader before Rachel falls in love with him (the conventional role of the comic lover being self-explanatory) and Luke, for his part, sets off on the visit where he will propose to Rachel without any set purpose of doing so. "It will, I fear," says the narrator, "be thought from this that he was light in purpose as well as light in heart," but in fact this is "the way of men," who can scarcely do other than follow "little words and little acts" to "their natural consequence . . . without much premeditation" (chap. 11). In a world centered on the pleasure principle this kind of folly is enough. Lord Lufton takes the same kind of almost involuntary leap in the dark in proposing to Lucy Robarts in *Framley Parsonage*:

> He hardly knew what it was for the saying of which he
> had so resolutely come thither. He had by no means made
> up his mind that he loved Lucy Robarts; nor had he made
> up his mind that, loving her, he would, or that, loving her,
> he would not, make her his wife. He had never used his
> mind in the matter in any way.
>
> (Chap. 16)

Not surprisingly, the forms of erotic and conjugal love that Trollope presents most approvingly and explores most deeply have little in common with romantic ecstasy. For one thing, he persistently highlights the imperfection and incompleteness of the love unions he praises most: those, for example, of Palliser and Glencora (neither of whom in the slightest deifies the other), Alice Vavasor and John Grey, Mary Lovelace and Lord George Germain in *Is He Popenjoy?*, Clary Underwood and Gregory Newton in *Ralph the Heir*, Margaret Mackenzie and John Ball, Lady Carbury and Mr. Broune. All these pairs represent genuine images of felicity or at least semi-felicity, but all are marked by severely curtailed passion, whether because of the advanced age and general disenchantment of one or the other partner, or because the match is explicitly a *pis aller*, a replacement for a failed love affair with someone else. In contrast to the insanely passionate (and thus destructive) intensity of the two main characters in *He Knew He Was Right*, Charles Glascock, having been rejected by Nora Rowley and thinking his heart broken, finds himself falling in love anew with Caroline Spaulding, to whom before long he proposes more successfully, and with Trollope's evident blessing. Theirs is a romance of warm and authentic but chastened, moderate feeling, free of ecstatic transfiguration, and as such it embodies a prime Trollopian ideal. Stories like these are scarcely comic in themselves, but they are outgrowths of the logic of comedy none the less.

We have hardly scratched the surface, however, of Trollope's disavowal of overwhelming sexual passion.

PERVERSITIES OF DESIRE

The appeal of the unsentimental comic view of love is surely strong: in emancipating us from the mythology of romantic passion, comedy works to reconcile us to our own imperfect natures, which have a way of always falling short of the ideal intensities posited in romantic literature. But we come to a point where the comic perception of desire not as transcendence but as natural folly may shade into a more disturbing vision altogether; and Trollope, following the logic of comedy where it leads, incessantly teases us beyond that point, giving us a troubling modernistic science of the psychology of love that again makes one think strongly of Freud and Proust. Love in this view is irrational and perverse, has little to do with the perception of admirable qualities in the object of love, and leads almost necessarily to disenchantment and suffering. To see such a view emerge in Trollope is to realize (if works like *A Midsummer-Night's Dream* or *The Man of Mode* had not made this clear long since) that traditional comedy is charged with nihilistic energy and that it maintains its celebratory mood only by summarily overruling the darker implications of its whole conception of love.

Probably no other pattern in Trollope's fiction expresses these implications more plainly than his recurring tales of women who fall in love with wholly unsatisfactory men, or men, in any case, plainly their inferiors. This is just the inveterate pattern of comedy, but Trollope invites us to notice its disturbing side. Frank Gresham is an amiable young man, but there is an unmistakable disparity of character between this "arrant puppy" and the strong, witty, sophisticated, self-possessed Mary Thorne that makes the reader of *Doctor Thorne* wonder how she could ever have fallen hopelessly in love with him. The anomaly of this pairing is the most distinctly underlined fact of the story. Comedy asks us to see it merely as a fable of the omnipotence of impulsive pleasure, but Trollope studies the realities of nineteenth-century social life in too concerted a fashion not to raise questions about the whole structure of cultural institutions, particularly those dictating certain hierarchical relations between the sexes (the institution of romantic love being one of these), that could induce a young woman like Mary to bestow herself upon such a man. Lying latent in Trollope's comic pattern, in other words, is the whole searching analysis of the culturally ordained victimization of women, especially in marriage, that emerges in fully articulated form in such a novel as *He Knew He Was Right*.

In the mild form that it takes in *Doctor Thorne*, the question is raised in a succession of other stories of unequal matches such as that of Violet Effingham and the obsessive foxhunter Lord Chiltern or that of Isabel Boncassen's love for Lord Silverbridge in *The Duke's Children*. The same motif takes more acute form, as we have seen, in Florence Burton's attachment to the hopelessly mediocre Harry Clavering, or in Lucy Morris's to her neglectful fiancé Frank Greystock. At the end of the most insightful study so far of Trollope's treatment of love, Robert M. Polhemus argues eloquently that the union of Phineas Finn and the ravishing Madame Max Goesler in *Phineas Redux* vindicates at the last the saving power of sexual love, that earlier in the *Phineas* books has more often than not seemed destructive ("Being in Love," 395). Once again, however, we have in this story the same dismaying fable of the superior woman bestowing herself on a patently inferior man. Trollope has underlined this pattern here with unusual distinctness, bringing forward Violet Effingham to explain in so many words why she chose not to accept Phineas's proposal of marriage. "Mr. Finn, when I came to measure him in my mind, was not small," she says, "but he was never quite tall enough. . . . Mr. Finn was just half an inch too short. He lacks something in individuality. He is a little too much a friend to everybody" (*Phineas Finn*, chap. 71). How is it that the usually so discriminating Madame Max fails to perceive the deficiencies of this man's character? In other analogous cases this discrepancy between the woman and the man is so sharp and dangerous as to create potential tragedy, as in Lady Glencora's infatuation with the charming ne'er-do-well Burgo Fitzgerald, Alice Vavasor's love for her violent cousin George, Emily Wharton's for the brutish Lopez, or Marie Melmotte's for Sir Felix Carbury, the most grotesquely worthless character in all of Trollope's fiction.

The tragic potential of this well-nigh obsessive theme is fully acted out for once in *Sir Harry Hotspur of Humblethwaite*. The noble-minded Emily falls in love with her fortune-hunting cousin George Hotspur although—could it be because?—he is "a brute, unredeemed by any one manly gift; idle, self-indulgent, false, and without a principle" (chap. 22). Her eventual discovery of his abject worthlessness does not, however, extinguish her feelings for him, even when he has married another woman: "she still loved in a way which she could not herself understand, loving and despising him utterly at the same time" (chap. 24)—yet another rehearsal, one can see, of the Amelia Sedley story, so full of mythic resonance for the nineteenth century as a whole. Emily's father, Sir Harry, who assumes that love is rational at bottom, or bears at least some intelligible relation to moral judgment, is entirely bewildered.

> "Why she has loved him, what she has seen in him, I cannot tell," said Sir Harry to his wife that night.
> We must presume Sir Harry did not know how it is that the birds pair.
>
> (Chap. 21)

The phrase crystallizes the way Trollope perverts the specifically comic paradigm of love (love as thoughtless instinct) into a frightening vision of desire as an irrational compulsion driven, it seems, by everything that is antithetical to one's conscious values. At the same time, he shows this pattern of love to be a widespread cultural malady that implicates the whole system of sexual interrelations in this society, where women's erotic life seems almost inescapably governed by their attraction to unworthy men.[9] The fundamental logic of this pattern, in which the most despicable men are the most compulsively loved, remains obscure in Trollope's novels, but it strongly suggests a violent psychic response to the Victorian idealization of the moral sensibility of women—an idealization that women (and men with deep intuitive sympathy with them, like Trollope) could only feel as ultimately sinister and imprisoning, a vast cultural mechanism for reflecting glory back upon men. Freud briefly speculates along very much these lines in his essay on "debasement" in love, where he suggests that in a culture obsessed with the sexual purity of women, the female libido is necessarily fixated upon "forbiddenness" in sex (p. 186).[10] Trollope clearly had uncovered this principle for himself, and had made it one of his chief narrative devices.

His fullest exploration of the perverse anomalies of erotic love comes perhaps in *The Small House at Allington*, which in its step-by-step re-writing of *Sense and Sensibility* epitomizes the way Trollope shifts comic patterns into a Proustian mode. We get a glimpse of such a mode in the subplot of Bernard Dale's odd courtship of his cousin Bell. He grudgingly proposes to her wholly in obedience to the squire's wishes, and is surprised to find that her refusal, rather than relieving him, makes him unhappy. "Having expressed a wish for this thing," comments the deeply analytical narrator, fascinated with the obliquity of sexual desire, "the very expression of the wish made him long to possess it." Bernard finds to his surprise and discomfort that he is un-able to shake off this attraction to Bell.

> Why had he subjected himself to this numbing weakness? His love had never given him any pleasure. Indeed he had never hitherto acknowledged it; but now he was driven to do so on finding it to be the source of trouble and pain. I think it is open to us to doubt whether, even yet, Bernard Dale was in love with his cousin; whether he was not rather in love with his own desire. But against himself he found a verdict that he was in love, and was angry with himself and with all the world.
>
> (Chap. 13)

Trollope seeks lamely here to salvage an idealized conception of love, but all his analysis reveals a passion that has little or nothing to do with the loved person herself, but rather is weirdly conjured into ex-istence as a reflex of one's own words, is recognizable only in the "trouble and pain" it precipitates (this is the entire negation of the pleasure principle), and is almost impossible to distinguish from a state of being in love simply with one's own desire—whatever that may mean. The erotic universe of Proust could hardly be more explic-itly or more concisely laid before us.

The paradoxes touched upon in this preliminary sketch are far more elaborately dramatized in the story of Lily's lifelong devotion to the worthless Crosbie. In Jane Austen's telling, the heartbroken girl at last reasserts her rational will and teaches herself to love the worthy and respectable Colonel Brandon, but this is the consoling event that never occurs in *The Small House*. Trollope is relentless in showing that even his gayest, sweetest, most shrewdly intelligent heroine—and Bell too, for that matter—is vulnerable to Crosbie's hollow charm. She marks him down at first glance, as we have seen, as a mere "swell," then proceeds to fall helplessly in love with him for exactly this rea-son. Johnnie Eames ruefully and lucidly analyzes what has happened. "He had that sort of manner, you know," he says to his friend the earl.

"He was a swell, and girls like that kind of thing" (chap. 32). Even without invoking the sexual *double entendre* lodged in the word "swell," this to my mind is one of the cruelest lines in Trollope's fiction, turning the exquisite heroine as it does into just another case history of postadolescent sexual pathology. Like Bernard, Lily seems to be "in love with [her] own desire," fixated, that is, on a sentimental myth of love that robs her of all control of her own will. Proust goes a step further and declares that this kind of delusive, deeply masochistic love of our own mental projections is the only kind there is. Trollope can hardly let himself go so far, but in *The Small House at Allington* only the union of Bell and Dr. Crofts (the Colonel Brandon of this novel) mitigates the prevailing view of love as a destructive labyrinth of irrationality.

For a writer long accused of trafficking in nothing but platitudes and conventional sentimentalities, it is surprising how insistently Trollope sets forth this disenchanted analysis of the tender passion. Frank Greystock in *The Eustace Diamonds* is another character who discovers how love may wholly violate one's moral sensibilities.

> In his very heart Greystock despised [Lizzie]; he had told
> himself over and over again that were there no Lucy in the
> case he would not marry her; that she was affected,
> unreal—and in fact a liar in every word and look and
> motion which came from her with premeditation. [He]
> . . . knew her to be heartless and bad. . . . And yet he
> loved her after a fashion, and was prone to sit near her,
> and was fool enough to be flattered by her caresses. When
> she would lay her hand on his arm, a thrill of pleasure
> went through him.
>
> (Chap. 65)

That loving and despising can coincide so closely, and that one can be intensely flattered by gestures that one knows to be wholly false, is a depth of irrationality to make the head spin. By the same token, Trollope in this novel, as often elsewhere, challenges the sacrosanct myth of love as a state of undivided fidelity. "If it were to be asserted here that a young man may be perfectly true to a first young woman while he is falling in love with a second," says the narrator, "the readers of this story would probably be offended. But undoubtedly many men believe themselves to be quite true while undergoing this process, and many young women expect nothing else from their lovers" (chap. 24). From the point of view of the moralized mythology of love (the mythology of purity, permanence, and ecstasy), the true, convoluted logic of sexual relations seems so absurd that the word "love" itself begins to appear nonsensical. There is a strong note of humor in Trollope's dwelling on this absurdity, but it is not a style of humor calculated to ingratiate him with the Victorian reading public at large.

Like Proust and like Freud, Trollope notes constantly that desire has roots in predatory instinct and especially in jealousy, which he calls (in an uncannily Proustian phrase) "one of the most common phases of the human heart" (*Framley Parsonage*, chap. 31).[11] This is the phase displayed, for instance, in the story of Lizzie Eustace's desiring to marry Lord Fawn only after she has been rejected by him and come to hate him as a result, or, in a more violent rehearsal of the same theme from *The Eustace Diamonds*, in the story of the courtship of Lucinda Roanoke by Sir Griffin Tewett. On Sir Griffin's side, desire is wholly detached from charm, being a compound of jealousy, resentment, and sadism. "He hardly knew why it was that he wanted her," observes the narrator. He is attracted neither by married life nor by Lucinda's personal qualities. "He had seen that she was a very handsome girl, and therefore he had thought that he would like to possess her. Had she fallen like a ripe plum into his mouth, or shown herself ready so to fall, he would probably have closed his lips and backed out of the affair. But the difficulty no doubt added something to the desire" (chap. 39). "There are men," says the narrator later, "in whose love a good deal of hatred is mixed—who love as the huntsman loves the fox, towards the killing of which he intends to use all his energies and intellects" (chap. 41). This is admittedly an extreme case—though Trollope is full of dramas of sadistic love, from Lord Ongar to Robert Kennedy to Louis Trevelyan—but the dark, drastically unsentimentalized view of love as a system of irrational torment and destruction emerges in these novels often in forms that comedy can hardly accommodate, forms that reveal, in other words, how fine a line separates the cool comic version of love from a nightmare vision of jealousy compulsively feeding upon itself. What we see throughout Trollope's fiction, in other words, is that when charm ceases to operate as the catalyst of desire, comedy can only turn chillingly inside out.

Celebrating Friendship

Another symptom of Trollope's disenchanted view of erotic love is his lifelong sponsorship of an ideal of tender nonsexual friendship, as well as of parental and filial affection, both of which seem to him potentially more rational and more authentic alternatives to the prospect of being "mutilated and tortured" (*The Small House*, chap. 11) by the impulsive emotions of romantic love. In this respect Trollope seems at

last to accept the severing of affection and desire as an inescapable
reality, not because love has been too idealized to consort with desire,
but for essentially the opposite reason: that romantic love, the cultural
institution supposed to give morally legitimate form to sex, has been
found to be a largely pernicious illusion. Friends, too, are spared that
almost inevitable pang of melancholy that in Trollope befalls even the
most genuine lovers as they go at last to the altar. "Is it not the fact,"
asks the narrator of *Framley Parsonage*, "that the sweetest morsel of
love's feast has been eaten, that the freshest, fairest blush of the flower
has been snatched and has passed away, when the ceremony at the
altar has been performed, and legal possession has been given?"
(chap. 48). The same predicament conjures up crueler imagery earlier
in the same novel, where young men are seen as moths fluttering
recklessly about the candle of desire, "till in a rash moment they rush
in too near the wick, and then fall with singed wings and crippled
legs, burnt up and reduced to tinder by the consuming fire of matrimony" (chap. 20). Trollope is obsessed with this moment of disillu-
sion because it is the moment when young lovers realize, too late, that
the mythology of ecstasy and permanence in love, rather than being a
true description of experience, is largely just a sociocultural mechanism (the maintenance of which is particularly the responsibility of
popular novelists) for perpetuating the institution of marriage; and he
constantly analyzes married life itself, therefore, as a strenuous process of attempting to reconcile oneself to the absence of the erotic euphoria that one had been taught to look forward to.

Friendship, then, runs throughout Trollope's work, charged with
the kind of compensatory significance that I have suggested, and
forms some of his most affecting material.[12] As early as *The Warden*,
for example, Eleanor Harding's odd folly of infatuation with a man unworthy of her, John Bold, is in effect compensated for by the evocation
of the real center of feeling in this novel, the deep, loving friendship
between Mr. Harding and the old bishop of Barchester. That this
friendship represents for Trollope a displacement of erotic attraction
into another—and a better—kind of relationship is suggested by Trollope's language here: "There was a gentleness about the bishop to
which the soft womanly affection of Mr. Harding particularly en-
deared itself, and it was quaint to see how the two mild old priests
pressed each other's hands, and smiled and made little signs of love"
(chap. 9). Deep, tender, all-forgiving friendships of this kind prolifer-
ate in subsequent Barset novels and throughout Trollope's career, in
the friendships of Arabin and Josiah Crawley, of Dr. Thorne and
Squire Gresham, of Johnnie Eames and Earl de Guest, and many
more. On at least a couple of noteworthy occasions in his later work

Trollope seems plainly to act out the displacement of erotic love by friendship. In *The Eustace Diamonds*, the "Corsair," Lord George de Bruce Carruthers, surprises Lizzie by his deeply felt speech about Mrs. Carbuncle, once, apparently, his mistress, but now his friend. Lizzie accuses him of caring more for "that odious vulgar woman down-stairs" than for her. "Ah, dear!" replies Lord George. "I have known her for many years, Lizzie, and that both covers and discovers many faults. One learns to know how bad one's old friends are, but then one forgives them, because they are old friends" (chap. 75). There is also the story in *The Way We Live Now* of Mr. Broune and Lady Carbury, whose ill-starred *amour* turns little by little into a deep, confidential friendship, and then gradually back into another kind of love: it is one of the most affecting passages in Trollope, and one of his tenderest, most poignant salutes to friendship. "There was something in the absolute friendship which now existed between Lady Carbury and [Mr. Broune]," comments the narrator, that makes this normally unscrupulous woman not dare to ask him for any improper favors (chap. 89). Friendship is Lady Carbury's salvation in a novel where salvation—that is, peace of mind—is next to impossible to achieve, especially if one looks for it in the labyrinths of erotic love.

Trollope's many moving portrayals of love between parents and children likewise counter the hazardous complexities of erotic love, and themselves, in fact, often seem just a subspecies of friendship. Sometimes parental love takes on the very aspect of erotic love, imitating its irrational jealousy and possessiveness or self-laceration—as in Mrs. Bolton of *John Caldigate* or Lady Carbury herself in her masochistic, half-amorous devotion to Sir Felix—and in these cases it becomes distorted beyond recognition. But in the relations of Mr. Harding and Eleanor, Dr. Thorne and Mary, Lady and Lord Lufton, or Mrs. Dale and her daughters, Trollope imagines friendship of a sublime (yet wholly credible) kind that momentarily takes us away from the perilous zone of charm and desire. At such moments we see Trollope, characteristically, injecting into the frivolous, artificial, pleasure-oriented world of comedy a strain of deep natural feeling that gives comedy new valences of emotion. It is this kind of inflection of the basic tonalities of comedy that constitutes, we are seeing, Trollope's incessant practice as a novelist.

4

Comic Design and "The Impression of Life"

Comedy is not the same thing as life.

W. P. Ker, "On Comedy"

The Realist's Paradox

In the patently artificial world of comedy, plots, we have seen, are geometrical constructions of parallelisms, repetitions, and inversions, all leading to the symmetrical patterns of a happy ending; the impression of naturally (that is, irregularly) unfolding trains of events is everywhere preempted by comedy's overriding sense of design. Comic characters often seem to have an intuition of this quality of the world they inhabit and to strive, with wild expenditures of energy, to break out into some freer mode of existence and a fuller selfhood. The rampant hedonism that forms such a prominent theme in comedy seems the symptom, for example, of a hunger for real experience that in the stylized comic world can never be gratified. This implication is particularly apparent in the perennial comic formula of pairs of lovers intercoupling (as they do in *A Midsummer-Night's Dream* or Iris Murdoch's novel *A Severed Head*) in one combination after another, as though in quest of a gratification that ever eludes them. Again, Freud's remarkable essay on "debasement in the sphere of love" sheds light on comic structures. Freud sees erotic life in civilized society as cursed with an inevitable failure of pleasure, and thus as falling into just the configurations of comic plot, "an endless series of substitutive objects none of which, however, brings full satisfaction." This hypothesis, Freud says, "may explain the inconstancy in object-choice, the 'craving for stimulation,' which is so often a feature of the love of adults" (p. 189) and is also, we may add, the almost invariable theme of comedy. The stylization of comic plot thus seems to have a deep connection with potentially hysterical anxieties about the unattainability of human desires—which may be why, as many have testified, comedy has as great a power to disturb as tragedy does, and why figures like Don Juan, Horner, and Dorimant occupy such a central position in our literary culture.

In this and in other sometimes elusive, almost subliminal ways, the principle of formalized patterning is linked to the whole range of comic themes and effects. To the extent that the sense of conscious stylization is diluted in a given work we feel ourselves estranged from comedy and from its implicit promise of pleasure—for, whatever anxieties it may conceal, the principle of geometrical plot design is inseparable from that of comic pleasure. The artificiality of comic plot is from one point of view an imprisonment, but from another a guarantee of temporary immunity from real-life contingencies, a guarantee, as we have seen, that is the primordial condition of comedy's world of holiday entertainment. To repeat this point is to stress again the discrepancy between comedy and "realism"—a vexed term central to critical discussion of Trollope, and one that I need briefly to comment upon, though without being drawn further than necessary into the philosophical quicksand surrounding this term at present.

Sophisticated theorists are inclined to take for granted nowadays that realism, far from being able to give a uniquely faithful picture of the real world, is merely a code of arbitrary stylistic conventions. Verisimilitude is merely an illusion, "a mask assumed by the laws of the text" (Todorov, 83) and in no way equivalent to "the big blooming buzzing confusion" (to borrow a phrase from Beckett's *Murphy*), the total absence of determinate patterns, supposed to constitute reality truly perceived. All realism, we are often reminded, necessarily constitutes "a violence done to the multiplicity and variousness of experience, to the elusiveness of reality" (Levine, 134). Given what he speaks of as "the infinite play of the world," Roland Barthes posits an "ideal text" that will be "absolutely plural," "a galaxy of signifiers, not a structure of signifieds." For such a text, of course, "there cannot be a narrative structure, a grammar, or a logic" (pp. 5–6). From the point of view not of metaphysics but of one interested in the rhetoric and history of fictional styles, however, the relevant point may be that all apprehension of art as art is predicated on our possessing—as, necessarily, we must—a distinct conception of the real with which particular works of art enter into complicated relations both of harmony and dissonance. What is at issue here is not the origin or the philosophical validity of this conception but just the way it functions to let us read works of art as attempts to imitate or extend it or, alternatively, to alter it by thrusting some new image between us and our habitual scene. The phantasmagoria of infinite multiplicity so often postulated in present-day critical theory is in fact a chimera that has never, I take it, been observed, and is of course wholly beyond the power of art to represent. By the same token, as I have been arguing, the central effect of comedy depends on our perception that the symmetrical patterns of its plot *are* stylized conventions that usurp natural causality; a reader or spectator unable to make such judgments could scarcely know what comic art is, much less enjoy it.

Realism, then, may or may not be able to align itself with reality (the point seems moot) but it does seek to present images of recognizable life, and it trusts its readers or viewers to be capable of recognizing them as such. However, realism is never neutral, passive, impartial, or disinterested, as it has sometimes been said to be; it is an active literary method that imitates ordinary perceptions of reality in order to achieve literary *effects*. It is always *expressive*. To understand this point one need only study some such document as the text of the Watergate tapes, which constitutes if anything could a faithful and direct transcription of reality and is full of information about the helter-skelter rhythms of actual speech and the workings of actual personalities, but at no point gives the reader the sense of aesthetically satisfying "realism." Why should this sense be exclusively the prerogative of *literary* texts, of imaginative imagery, of metaphors? The answer is that what we call realism lies not in a static "true-to-life" image, as the often-invoked analogy of photography would imply, but in a felt act of imagination. Its function is not simply to present an image corresponding in some way to reality, but to give us the sense of witnessing an extension of art, a capturing of some hitherto unrecorded facet of real experience. Realism, in other words, involves a simultaneous commentary both upon reality and upon art. As George Levine has stressed in his illuminating discussion of this issue, it manifests itself in the ironic rectification of some pseudo-realistic notion of life, some literary convention, that is now to be displaced. This effect is just what a tape recorder can never achieve, for it knows nothing of representational conventions to begin with. Significantly, realistic fiction centers often on the fable of the slow discovery of some character's true nature that at first is obscured by conventional preconceptions (the discovery of Charles's true nature in Balzac's *Eugénie Grandet* or of Casaubon's in *Middlemarch* or of St. John Rivers's in *Jane Eyre* will suggest the pervasiveness of this paradigmatic story), a fable that projects the essence of the realistic imagination itself, always *finding things out*. This is why realism can never achieve a fully perfected form, but must perpetually exist in a transient, evolving mode, and why it is the unavoidable fate of realistic experiments (like Trollope's, or even more, like Hemingway's) that at first are striking for their verisimilitude to come to seem mannered and stylized, anachronistic, and to be displaced in turn by the new realism of a succeeding generation. Realism is always seen in the act of undoing its own tradition.

The realist achieves his special effect, therefore, not so much by fixing on reality itself as by inventing a new "paradigm" (to use Thomas S. Kuhn's term) to displace an older one hitherto taken as natural: the one, say, that depicts heroes as bold and glamorous, or endings as decisive, or sexual relations as devoid of physical detail, or actions as always significant, or motivation as clear-cut and logical. Realism always reveals the same thing, that habits of artistic representation have falsified this or that aspect of real experience. But in order to heighten that sense of fresh seeing that realism seeks to give, artists in this mode habitually dramatize the very paradigms they mean to invalidate; in a sense they *must* do so if the realistic effect is to be fully achieved—that is, if we are to be fully struck by the potency of this or that newly invented artistic device. *Don Quixote*, the original pattern of modern realism, epitomizes this principle in its elaborate invocation of the chivalric romances, whose vision of life is sharply contradicted at every stage of the hero's adventures. Realistic fiction of later centuries duplicates this process, constantly invoking images from sentimental, heroic, Gothic, Byronic, and other species of romance, only to replace these images by others closer to the lineaments of everyday life. Realism thus is always an ironic, adversarial mode, but almost by definition has a strong symbiotic relationship with the conventions that it purports to do away with.[1]

The problem that it must confront is that by defining itself negatively as a systematic program of elimination of all conventions that lend spurious heightening or dramatic interest to experience, it threatens at every moment to lapse altogether into the humdrum banality that it sets up as the standard of authenticity. I have referred once already to Mr. Biffen, the avant-garde novelist in Gissing's *New Grub Street*, who states the problem succinctly in describing his ambition of attaining "absolute realism," a project bound to produce, as he says, "something unutterably tedious" (p. 120). No real-life novelist illustrates this dilemma more plainly than Trollope himself, often praised for the almost uncanny "air of reality and truthfulness" that he achieves in his fiction, but no less often denounced for what one reviewer called his addiction to "the weary trivialities of common life" (Smalley, 279, 214). All realist novelists (those at least who seek to earn a living by their work) need to disarm such criticism by making the world they represent not only true-seeming but interesting. Thus the history of realism proves to be a history of devising strategies for cheating tedium by insinuating back into fiction the imaginative richness of the nonrealistic modes supposedly being repudiated. The definitive example of this method, again, is *Don Quixote*, where the preposterous idealism of chivalry is subjected to unrelenting parody, yet is glorified ever more poignantly by contrast with the sordid realities of the world the deluded knight inhabits. Even in *Madame Bovary*, where "realism" corresponds to an attitude of unrelieved scorn and cynicism, Emma's fatuous romantic daydreams, at first the signs of her poverty of mind and spirit, take on value the more fully we perceive the sterility of the provincial world she inhabits: at least they show a flicker of imaginative life, however tawdry, and this is more than nearly any other character in Flaubert's tale is capable of. In these and many equivalent cases the realist ends by authenticating the imaginative hyperbole that realism supposedly forbids. Realism, in other words, proves to be bound almost inseparably to the whole range of fictional conventions that it professes to demolish, and to take much of its energy directly from them.

Trollope and Lifelike Plotting

Trollope subscribed wholeheartedly to the theory of realism, declaring in a hundred places that the highest criterion of excellence in fiction was that of lifelikeness or "truth to nature." He insisted, however, that this quality was achieved not by passive or mechanical copying but by the exertion of an imaginative power that has almost occult overtones. Generally self-deprecatory in his accounts of his own novelistic methods, he surprises us by how fervently he describes his gift for creating visible, tangible, audible realities in his imagination, that "singular faculty" for bringing fictional characters to life that one admiring reviewer said could be accounted for "only by the doctrine of metempsychosis" (Smalley, 165). When Trollope turns to this theme, his notorious equation of the novelist and the diligent shoemaker is forgotten, and the writing of realistic fiction in the most prosaic style is seen in its true light as a kind of wizardry, an act of extrasensory perception enabling him actually to inhabit "a world altogether outside the world of [his] own material life" (*Autobiography*, 43) and to "live with [fictional characters] in the full reality of established intimacy" (ibid., 233). "To me," he declares in the concluding paragraph of *The Last Chronicle of Barset*, "Barset has been a real county, and its city a real city, and the spires and towers have been before my eyes, and the voices of the people are known to my ears, and the pavements of the city ways are familiar to my footsteps."

It is because Trollope believes so keenly that his imagined world is in some sense "real" that he disavows plot as a principle of composition, declaring that he deliberately begins novels without designing the action ahead of time, lest such a design falsify the natural development of his characters' motivations and circumstances (*Autobiography*, 175).[2] Plot, he says, is "the most insignificant part of a tale" (ibid., 126). In setting forth this dictum he exactly illustrates the claim of Robert Scholes and Robert Kellogg that realistic fiction tends inevitably toward the elimination of all sense of patterned design and toward a kind of structureless story that is, in their phrase, "virtually an 'unplot'" (p. 232). Trollope's critics have stressed the relevance of this principle to him in particular, emphasizing his propensity for natural-seeming, fluid, "open" story lines that seem unpremeditated. In Trollope, says Ruth apRoberts, we see "the high correlation of realism with the loose plot" (p. 28); James R. Kincaid treats this point at length, claiming that even when Trollope uses this or that conventional plot pattern we are given "a concurrent sense of the artificiality, even falseness of that pattern, a sense that genuine life is to be found only outside all pattern" (p. 40)—a comment strongly reminiscent of Bergson's idea of comedy as a parodic affirmation of "the fundamental law of life, which is the complete negation of repetition" (p. 81). An essayist in *The North British Review* of May 1864 makes the same point, arguing that novels like Trollope's represent a gain in verisimilitude over the drama since in novels people can "hang together as loosely as in real life" (quoted in Stang, 124). But the oft-invoked relationship between "looseness" and Trollopian realism is perhaps more intricate than these comments suggest, and his concern with plot more developed than his own disclaimers admit.[3]

Trollope's stock in trade as a novelist is a constant, mischievous revision of conventional patterns in fiction, but nowhere, I believe, does he suggest that verisimilitude means dispensing with "all pattern," an idea that again silently sets up the big blooming buzzing confusion as the authentic paradigm of the real. Trollope presumes, on the contrary, that any convincing imitation of real experience must be distinctly patterned, and that any attempt at an "absolute realism" apart from literary conventions would contradict itself. His sophisticated awareness of the structural limitations of realism is suggested by a now-familiar passage in the *Autobiography* where he declares that in order to achieve verisimilitude in dialogue a novelist must use a more coherent style than the disjointed syntax of true speech, in order to coincide with readers' preconceived though faulty notions of how coherent natural speech is (p. 240).[4] The disruption of paradigms that is the essence of realism needs to be carried out, in other words, with the finest gauging of effects. So, too, with regard to the structuring of plot, a problem to which Trollope devoted some of his keenest critical thinking.

A main point of reference here is the case of Trollope's mentor in the art of fiction, Thackeray, whose novels, especially *Pendennis* and *The Newcomes*, provided Trollope at the beginning of his career with examples of realistic fiction based on the principle of maximum looseness of plot. What Trollope could see clearly in these works was just the flaw that Henry James pointed to in dismissing them as "large loose baggy monsters": that instead of capturing a poignant sense of lifelikeness they convey primarily the impression of looseness itself, of slovenly construction—and that the final result is the one foreseen by Gissing's Mr. Biffen, invincible boredom. The sense of plotlessness and disconnectedness, Trollope saw, once allowed to dilate beyond a certain point needing to be artistically calculated with utmost precision, could only impair the illusion of lifelikeness in just the way that unimproved speech does. Hence his repeated stress in *Thackeray* and elsewhere on the importance of organic unity of plot, that is, on a strongly sustained sense of movement toward closure. Because Thackeray was so ready to give rein to his lazy "propensity to wandering" in fiction, all his novels except *Henry Esmond*, says Trollope, "contain rather strings of incidents . . . than a completed story"; they are "vague narratives" (*Thackeray*, 134, 121, 134–35). George Levine has eloquently praised Thackeray's attempts to imitate in fiction the vagueness that supposedly inheres in real life; but one feels that this defense is too much in thrall to current critical preconceptions, particularly the ones that say that "subverting" conventions is the highest function of art, and that realism equals maximum formlessness. Trollope is right about Thackeray: he neglects conventions of patterned narrative at the peril of his whole attempt at realism, and with only a couple of exceptions his novels founder in vagueness, squandering an immense talent.

The key to Trollope's own artistic method, in contrast to Thackeray's doomed attempt at a radically neutral realism, lies in the principle of the interdependence of realism and other modes, especially the comic. In a couple of places Trollope goes out of his way to articulate precisely this principle (though in the passages that I am about to cite, comedy is not the antithetical mode in question). In *Thackeray*, in the *Autobiography*, and again in his lecture "On English Prose Fiction as a Rational Amusement," Trollope considers the notion that the novelist aiming at realism must strictly abjure romance, the sublime, the sensational, and all such attempts "to soar above the ordinary actions and ordinary language of life" (*Thackeray*, 185). Though such styles seem incompatible with Trollope's own realistic style of low-key, prosaic storytelling, he argues that just as romance not deeply informed by realism "is apt to become cold, stilted, and unsatisfactory," so realism cut off from romance is doomed to mediocrity. "It is thus," he declares, quoting some oratorical passages from Scott's novels, that the sublime may be mingled with the realistic, if the writer has the power" (ibid., 186–87). "A good novel should be both [realistic and sensational], and both in the highest degree" (*Autobiography*, 227). The problem of a realist seeking to avoid the high-minded artistic suicide proposed by Mr. Biffen, Trollope declares, is not that of purging antirealistic elements but rather of discovering ways to salvage and incorporate them. In Trollope's work, Walter M. Kendrick cogently observes, sensationalism, "the theoretical opposite of realism[,] was not external to realism but its inseparable companion" (p. 52). The antirealistic mode that Trollope most often and most subtly experiments with, however, is not sensation romance but comedy. Ultimately his artistic goal is one that can scarcely be attained: to fuse the two antithetical modes, and in the fusion to enhance each. This I think was the philosopher's stone that Trollope sought, not in abstract theory but in concentrated artistic practice, throughout his career—and occasionally, in some of the finest passages of his fiction, actually seemed to find.

Given the focus of this study, we need only touch in passing on examples of Trollope's brilliant experiments in "loose" realistic plotting, experiments, that is, in somehow freeing story lines from the constraints of formula and pattern (including the basic pattern of suspense and dramatic climax), yet keeping them also from degenerating into "vague narratives" that are merely "strings of incidents." The main point here is that in Trollope's fictional world unravelings of narrative patterns are as a rule correlated with major breakdowns of the principle of comic pleasure. This effect is distinctly highlighted, for example, in *He Knew He Was Right*, where the ever-escalating quarrel between Louis and Emily Trevelyan serves as the vehicle for an elaborate exercise in "unplot": in this story causes and effects are always wildly out of joint and personal motives on the parts of both warring spouses are hopelessly divided and confused. The result is a succession of ambiguous, self-contradictory ultimatums that seem forgotten as soon as they are pronounced, perpetual, seemingly aimless oscillations of purpose, and a growing awareness on the part of readers as well as of bystanders within the story that the whole devastating quarrel has arisen from no substantial cause at all. One reviewer, used to the heavy plotting of Victorian popular fiction, remarked in exasperation, but quite acutely, that this story was "as shapeless as a boned fowl, entirely without any skeleton of plot or incident" (Smalley, 329). This effect of realistic shapelessness is heightened by contrast with the novel's group of comic subplots, each strongly marked by the geometrical form (here mainly triangular) basic to comedy: the farcical story of Mr. Gibson the clergyman in his dilemma with Camilla and Arabella French (he becomes engaged first to one, then to the other, then to the first again), or of Nora Rowley and her two suitors Mr. Glascock and Hugh Stanbury, or the story of the courtship of Dorothy Stanbury by Gibson and Brooke Burgess. All these subplots of *He Knew He Was Right* are shaped by the ever-repeated figure of lovers coupling in the usual comic minuet; the main plot is dominated by the opposite image of the couple erratically unraveling. Narrative shapelessness, the sense, that is, of a story deprived of the order and clarity of traditional plot patterns, forms a primary metaphor for the disorder in contemporary sexual relations and the resulting annihilation of pleasure that the novel explores.[5]

This contrasting of comic and tragically realistic story lines forms one of Trollope's commonest devices. Evidently he found it, as Robert Tracy has said, where he found so much, in seventeenth-century drama. Still, it is a very surprising practice for a writer professing a credo of lifelikeness and stylistic transparency, for with each shift from one vein to the other the reader is reminded as forcibly as possible of the arbitrariness of literary modes, causing the felt interplay between text and life to be largely eclipsed by the jostling of styles within the text. Most readers will agree that this juxtaposing of modes is an unfortunate distraction in *He Knew He Was Right*, robbing the novel of too much of its dramatic force, but the very awkwardness of the device draws attention to the subtle commentary that it makes on the problem of fictional plot. On the one hand, the comic subplots set off by contrast the remarkable experiment in "loose" plotting of the Trevelyan story. But they show at the same time that this looseness is fundamentally illusory, being itself a contrivance, a formal design. The covert pattern of the main story is in effect that of the comic stories turned inside-out. The more closely we look at it in this perspective, indeed, the more evident it becomes that the tragic Trevelyan story, one of Trollope's most extreme exercises in "realism," needs to be seen, with its long succession of misunderstandings, crossed purposes, and reversals, as a weirdly inverted comedy, full of suppressed humor. Realism, this novel implies in its whole formal design, is not a simple mirroring of real life but a mirroring of certain literary patterns in a kind of wavy, clouded, distorting mirror.

Given Trollope's commitment to natural-seeming fiction, he instinctively avoids the outlandishly artificial geometry that characterizes plot design in classic comedies; this kind of design makes frequent appearances none the less in his fiction, and rarely lies far beneath the surface if we look for it. To claim that Trollope "made war on symmetry" (Kincaid, 61) is to deny some of his most cunning effects. One example among others occurs in *Is He Popenjoy?*, where the severe, priggish Lord George Germain, who is involved in a budding love affair with Adelaide Houghton, is filled with horror at the suspicion that his wife Mary is having an affair of her own with Jack De Baron. Trollope stresses the symmetry of the situation, and in the process makes it funny. "[Lord George] had been unhappy before because he was conscious that he was ill-treating his wife, but now he was almost more disturbed because it seemed to him to be possible that his wife was ill-treating him" (chap. 19). The parallelism of the two stories is an authorial joke at Lord George's expense, and functions to mete out comic chastisement of a familiar kind: it reassures us that the novel—itself full of ominous parallels to *He Knew He Was Right*—is sure to end happily.

The comic pattern most consistently stressed in Trollope's novels is the presiding one of comedy: that of the concluding marriage, full as it is of implications of social reunification and the glorification of pleasure. Few of Trollope's novels fail to end in marriage—except those, like *The Small House at Allington*, that pointedly do not—and often he makes a point of calling attention to the convention, in just the kind of self-confessed artificiality that shocked Henry James. This he does both by direct commentary to the reader on this theme and by having one novel after another end not with one marriage but with a binge of them. At the end of *Ayala's Angel*, for instance, not only does Ayala marry Captain Stubbs, but her sister Lucy and Gertrude Tringle marry Isadore Hamel and Captain Batsby in a double ceremony, Imogene Docimer is joined to the scampish Frank Houston, and even the scoffer at matrimony Lord John Battledore is marched to the altar. "Now we have come to our last chapter," says the narrator,

> and it may be doubted whether any reader,—unless he be
> some one specially gifted with a genius for statistics,—
> will have perceived how very many people have been
> made happy by matrimony. If marriage be the proper
> ending for a novel,—the only ending, as this writer takes
> it to be, which is not discordant,—surely no tale was ever
> so properly ended, or with so full a concord, as this one.
>   (Chap. 64)

The stress on patterned contrivance, on the writing of fiction in accordance with stylized comic formulas, could be no stronger than this. Nor could the implicit equation between artificial patterning and fictive pleasure, a purely conventional equation, to be sure, but one that owes its persuasive power to the deeper-lying implication of comedy that pleasure itself is always a function of formalized patterns.

Given Trollope's proneness to ostentatious displays, even announcements, of the artificial patterns in his work, it seems an almost incomprehensible paradox that he should often have been credited with imitating real life so faithfully as to make the dividing line between real and fictional disappear. The broad answer to this paradox lies in the tendency of fundamental conventions of representation to seem automatic and natural rather than, as they are, essentially arbitrary. But the more particular answer is that the effects and formal devices that I have been treating as unambiguously comic rarely are, after all, in Trollope. His comedy is full, for readers attuned to them, of ironic crosscurrents, of devices for artfully undoing the bond between certain comic formulas and comic effects and then recombining them in unexpected ways. His career is punctuated with essays in relatively "pure" comedy like *Barchester Towers, Rachel Ray,* or *The Belton Estate,* as though periodically to refresh our memory of what this anachronistic mode, so out of place in the world of Darwin, Marx, and Flaubert, looks like in its original form. Elsewhere, though, his comedy is equivocal, compromised, alloyed with impurities, as the condition of keeping it alive.

I have emphasized from the beginning that the stylized geometrical patterns of comedy are inseparable from the exhilarating sense of emancipation from real-life necessity that comedy depends on. But in Trollope these patterns take on another function too, one tinged with deeply anticomic attitudes. The ever-recurring formulas to which he is so devoted are not, in fact, devices to create a mood of dancelike gaiety as much as they are the devices of an empirical scientist of human behavior carrying out in fiction a long, carefully controlled series of experiments in which real-life contingencies are not abolished after all, just selectively varied. Hawthorne's description of Trollope's characters as specimens lifted unknowingly out of their daily lives and placed under glass for purposes of observation is precisely to the point (*Autobiography*, 144–45). It is the scientist's voracious appetite for data that underlies the amazing volume of Trollope's fiction; and it is exactly the impulse of scientific study that governs his passionate insistence on fidelity to nature as well as his studiously flat, unpoetic, "objective" writing style. But especially we are struck by the schematic repetitiveness of his plots, for which, of course, he has often been condemned. He takes as one important experimental situation, for example, the case of a young man attracted by a second girl while committed, formally or otherwise, to a first; in his imaginative laboratory the novelist then runs through this situation over and over in successive stories, subtly varying each time the personal characters and social circumstances of the protagonists, noting and correlating in great detail the effects produced by each new combination of variables—including, importantly, the alterations in our own moral evaluations. The laboratory animals who serve as subjects in this particular experiment are named, among others, Frank Gresham, Ralph Newton, Frank Greystock, Adolphus Crosbie, Johnny Eames, Harry Clavering: and one wonders how they would feel toward their creator if they knew the uses to which their lives were being put, sacrifices as they all are to Trollope's inexhaustibly patient inspection of the subtleties of moral fiber and of the limits of comic tolerance.

We have come full circle here to touch again, more deeply this time, on the basis of Trollope's disavowal of plot. "When I sit down to write a novel," he declares in a typical passage, "I do not at all know, and I do not very much care, how it is to end" (*Autobiography*, 256–57; see also 126, 175)—a hard statement to reconcile with others in which he asserts that marriage is the only proper ending or that the novelist must above all "make himself pleasant" (p. 234). The rejection of prescribed endings, which puts the author in the position of awaiting the outcome of the current experiment with as much curiosity as the reader, implies that it is a matter of professional integrity not to falsify the experiment by prearranging the results. What is most provocative in this statement, however, is its tone, which certainly does not support the impression that Trollope shows a peculiarly tender and magnanimous feeling for his imagined people, even, as critics are fond of observing, the more scurrilous ones like Augustus Melmotte or Burgo Fitzgerald. A. O. J. Cockshut speaks rather grandiloquently of his attitude of "universal pity" (p. 195), William A. West declares that Trollope is "always warm, humane, kindly" (p. 126), and James Gindin states that "compassion dominates [Trollope's] novels" (p. 50). But is there not a note of something surprisingly pitiless in that "and I do not very much care"? If numbers of appealing and intelligent lab animals fail to survive the painful experiments devised for them, he seems to say, well, that too will furnish interesting data. E. S. Dallas pointed to just this quality in an 1859 discussion of *The Three Clerks*, which he sees as dominated not by compassion but by the enactment of a disaster "which apparently it requires but a word or a sign to prevent" and yet is shown to be inescapable. "The author," he notes, "is inexorable" (Smalley, 108).

This stony-hearted authorial refusal to intervene and make the tiniest readjustment so as to allow a happy ending is exactly what the reader feels in watching Lily Dale and Johnny Eames repeatedly fail by a hair's breadth to come together, or Lady Mason and Sir Peregrine Orme; or in seeing that Mountjoy Scarborough's good heart will not spare him from the fatal ravages of his mania for gambling, or that Palliser and Glencora, despite their own good hearts, will never quite be able to find happiness in their marriage, or that circumstances implacably forbid the happiness of characters like Mr. Whittlestaff (*An Old Man's Love*) or Sir Harry Hotspur. One of the commonest developments in Trollope's stories, in other words, is that psychological and social laws bring the most endearing and deserving characters up short mere inches from happiness, like white rats kept from food or their mates by thin panes of glass. The truth is that Trollope, often scorned for his alleged comfy benignity, has in his fiction a streak of concentrated cruelty toward what one shrewd reviewer called his "specimens" (Smalley, 151) that no other English novelist of his period except, probably, Hardy, can come near. It is a cruelty based not on misanthropy, but just on a principled refusal to fudge the laws of that entity that he forever points to as the touchstone of worth in fiction, "human nature." His principle—to quote Ford Madox Ford on Flaubert—is that of "carrying the subject . . . he has selected for rendering, remorselessly out to its logical conclusion" (*The English Novel*, 129). Why doesn't Lily marry Johnny? asks Ruth apRoberts: "Because she wouldn't have" (p. 43). The special vividness of this effect in Trollope is inseparable from his persistence in basing his fiction upon comic and pseudo-comic patterns, which continually remind us of the author's sovereign ability to step in at any moment, exercise mercy, and terminate the experiment if he chooses—as indeed he does in a novel like *The Belton Estate*, if only to exhibit the power that he often declines to use. It is inseparable, too, from his presentation of his narrator as "a very human presence, concerned for the trust and loyalty of his audience" (McMaster, 209). To trace the implications of comic stylization in Trollope's work is thus to move along the widening rift—the locus of his genius—between his declared goal of manufacturing "pleasant" novels "enlivened by humour and sweetened by pathos" (*Autobiography*, 126) and his determination to record the dynamics of human life with exact, uncompromising accuracy.

Another primary site of ambiguity where comic and anticomic effects collapse together in Trollope is the point at which geometrical symmetries, the supposedly unmistakable constituent of comic structure, blur into the realistic fluidity and amorphousness of a mere "string of incidents." I have treated the two opposite principles so far as though they were readily distinguishable (as in practice they usually are), but in fact Trollope often treats them in such problematic terms that the border between comedy and realism wavers, an effect too consistent in his work to be other than the result of a concerted design. He devises many intricate variations, especially, on the traditional comic paradigm of the amorous merry-go-round, which he employs in ways that both evoke and subtly undermine the sense of comic convention. The effect is reminiscent of the perceptual tricks made so much of by E. H. Gombrich in *Art and Illusion*: we feel, so to speak, two alternative readings of the same text overlapping, one reflecting a dancelike comic merry-go-round of interchanging lovers, the other, naturalistic flux, mere "strings of incidents." Harry Clavering's back-and-forth amorous progress from Julia to Florence to Julia to Florence, for example, certainly evokes the stylized comic dance of works like *A Midsummer-Night's Dream* or *Così fan tutte* and thus prepares us, to the extent that we are aware of it, for the attitude of tolerance that finally is taken toward Harry's near-shotgun union with Florence: yet this reading is so nearly submerged in other impressions generated by *The Claverings* that it is hard to keep clearly in focus. The plot, for one thing, is spread over such a long novel, and is accompanied by such elaborate concern for the complexities of motivation and circumstances of the main actors in the drama, that the sense of comic artifice is greatly dissipated after all. The effect of this calculated ambiguity, which is the stylistic principle of *The Claverings*, is to bring about for a moment that fusion of comedy and its antagonist, realism, that much of Trollope's work moves toward—a highly unstable fusion, and one only achieved by an act of fictional legerdemain.

Trollope plays just as cleverly with the same effects in *The Eustace Diamonds*, another elaborate exercise in modal ambiguities. Lizzie Eustace's whole career consists of her weaving her way from one lover or potential lover to the next: Sir Florian, Lord Fawn, her cousin Frank Greystock, Lord George de Bruce Carruthers, Mr. Emilius; for a fleeting moment she even imagines finding happiness with Major Mackintosh, the police officer who comes to bring her to book about the diamonds—not being aware that he has "a wife at home and seven children" (chap. 68). Frank, for his part, oscillates uncontrollably, Harry-Clavering-like, between Lizzie and Lucy Morris. Again, the longer we look at this story (where the comic ambience is much more distinct than in *The Claverings*) the more the configuration of the comic merry-go-round seems to half-dissolve before our eyes and to assume the shape of mere flux that might, rather than coming at last to the decisive final integration of comedy, simply prolong itself indefinitely, or until the characters become too fatigued to carry on. Again we can hardly decide whether we are looking at the stylized geometry of comic plot or the utterly open and fluid shapelessness of "real life." We feel ourselves, in any case, experiencing the characteristic texture of Trollopian fiction.

These schematic synopses give only a very inadequate idea, however, of the fictive interest generated by Trollope's experiments with comic geometry. Let us look in slightly more detail, therefore, at two of his most elaborate and impressive, and in some ways most perverse, formal exercises, *Ralph the Heir* and *Mr. Scarborough's Family*.

"RALPH THE HEIR": THE DISTEMPERING OF COMIC FORM

This brilliant, modernistic, rather cold and unappetizing novel is conceived from the outset as a concerted study of the formal elements of comedy. It is as though Trollope consciously restricts the factors of personal charm and warmth in his cast of characters in order to concentrate his and our undivided attention upon a mischievous experiment that can be described as a detaching of comic effect from comic design. *Ralph the Heir*, which in many ways prefigures the sensibility of a writer like Samuel Beckett, thus is a leading example of that large class of Trollope novels that embody and seemingly disavow comedy at the same time, and that I am calling "noncomedies."

The book's strong grounding in traditional comedy is signaled by its evident borrowing of main elements of its story lines from a pair of early plays. The love story centering on Ralph Newton's abortive courtship of Polly Neefit fairly clearly originated in Beaumont and Fletcher's early comedy *The Knight of the Burning Pestle*, where one finds the whole scenario, duplicated in *Ralph the Heir*, of the merchant seeking to marry his daughter to a half-reluctant, socially superior young man, but whose plan is frustrated by the apprentice who wins the girl in the end. The identification of this play as Trollope's source is strengthened, one might notice, by the fact that he read it (thinking it "very poor") for the second of three recorded times on 9 March 1869, [6] and began writing *Ralph the Heir* less than a month later, on 4 April. For the plot line of the heir relinquishing his inheritance under duress, the focus of the story of the two Ralphs, Trollope could have drawn on two classic comedies well known to him. The first of these is Fletcher's (and probably Massinger's) *The Elder Brother*; but the play in which the relinquishment plot so consistently parallels Trollope's version as to make the direct connection between the two texts unmistakable is Congreve's *Love for Love*—of which Trollope owned the eminent actor Charles Macready's prompt copy, suggesting that this comedy had a special importance for him. I shall refrain from discussing the detailed similarities between *Ralph the Heir* and its apparent sources, but readers can easily confirm for themselves how closely Trollope's story follows these comedies.

Weaving together the two borrowed strands of his story, Trollope creates a work that reaffirms its origins in stage comedy by focusing upon the great comic principles of pleasure and charm. One group of characters is set up in effect as the party of the comic ethic: Clary Underwood, "fond of pleasure" (chap. 2), Ralph Newton the heir, "idle, extravagant, fond of pleasure" (chap. 3), and Polly Neefit, a vivacious, pure-hearted girl unabashedly fond of young men and of dancing, which seems to her a "Paradise" (chap. 5). Arrayed on the other hand, in accordance with the conventional design of comedy, are the embodiments of seriousness and self-restraint: the spinster Patience Underwood, the other Ralph Newton, the "sombre" parson Gregory Newton, the reclusive scholar Sir Thomas Underwood, and Mary Bonner, for whom "lovemaking [is] but an ugly amusement" (chap. 32). As we noticed in the last chapter, it is clear from the first that *Ralph the Heir* is aligned with the ideal of seriousness, and that the love of pleasure is everywhere treated, except in Polly Neefit, who plays an eccentric role somewhat analogous to that of Micawber in *David Copperfield*, as a debilitating vice. Clary, for example, at last overcomes her infatuation with Ralph in favor of the worthy but drab Gregory, realizing remorsefully that "a grave manner and serious pursuits had been

less alluring to her than idleness and pleasure" (chap. 47). The anticomic attitude could not be more succinctly expressed.

The main sign that Trollope has designed *Ralph the Heir* as a kind
of comedy turned inside-out, however, is the way its plot falls into
the strongly marked symmetrical patterns of comic action. The very
idea of a story centering on a pair of rival Ralph Newtons suggests the
farcical confusions of the Antipholuses and Dromios of *A Comedy
of Errors*, an effect renewed each time the narrator laboriously distinguishes between Ralph Newton "who was the heir" and Ralph
Newton "who was not the heir"; but this after all is only a detail
symptomatic of the patterned design of the whole plot, constructed as
it is in terms of an elaborate courtship dance involving several pairs of
partners. These pairs, in the purest comic fashion, are out of sequence
all along the line. Gregory loves Clary, but Clary loves Ralph (the
heir); Ralph first woos Clary, then Polly (who, for her part, really loves
the bootmaker's son Ontario Moggs), then the beautiful Mary Bonner,
then Gus Eardham; Mary Bonner, wooed by the first Ralph, favors the
second. Well may it seem to Sir Thomas that "all the young people
were at cross purposes" (chap. 38)—a nice description of the formula
that underlies much comedy. All the significant action of the novel
involves linking these multiple pairs of lovers up in the proper com-
binations. Trollope plays this patterned scheme for all it is worth, especially at the end, when Ralph receives his comic chastisement by
being rejected in swift succession by Polly, then Mary, then Clary, before being bullied at last into marrying the unappealing Gus.[7] The
stylization of this design, in which all the lovers click at last into their
destined pairs, is as pronounced as possible; we are far indeed from
the "vague narratives" of Thackerayan realism.

Trollope sets up this elaborate comic design, however, only to further a perverse-seeming experiment in constructing a work that is formally a comedy, that incorporates materials taken from classic models
of comedy, but yet is lacking in any but the most attenuated comic
spirit. The aim seems to be to try to resolve the issue that has often
perplexed theorists of comedy: How essential a factor in the constitution of this mode is the intangible element of "spirit," of comic exhilaration? Throwing this question into high relief, Trollope stifles
comedy in *Ralph the Heir* by loading the story with serious emotions,
particularly in the melancholic figures of Sir Thomas, Squire Newton,
and the squire's illegitimate son Ralph. But more fundamental in disturbing the flow of comic pleasure is the special turn given by Trollope
to his guiding theme of purposelessness and irresoluteness, the theme
centering on Ralph the heir. Ralph may look at first glance like that
archetypal figure of comic literature, the "wild extravagant fellow of

the times" (to borrow a line applied by Etherege to his hedonistic hero Dorimant in *The Man of Mode* [4.1.372–73]), but the resemblance is entirely misleading. Trollope's mischievous joke is to portray this new-style hero simply as a spineless nonentity beneath his patina of charm, and thus to make him a walking image of the decay of comic energy.

Ralph's flaw is that he has been so spoiled that he has lost the capacity for the slightest resoluteness or self-discipline, and thus has frittered away his expectations. What especially interests Trollope, and what he makes into the main comic motif of the novel, is the way each new predicament in finances or in love immediately reduces poor Ralph to helpless irresolution and inertia. His sole mode of movement is rudderless, self-indulgent drift; when called on to take a purposeful step of any kind he is stricken with paralysis. Lest we miss them, the existential implications of such a state are displayed in an altogether serious vein—though the affiliation with comic hermits like Jonson's Morose and Molière's Misanthrope is plain to see—in the Beckettian Sir Thomas, who has condemned himself to a reclusive life in his gloomy London chambers, ignoring his duty to his daughters and making no progress whatever on his great project, a life of Bacon obviously destined to remain forever incomplete. "For years past he had sat intending to work, purposing to achieve a great task which he set for himself, and had done—almost nothing" (chap. 58). The hint of absurdist humor in the treatment of Sir Thomas's short-circuited will comes to the surface in the companion portrait of Ralph, constitutionally incapable as he is of forming, still less of executing, any serious or even trifling resolve. In him, it is motives and actions that are forever comically at cross-purposes. "Ralph, as a man of property, with many weighty matters on hand, had, of course, much to do. He desired to inspect some agricultural implements, and a new carriage,—he had ever so many things to say to Carey, the lawyer, and wanted to order new harnesses for the horses. So he went to his club, and played whist all the afternoon" (chap. 43). The special agony of his financial emergency, which calls on him either to sell his claim on the family estate at Newton, to marry Polly Neefit for her father's money, or to impose severe economy measures on himself, is that he can never come to a settled decision among these unpalatable alternatives; instead he oscillates helplessly from one to the other and back again. He concludes that raising sheep in Australia, cattle in South America, or corn in Canada require

> an amount of energy which he no longer possessed.
> There were the four horses at the Moonbeam;—and he
> could ride them to hounds as well as any man. So much
> he could do, and would seem in doing it to be full of life.
> But as for selling the four horses, and changing altogether

the mode of his life,—that was more than he had vitality
left to perform.

(Chap. 13)

At one typical point his namesake, doubting his resolution, reminds
him that he has written to his lawyer to indicate an interest in selling
his claim to the reversion of the Newton estate:

"Yes; I wrote the very moment I had made up my
mind."
"You had made up your mind, then?"
Ralph had certainly made up his mind when he wrote
the letter of which they were speaking, but he was by no
means sure but that his mind was not made up now in
another direction.

(Chap. 24)

The same joke at Ralph's expense (underlined in the above passage by
the befuddled phrasing of the last clause) marks his final capture by
Gus Eardham and her predatory mother. "It can hardly be said that he
had made up his mind to offer to her before he started for Cookham,—
though doubtless through all the remaining years of his life he would
think that his mind had been so fixed" (chap. 55).

The perpetual discomfiture that Ralph's feebleness of will causes
him functions, then, as an ever-repeated comic chastisement of a kind
that is fully consonant with the novel's comic structure. In this state he
forms the perfect image of that important species of comedy named
by a character in Jonson's *Silent Woman* the "comedy of affliction"
(2.6.34–35). But Trollope's heavy stress on directionlessness, on images of helpless drifting and vacillation, introduces into the story a
narrative rhythm that is the plot equivalent, so to speak, of the syntax
of "but he was by no means sure but that his mind was not made up
now in another direction." This rhythm, altogether at odds with the
dancelike regularity of comic plot, is closely allied to the "looseness"
and mere flux that is the hallmark of fictional realism. Precisely at the
center of this novel's elaborately geometrical structure, in other words,
we discover the wavering line of a plot like that of *He Knew He Was
Right*, "as shapeless as a boned fowl, entirely without any skeleton of
plot or incident." In this way (in addition to other ways) Trollope devises in *Ralph the Heir* his characteristic effect, an ambiguous running
together of comic and anticomic elements.

What Trollope specifically undoes in this novel, in other words, is
the impression of inexhaustible vitality and exuberance that is central
to the environment of comedy. Ralph's eternal perplexity reflects a
state of deep, incurable enervation that could only sustain a very
weird and entropic, dispiriting comedy like Beckett's. That resonant

ironical phrase declaring that Ralph rides athletically to hounds despite his extreme depletion of "energy" and "vitality" because he "would seem in doing it to be full of life" makes the point well. Ralph turns out only to be *simulating* a life of pleasure-seeking; in fact, his abiding purpose is just to give the impression, which he himself knows to be false, of being genuinely alive, of having any purpose at all, even the frivolous one of enjoying himself. In this, Trollope clearly shows, there is little pleasure. Ralph therefore is not finally cast as a comic transgressor of a classic kind (the kind we irresistibly identify with despite moral disapproval) but rather, like Lizzie Eustace, like Ferdinand Lopez, like Sir Felix Carbury, like George Hotspur, like the marquis of Brotherton—Trollope's fiction of 1870s, where all these characters appear, is full of variations on this theme—a kind of hollow man whose outward activity is all a screen for abject inner nullity. *Ralph the Heir* needs finally to be read therefore as an essay on the problematic fate of comedy and its elaborate pleasure-giving formality when modernistic figures like Ralph displace the likes of the vivacious Neefits at the center of the stage: the stylized comic devices are likely to seem as lacking in life as the protagonist himself and to project, in Kincaid's phrase, "a strange emptiness and lack of vitality" (p. 160).

Seen from a slightly different angle, Trollope's artful play with comic forms in *Ralph the Heir* takes the shape of a study of principles of order and disorder. All the liberated gaiety of comedy is directly a function of the ordered formality that creates and preserves an artificial world devoted to celebrating pleasure. In *Ralph the Heir*, the structural symmetries that we noticed above seem increasingly threatened by images of spreading confusion and disintegration. The plainest locus of this in the story is the episode of the Percycross election, a spectacle of rampant civic disorder. But the most pervasive and finally most significant strain of disorder in *Ralph the Heir* is the one we have seen, the tendency of the geometrical plot configurations of comedy to blur into the amorphousness, entropy, and inertia that envelop the careers of Ralph (the heir) and Sir Thomas. Comedy seems in this novel to be losing the force to sustain its own essential shape, or to generate its own essential energies—which turns out to be much the same thing.

"Mr. Scarborough's Family": Comedy's Deathbed

One might not at first notice the close links between *Mr. Scarborough's Family* and *Ralph the Heir*, but in fact the former takes up and develops the significant patterns and aesthetic preoccupations of its predecessor of twelve years before in quite direct ways: this is a pairing of works that shows impressively Trollope's fertility and subtlety of invention in his perpetual activity as a novelist, recreating already-used formulas. As in *Ralph the Heir*, the plot of the later novel deals with the inheritance of an estate, with adjudicating the claims of potential heirs one of whom is (or seems to be) illegitimate, and with the efforts of a father to circumvent the law of entail and primogeniture. "The old Squire," says the narrator of Squire Newton in *Ralph the Heir*, making clear his kinship with the more devilishly ingenious Scarborough, "had understood well how to supersede the law, and to make the harshness of man's enactments of no avail" (chap. 34). Underlining the resemblances of the two stories, Trollope again in *Mr. Scarborough's Family* plays on the joke of the trouble of finding a name to distinguish the heir from him who is not the heir. "'Augustus has always proved himself to be affectionate and respectful to his elder brother, that is, to his brother who is—is older than himself,' added Mrs. Mountjoy, feeling that there was a difficulty in expressing herself as to the present condition of the two Scarboroughs" (chap. 10). The joke points to the deepest resonances of the two plots, which at heart are fables of ambiguous identity and of mounting existential anxiety. In *Ralph the Heir* the question of legal identity and proper inheritance throws ever clearer light upon the underlying issue of Ralph's utter vacuousness: the law declares peremptorily that he is not only a person but one of special privilege and status; the story, however, dramatizes his catastrophic lack of selfhood. The same ironic pattern comes to the fore, more deeply tinged with existential despair, in *Mr. Scarborough's Family*.

The main plot of *Mr. Scarborough's Family* follows *Ralph the Heir*, too, in carrying out another steady repudiation of the pleasure ethic; indeed, it contradicts the principles of comedy at every point. The main proponent of pleasure here is Mountjoy Scarborough, another extravagant Dorimant-type, but wholly lacking Dorimant's gaiety and his effortless success in amorous and other intrigues, and—worst liability of all—burdened with a moral sense and a bad conscience. Mountjoy's sorry career, like Ralph Newton's, illustrates the principle that unbridled self-indulgence leads straight to perdition. Subject as he is to this inevitable trajectory,Mountjoy appears as a stark contradiction of comedy's animating myth of personal limberness: in the unshakable fixity of his psychosis he forms one of the nineteenth-century novel's most vivid images of tragic determinism, and determinism, as George Levine says (p. 56), is of the essence of realism in fiction. And if comedy is propelled by its themes of youth and revitalization, the main plot of *Mr. Scarborough's Family* dwells relentlessly on decrepitude and on slow, agonizing death. We could hardly, it seems, be further estranged from the charmed world of comic pleasure.

Once again, however, comedy emerges amid the most uncongenial surroundings, signaling its presence by means of stylized artificialities of form. Nothing could be more striking than the artificiality of a novel divided as sharply as this one is into two halves, the tragically realistic and the comic: for the subplots of *Mr. Scarborough's Family* are for the most part as comical as the main plot is the reverse. Mr. Prosper, Harry Annesley's pompously old-fashioned, dimwitted uncle, is a foolish "humor" character descended directly from classic models like Morose and Malvolio; he is "a man made up of forms and commonplaces," to borrow another apt phrase from *The Man of Mode* (4.1.374–76), "sucked out of the remaining lees of the last age." In his abortive engagement to Matilda Thoroughbung, an engagement entered into purely out of pique toward his young heir Harry and soured by his discovery that the intended "quiet companion" for his "declining years" (chap. 27) is a strong-willed woman with a taste for conviviality, champagne, and ponies, Mr. Prosper gets a comic comeuppance that seems derived directly from the ordeal of Morose in Jonson's *Silent Woman*, who also seeks unwisely to disinherit his nephew by a late marriage to a woman guaranteed not to disturb his peace and quiet. (Trollope read Jonson's comedy—surely not for the first time, or perhaps for the last—in January 1876, four years before writing this novel.) The story of Florence Mountjoy and her courtship by the would-be gallant Mr. Anderson in Brussels, though probably based on no specific model, is a comic sketch of a familiar kind. It is true that Trollope's almost vindictive stress on the feebleness of Harry Annesley's character (he is a close relation, as far as moral fiber goes, of Harry Clavering and Ralph Newton) lends a jaundiced mood to these parts of the novel. Still, the salient formal feature of *Mr. Scarborough's Family* is this sharp juxtaposition of opposite modes of fiction.

And yet, the closer we look at the Scarborough plot, the more clearly we are likely to see the outlines of a kind of latent comedy emerging from its tragically realistic materials. For one thing, we become aware at least subliminally of its ties to a surprising number of stage comedies. As I mentioned in the Introduction, Bradford Booth suggested in passing the affinities between *Mr. Scarborough's Family* and several seventeenth-century plays including Massinger's *A New Way to Pay Old Debts*, Middleton's *A Trick to Catch the Old One*, Beaumont and Fletcher's *The Elder Brother*, and, especially, Jonson's *Volpone* (Booth, 129, 131). Robert Tracy has since discussed Booth's suggestions in more detail (pp. 305–7). For the part of Trollope's story involving the relations between the two brothers, Mountjoy and Augustus Scarborough, an especially striking parallel is found, as Bill Overton notices (p. 192), in Sheridan's *School for Scandal*, where the story of Joseph and Charles Surface and their rich uncle Sir Oliver, a trickster seeking to decide which nephew to make his heir, prefigures Trollope's novel in many details. But the most direct source for much of the Scarborough plot is found in George Wilkins's comedy *The Miseries of Enforced Marriage* (1607), which Tracy says Trollope may have used for "the names of his characters, and one or two other hints" (p. 307). In fact, his indebtedness to this play was extensive. Wilkins's protagonist William Scarborow, who becomes Trollope's Mountjoy Scarborough, is driven by the suicide of his fiancée into a mood of remorse and self-destructive despair. Leaving the family estate in Yorkshire, he goes to London, where, clearly prefiguring Mountjoy, he sinks into a life of debauchery and gambling and falls into the hands of rapacious usurers. In Ilford, Wentloe, and Bartley, the three low-life characters who plunder their supposed crony Scarborow, we have clear foreshadowings of Captain Vignolles and Major Moody, who plunder Mountjoy in just the same fashion (chap. 42). And Mountjoy's conflict with Augustus is foreshadowed no less clearly in Scarborow's strife with his own younger brothers, who bitterly accuse him of squandering their patrimony.

What is missing from Wilkins's scenario is the central figure in Trollope's version of the tale, the trickster father who engineers a secret marriage in order, first, to disinherit his elder son, and then to punish the rancorous younger son by amazingly reinstating the elder. Many characters from stage comedies make striking analogues to Scarborough, notably Sir Oliver Surface and Volpone, an old rogue on his pretended deathbed (Scarborough is of course dying in earnest) devising ingenious schemes for defrauding the predators who hover expectantly about his house, hoping to get their hands on his inheritance; Tracy (p. 306) nominates Polymetes from Thomas May's *The Heir* as another possible Scarborough prototype. The most convincing one of all is perhaps found in another comedy of Fletcher's, *The Spanish Curate*, a play that Trollope had read at least twice. In this story the wealthy Don Henrique, angered at his venomous brother and supposed heir Don Jamie (whose character exactly coincides with Augustus Scarborough's), astounds everyone by suddenly announcing a secret earlier marriage that disinherits Don Jamie and makes Ascanio his legal heir (3.3). Don Henrique had married two different women, whereas Scarborough had married the same woman twice; otherwise their schemes are the same, and have the same result. Like Augustus, Don Jamie protests bitterly that his sudden disinheritance is fraudulent, but his protests are as futile as Augustus's. Circumstantial evidence suggests, then, that Trollope owed much of *Mr. Scarborough's Family* to *The Spanish Curate*, *The Miseries of Enforced Marriage*, *Volpone*, and other plays. The novel evidently draws so freely on early comedies, indeed, that its plagiarisms seem almost impossible to disentangle from one another. However, one need not conclusively identify the provenance of each segment of Trollope's plot to grasp his method of systematically building up the tragic Scarborough story from comic borrowings. The contemporary reviewers who often exclaimed over Trollope's "daring" experimental devices in fiction could have singled out this elaborate transposition of comedy into tragic realism as the author's most extraordinary performance, a trick as audacious, and as brilliantly pulled off, as Scarborough's and Volpone's ingenious swindles.

In its affinity with *Volpone* Trollope's novel exactly reverses the comic mechanism of *Ralph the Heir*, where the focus falls so sharply on the image of the weak-minded hero freezing into helpless inertia. If, as I have argued, disguises, ruses, and cunning stratagems form an almost indispensable element of comic plot, Ralph's half-hearted courtship of Polly Neefit (devised in the first place by Polly's father, who has to bully him into attempting it) presents an image of comic scheming reduced amusingly to its most attenuated possible form. But in *Mr. Scarborough's Family* the Jonsonesque hero is strong-minded, resourceful, and inventive to a fault, displaying as the story goes on the kind of ingenuity, and the pleasure in the exercise of it, that is the inveterate theme of comedy at least as far back as the figure of Master Pathelin in the fifteenth-century farce, exuberantly outwitting the law. Trollope usually avoided this type of plot for the reason that he sums up in a manuscript comment on Fletcher's comedy *The Wild-Goose-Chase*: "the scheming of the play is antagonistic to one's realistic sense."[8] But in *Mr. Scarborough's Family* he uses the stratagem plot, normally fatal to realism, with a vengeance.

The narrative pattern corresponding to the figure of the wily schemer is that of the far-fetched peripety, and this, of course, is the principal device of *Mr. Scarborough's Family*, where the mind-boggling implausibility of events forms the story's constant theme. Trollope clearly means to test in this book just how far fictional realism is subject, as one assumes it to be, to the rule of plausibility. Thanks, then, to Scarborough's device of marrying his wife in two separate clandestine ceremonies, Augustus with magical suddenness is made to replace his brother Mountjoy as the heir to the family estate at Tretton. Scarborough's original supposed marriage evaporates as suddenly as does the one in *The Silent Woman*, where Morose discovers that he has actually married a boy in disguise. Trollope devotes all his skill to giving this wild turn of events an air of verisimilitude, to convincing us that once again we are observing the daily lives of ordinary people as though they had been placed under glass; and just as he has allayed our skepticism (and that of Mr. Grey the lawyer), he triggers the second great *coup de théâtre* in which Augustus and Mountjoy suddenly change places all over again. It has all been a diabolically intricate fraud in which no law has technically been broken and which utterly confounds Mountjoy's voracious creditors. No law of realism has technically been broken either, but we as readers are bound to feel that we have been manipulated by an unprincipled novelist as grossly as Mountjoy's usurers have been, unless we have realized that we have been, tragic implications notwithstanding, in a comic world all along, where such machinations as Scarborough's are entirely in keeping. In *Mr. Scarborough's Family*, in any case, there seems to be no trace of that "looseness" of construction implicit in realism: symmetrically patterned plot (in the two congruent senses of the term "plot") dominates the story to an extravagant degree from the beginning.

The hallmark of Trollope's novel is the ironic inhibition of the comic effect that ought to flow from this elaborate, stylized design. We are treated in *Mr. Scarborough's Family* to not one but two amazing happy endings where ingenious stratagems ward off seemingly sure disaster—but the anticipated happiness is stillborn in each case. Trollope decisively veers away from his comic models by focusing attention less on the trickster's contrivances than on the unforeseen effects that arise from them—an intent he signals by springing the first of the story's two great reversals in the very first sentence of his narrative. The emphasis falls on all the factors in the situation, mainly psychological ones, that even the preternaturally clever Scarborough is utterly unable to control, and that cause his schemes at last to fail dismally. "Hero that he is," says Kincaid, "he is able to accomplish nothing" (p. 254). His original revelation seems miraculously to rescue from the usurers the estate that Mountjoy's gambling had squandered: but Mountjoy is implacably bitter at being made into a bastard, and vows to contest his father's claims; Augustus, for his part, rather than being filled with gratitude, plainly is filled with hatred toward his father, who has, he believes, up until now fraudulently given Mountjoy his, Augustus's, proper place as elder son and heir. (This is never spelled out, and ostensibly Augustus in his mounting cruelty and insolence toward his dying father is merely revealing his malignant nature; but his reactions are in fact deeply understandable. Under the circumstances, how could he do other than regard his father as his secret lifelong enemy?) Mr. Grey the lawyer, rather than applauding his old client's audacity and cleverness, is appalled by his dishonesty, and moreover is destroyed professionally by his implication in the case. Thus comic effects become snarled in complicated, unforeseen contingencies, and the movement of the plot takes on after all that inefficient, redundant, self-contradictory quality characteristic not of comedy but of realism. The schemer's ingenious plots, rather than yielding a decisive resolution, merely seem to generate a new set of festering problems. The same is truer still of Scarborough's second great revelation—that Mountjoy is legitimate after all. The moneylenders are decisively cheated and Augustus decisively punished. But Mountjoy, after making only the briefest pause, returns to his headlong course of ruin, and Trollope, with malicious cleverness dismantling the comic pattern that he has so painstakingly constructed, makes clear that nothing this time will be able to save the estate from annihilation. The whole convoluted story comes at last to the ironic discovery that nothing at all has been achieved, and that the affairs of the Scarboroughs have simply come full circle to where they were just before the opening of the novel six hundred pages earlier—an exercise in narrative inefficiency (that is, the expenditure of effort to no purpose) that must have few equals in fiction. The prospective image of the estate disintegrating thus makes an apt metaphor for what happens to comic form in the course of this tortuous novel, where all Scarborough's artful symmetries fall apart at last.

Trollope's pseudo-comic design only serves in the last analysis to highlight an array of implacable influences that operate too powerfully in this world to be neutralized even by the most ingenious contrivances. This is noncomedy with a vengeance, in other words, comedy perverted to perform the reverse of its proper functions. Chief among the novel's implacable influences is Mr. Scarborough's illness, presumably cancer, that kills him inch by inch as the story proceeds; he can make and unmake elder sons in the twinkling of an eye like a magician or a deity, but his power is helpless against his disease. It is helpless too against the effects of the corrupt characters of his two sons, who have each gone bad despite his lifelong efforts on their behalf: Mountjoy the compulsive gambler is psychically diseased as his father is organically, and Augustus is a mass of malevolence. Another main reflector of the failure of comic effect in this novel, as Robert Tracy has stressed (pp. 304–5), is Mr. Grey the lawyer, whose reverence for rectitude cannot protect him from becoming embroiled in Scarborough's plots and being effectively destroyed by them. Mr. Grey is a figure of realism caught to his pain in a would-be comedy, playing the traditional role of characters like Jonson's Surly, Shakespeare's Prince Hal, Wycherley's Plain Dealer, or Jane Austen's Mr. Knightley, refusers of the comic libido, which promiscuously authorizes all forms of amusement. Mr. Grey clings stubbornly to unbending principles of propriety, refusing to make that supple readjustment that the comic spirit requires, and so comedy in his case becomes something close to tragedy. Existential loneliness and despair, in fact, envelop at last not just Mr. Grey but all three Scarboroughs, confirming the eclipse of comedy by realism that the whole novel has enacted.

Formally, instead of moving toward that crystallization of a new society that Frye calls the distinctive motive of comedy, *Mr. Scarborough's Family* moves strongly in the opposite direction, showing all the principal actors in the main plot flying apart. Morally, the tale remains equivocal at the end (most modern-day criticism has dwelt on the vexing question of how much praise or blame Scarborough deserves), but it is clear that the blanket anmesty generally bestowed on comic characters has been revoked in this novel, and that readers are meant to try to mete out serious moral judgments, albeit of a very mixed and tentative kind. Trollope has Dr. Merton, one of the story's most sympathetic bystanders, make this point with great clarity at the end. True, says Merton, Scarborough was a lawless rogue. "But if you can imagine for yourself a state of things in which neither truth nor morality shall be thought essential, then old Mr. Scarborough would be your hero" (chap. 58). This hypothetical state of relaxed moral dictates is precisely the world of comedy, and if Merton's comment makes clear how strongly such a world is intimated by Scarborough's mischievous career, it makes just as clear that these intimations at last prove delusive. Truth and morality necessarily do matter in a world like this one where acts prove to have drastic, inflexible consequences, and seem to portend the inevitable downfall of comedy.

I began this chapter by stressing the interdependency of opposed fictional modes. But the implication pervading *Mr. Scarborough's Family* is that comic style and the modern usurper, realism, are in conflict, and belong to an evolutionary process in which one will ultimately overwhelm the other and make it extinct. The process of evolutionary decay in society and culture forms, significantly, an important subtheme of the novel. "Old times are changed," laments Mr. Grey to himself, "old manners gone" (chap. 58). What has gone with them, he might have added, is the comedy *of* those manners, for comedy finally survives in this novel only in mutant and, we feel, vestigial forms. Mr. Scarborough's cancer is at last, among other things, a metaphor for the way in which grim realism with its deterministic laws, its formal looseness, and its charge of existential distress has invaded the stylized pleasure-world of comedy and condemned it to death.

5

Tragic Fixity, Comic Ripening

We must go after our nature, Plantagenet.
Lady Glencora Palliser in *Phineas Redux*

What I have been calling comic "limberness" implies a theory of character deeply at odds with the one prevalent in nineteenth-century realistic fiction. We need to explore this difference now, for it is in relation to these two antithetical systems that Trollope's fiction (focused as it is on the treatment of character) largely composes itself.

As we saw in chapter 1, comic limberness is chiefly expressed in comedy's devotion to what Huizinga calls the "strange business of masks and disguises," which he sees as the essence of the spirit of play (p. 13). The obsessive concentration of comic drama on this motif goes a long way toward confirming Huizinga's thesis: a comedy lacking some more or less elaborate disguise theme is almost a contradiction in terms. Comic characters (those blessed with the special genius of comedy, that is) move from one identity to the next, shifting names, personalities, social stations, ages, and sexes with effortless ease. Sometimes, as happens to Rosalind in her masquerade as Ganymede in *As You Like It* or to the young gallants in *Così fan tutte*, comic masquers may momentarily become so engrossed in their assumed roles that they have trouble returning to their original ones. *A Midsummer-Night's Dream*, with its love potions and magic spells that variously transform the young lovers, Bottom, and Titania, is in effect based on this idea of the potentially coercive power of comic metamorphoses. But typically the fluidity of identity in comedy is a pure expression of euphoria, of "the dear pleasure of dissembling," to quote again the phrase from that compendium of comic imagination, *The Man of Mode*. Thus the presiding figure of comedy, the one that captures better than any other the *extravagance* of comic pleasure, is that of the polymorphous, of protean, shape-shifting character. "Wit is become an antic," declares the prologue to a revival of Fletcher's (and Beaumont's or Rowley's) comedy *The Noble Gentleman* and printed in Trollope's copy of the play, [1]

and puts on
As many shapes of variation,
To court the times' applause, as the times dare
Change several fashions; nothing is thought rare
Which is not new. . . .

This statement of a main comic principle hints at the affinity between comic limberness of character and the verbal idiom of comedy, and also between the conception of protean character and the fantasy of infinitely varied carnal pleasures that is persistently evoked, as we have noticed, in comedy: the potential to play an infinite number of roles and the potential to enjoy infinite playful pleasures amount in comedy to much the same thing.

The idea of character that operates in Victorian realistic fiction appears superficially to resemble the one that I am ascribing to comedy, for it too focuses on the potential for change. In fact, the two ideas are antithetical, and demonstrate once again the incompatibility of comic and realistic modes of fiction. If there is a main animating principle in Victorian realism, it is the moral scheme whose cardinal assumption is that individual character is not only permeable (chiefly to good influences) and capable of change but indeed, in accordance with Protestant formulas of sudden conversion and the descent of grace, is virtually required to undergo dramatic change, typically through an acute personal crisis, in order to attain full moral development and thus (the two being assumed to be one) happiness. Exceptions to this principle are many: obviously, for example, it is often bypassed on behalf of emblematic figures like Oliver Twist, Colonel Newcome, or even Jane Eyre, and in rare cases it is nullified altogether, as in Anne Brontë's *The Tenant of Wildfell Hall*, which centers on the shocking discovery that the dissolute Arthur Huntingdon, a character not without good instincts and the object of potentially redemptive influences, not only will never change his spots but can only move—like his real-life original, Branwell Brontë—in an ever-steeper trajectory toward ruin. Despite these exceptions, no pattern of dramatic action is more common in Victorian fiction, or more indicative of its guiding spirit, than the story of the change of heart—that is, of moral renewal. Thus, in *Adam Bede* the controlling theme is fulfilled as Adam at last overcomes his constitutional self-righteousness and forgives his enemy Arthur Donnithorne; in *Vanity Fair*, as old Osborne finally discards his hatred of Amelia; in *Great Expectations*, as Pip the snob at last embraces the lowly transported convict, Magwitch; in *Wuthering Heights*, as the implacable Heathcliff finally renounces his campaign of vengeance against Cathy and Hareton. Such episodes are pivotal in the works of George Eliot, Dickens, Thackeray, Emily Brontë, and others because they dramatize the assumption that human nature is ultimately flexible, always at least potentially open to redemption; and it is this assumption—at once a theory of human nature and a convention of narrative form—that underlies the Christian and humanistic conception of man that is the life's blood of the Victorian novel.

The comic pattern of change is obviously antagonistic to the one just described, and not only because it lends itself so readily to the stories of rascally duplicity and hedonism in "many shapes of variation" that were repugnant to Victorian sensibilities. Comic quick-change artists switch from one role to the next but never, or rarely, undergo genuine remolding of their personalities: comedy continually intimates, indeed, that personality may be nothing *but* the roles that one assumes from time to time. To the extent that nineteenth-century realism is based on the assumption of deep selfhood, it can only regard comedy as aberrant. The comic paradigm of virtually unrestricted limberness forecloses any prospect of a true, that is, permanent, change of heart. Put the other way around, the true change of heart abolishes for good all potential limberness. Once Pip has cast off his snobbery, his character is presumably set for life.

This fundamental contradiction between realism and comedy presented a nearly insoluble predicament for Trollope, who knew that his career as novelist depended on his affiliations with both. Nothing if not a man of his age, he had a natural affinity for fables of the redemptive remolding of character: they suited his generous, humane moral sense (which coexisted with what I have called his "cruelty"), and they suited, he knew, the tastes of his reading public. Deeply as all his fiction was influenced by comedy, on the other hand, the comic paradigm of the self as a sequence of virtuoso disguises was unsatisfactory to him both because it offended his moral sense and because it failed to tally with his observations of human nature. These observations also contradicted the paradigm of moral rebirth, for they very distinctly revealed to him that human nature, contrary to the conventional fable that was so deeply embedded in the thinking of his day as to seem axiomatic, was inelastic, virtually unalterable. The change of heart was a fairy tale that a scrupulous realist had to expunge from fiction. "In Dublin when he set to work on [*Stephen Hero*]," writes Stanislaus Joyce of his novelist brother, "the idea he had in mind was that a man's character, like his body, develops from an embryo with constant traits" (p. 17).[2] This idea, for the reasons set out above, calls the whole structure of traditional so-called realistic fiction into question, and it was one that Trollope deeply explored long before Joyce. To trace this exploration is to view from another angle Trollope's equivocal relationship to the moral ideology of his day.

THE MYTH OF THE CHANGE OF HEART

In the world of Trollope's novels hearts do upon occasion undergo dramatic change. Unlike the examples from other novelists cited above, such occurrences in Trollope's fiction almost always have the complexion of comedy—a Jane Austenian vein of comedy primarily, in which stubborn pride and prejudices, prejudices running so deep as almost to seem permanent features of personality, are at last overthrown. In *The Last Chronicle of Barset*, for example, Josiah Crawley's long-standing isolation from the worldly clergymen of his diocese at last appears to give way following his elevation to the living of St. Ewold's. We can rest assured that he will never go so far as to feel any interest in the great question of foxes ("It is an animal," he once grimly observes, "whose habits I have not watched"), but in the last chapter he is rumored to have submitted to being poked merrily in the ribs by the archdeacon, and this submission to the claims of ordinary human society is the sign, finely understated, of a saving change in him, a renewal of spirit. (The contrasting image in *The Last Chronicle* is that of Mrs. Proudie's grotesquely rigid corpse, which symbolizes the self-destructive rigidity and inhumaneness of all her attitudes when alive.) This kind of comedy, turning on the saving discovery of flexibility, sympathy, and good sense, is a moralized and sentimentalized modern hybrid that has little in common with traditional comedy in its usual guises. Nor does it have much in common with the dramatic moral transformations of the usual Victorian change-of-heart fable; Trollope carefully calibrates the amount of change that stories like *The Last Chronicle* demonstrate, and usually they involve little more than the reaffirmation of qualities perfectly visible, though in eclipse, long before. Within these limits, the pattern that I have described is an essential component of Trollope's artistic world. One of its commonest forms involves young ladies gradually changing their minds and accepting at long last some worthy, oft-rejected suitor. The cluster of tales built upon this story line includes some of Trollope's most thoughtful comedy and gives us heroines like Clara Amedroz in *The Belton Estate*, Polly Neefit in *Ralph the Heir*, and Ayala Dormer in *Ayala's Angel*. The potentially trivial motif of the girl changing her mind is thus important to Trollope, and is able to yield so many excellent stories, because it expresses a basic proposition about human nature: that individuals (at least some whose underlying good nature

and good sense are clear from the first, however they may be momentarily obstructed) are malleable—are able, when they must, to learn
and to change.

These truly joyous comedies, which play a large role in Trollope's
work, go far to explain Ruth apRoberts's sense of his "ultimate optimism" (p. 52). But the poignancy of these stories and of the view of
human nature they impart can be fully appreciated only when they
are seen to be in tension, throughout Trollope's work, with the opposite view that I have stated above: the view that character, wishful
thinking aside, is impervious to change, and that fiction describing
personal transformations is untrue to "nature."[3] This issue, significantly, forms a constant motif in his annotations of early plays. In a
comment on Massinger's *The Fatal Dowry* he notes, for example, that
the plays of the end of Fletcher's period are all damaged by their addiction to images of "unnatural repentance." "Women are whores in one
act and are ready to sacrifice their lives to ideas of chastity in the
next."[4] His determination to keep his own fiction free from any such
absurdities turns out to be one of his decisive motives as a novelist.

His attitude toward human change is influenced, for one thing, by a
typically Victorian awareness of change itself. It seemed clear and significant to him that personality (in common with human societies,
natural species, the earth's crust itself) evolves continuously, and he
makes this a key point in his code of fictional realism. "As, here in our
outer world, we know that men and women change," he says, "so
should [a novelist's characters] change, and every change should be
noted by him. On the last day of each month recorded, every person
in his novel should be a month older than on the first" (*Autobiography*,
233). When Trollope speaks in this way of "marking the changes in
men and women which would naturally be produced by the lapse of
years" (p. 318), he identifies the idea of change with a process of continual historical flux, and in some of his fiction—notably the vast Palliser series—he dramatizes this species of change with an amplitude
of detail that Proust himself can hardly be said to attain. Both these
writers, in any case, make clear the central point that change of this
kind nullifies the idea—the hope—of *decisive* change, the true change
of heart, for what it necessarily implies is that if all is flux no personal
renewal can be other than tenuous and temporary. Dickens's Pip may
renounce snobbery today, but what will he be like five years hence?

Underlying Trollope's awareness of constant flux, then, paradoxically enough, is the idea that individual character is absolute and
constant after all. Writers in the modernistic line of Rousseau, De
Quincey, and Dostoyevski had already, by Trollope's day, vividly pictured the self as a welter of irrational forces so incoherent as nearly to

abolish the concept of identity itself. Trollope, for his part, often calls attention to weird disjunctions in the acts and motives of his characters, but his point of departure is a presumption that personality is essentially monolithic at the core and possesses indeed almost the solidity, the distinctness of contour, the "constant traits," of a material object. Thus it is possible, for example, to get a good reading of character in the world of Trollope's fiction from wholly external signs. "He was a handsome man," says Trollope of George Hotspur, the ne'er-do-well cousin in *Sir Harry Hotspur of Humblethwaite*. "There lacked, however, to him, that peculiar aspect of firmness about the temples which so strongly marked the countenance of Sir Harry and his daughter" (chap. 5). This is not merely a passing device: the entire dynamics of this story and of Trollope in general are keyed to the idea that the various characters in the drama possess such definite mental and moral qualities that they carry them plainly stamped upon their faces.[5] Character is a *donnée*, not, as in Proust, some elusive, subterranean, deeply enigmatic thing that the fiction will strive to ferret out and at last to disclose.

Trollope's characterological assumptions spring from a theory of human nature to which he devoted serious thought, and indeed, although his critics have sometimes taken for granted that he "had no ideas" (Mizener, 161), one can hardly make sense of his work without understanding what the premises of the theory are. Some of these are set out in a notable passage from *The Eustace Diamonds*, and foremost among them is the assumption that character is not only coherent but *static*:

> Within the figure and frame and clothes and cuticle,
> within the bones and flesh of many of us, there is but one
> person, a man or woman . . . whose conduct in any
> emergency may be predicted with some assurance of
> accuracy. . . . Such persons are simple, single. . . . They
> walk along lines in accordance with certain fixed instincts
> or principles, and are to-day as they were yesterday, and
> will be to-morrow as they are to-day.
>
> (Chap. 18)

Trollope here articulates the idea of the self that presides, usually in an implicit way only, over the whole range of his fiction. He goes on to qualify it by acknowledging a second category of persons: "human beings who, though of necessity single in body, are dual in character; in whose breasts . . . evil [is] always fighting against good." But in fact these dual personalities tend in Trollope's fiction to emerge as only the most conspicuous examples of how people are governed from first to

last by their own "fixed instincts or principles." Adolphus Crosbie in
The Small House at Allington, for example, finds himself torn between
his new and revitalizing love for Lily Dale and his long-ingrained and
deadening devotion to luxury, independence, and social success.
Crosbie can clearly see that such values are in the long run—indeed in
the short run too—inimical to his happiness. All his conscious motives impel him toward Lily and toward renewal, but in the end he is
hopelessly blocked by his unconscious habitual self; his "duality," we
discover, never contained a real potential for change after all, only a
teasingly delusive one. In defiance of all conventional notions about
the regenerative power of love, Trollope leaves us in *The Small House*
with the lesson that Crosbie can only end up behaving, in spite of
himself, like Crosbie.

The principle underlying this story—the principle, that is, that
singleness and fixity are the grand laws of human nature—is alluded
to so often by Trollope as to become a kind of artistic signature. His
insistence on the novelist's need to portray gradual change in his characters, quoted above, is itself almost nullified elsewhere: "There are,
perhaps, but few of us who, after the lapse of ten years, will be found
to have changed our chief characteristics. The selfish man will still be
selfish, and the false man false." Those progressive changes that the
realistic novelist is enjoined to capture with such exactitude do not, it
seems, go very deep after all; they merely involve one's "manner of
showing or of hiding these [essential] characteristics" (*Autobiography*,
183). In *The Vicar of Bullhampton* the heroine bravely asserts that human nature is pliable and can be consciously refashioned. "I do not
believe but what people can manage and mould their own wills if they
will struggle hard enough," she says (chap. 33), but in the subplot of
Carry Brattle, the half-reclaimed prostitute, Trollope's stress falls on
the near impossibility of altering character: "humble, contrite, and
wretched as was the girl now," he says at one point, resisting any fac-
ile moral allegory, "the nature within her bosom was not changed"
(chap. 40). In *Lady Anna* the stress falls more upon the indelible effects of environment: Anna, though suddenly raised from poverty
and made a great heiress, "was as her bringing up had made her,"
says Trollope, defining the novel's main theme, "and it was too late
now to effect a change" (chap. 11). In *The American Senator* the adven-
turess Arabella Trefoil is filled with the desire to mend her ways but,
like other Trollope characters, finds that the personal metamorphosis
she longs for is impossible for her. "The girl's nature, which had become thoroughly evil from the treatment it had received, was not altered. Such sudden changes do not occur more frequently than other
miracles" (chap. 55). The same rule applies to Sir Thomas Underwood

in *Ralph the Heir*, a character whose fixity of nature is the most obvious fact about him. Sir Thomas "would . . . have given much to be able to be free and jocund as are other men. He lacked the power that way, rather than the will"; and so he is "doomed by his nature"—a telling phrase—to a life of incurable solitude (chap. 1). Phineas Finn, sunk in despondency after being tried for murder in *Phineas Redux*, is similarly, as he feels, a victim of his own unchangeable character. "One is only what one is," he says, putting Trollope's principle cogently. "I can't alter my nature" (chap. 68). In *Rachel Ray* Trollope at one point contrasts the apparent inflexibility of individual personality with the apparent adaptability of mankind at large. "A man cannot change as men change," he states here. "Individual men are like the separate links of a rotary chain. The chain goes on with continuous easy motion as though every part of it were capable of adapting itself to a curve, but not the less is each link as stiff and sturdy as any other piece of wrought iron" (chap. 18). And in *An Old Man's Love*, to give just one more example, Mr. Whittlestaff's housekeeper, Mrs. Baggett, upbraids him for his sentimental softness in the matter of his engagement—not realizing that it is simply beyond his human power to behave otherwise. "As was his character, so must he act," says the narrator. "He could not alter his own self" (chap. 11). The constant recurrence of phrases like these in Trollope's work should leave little doubt that the fixity of the self, made as it is of "wrought iron," was for him a firmly held conviction, almost an obsession. Thus his cardinal function as a novelist, as Henry James put it in a lapidary phrase (embedded, unfortunately, in a mass of misinformation), is "to tell us what certain people were and what they did in consequence of being so" (Smalley, 530).

This deterministic conception of character (which leaves largely in abeyance, we should note, the great question of the relative importance of environmental as opposed to innate factors in shaping personality) carries both positive and negative implications. On the one hand, its strong affirmation of individuality not only shields one from Dostoyevskian or Proustian existential panic (the terror of seeing identity dissolve or turn suddenly inside out) but also promotes an art based, as Trollope's and comedy's so conspicuously are, upon a plenitude of varied, vividly particularized characterizations. On the other hand, as characters like Arabella Trefoil and Sir Thomas Underwood learn to their pain, it makes into a potentially tragic enterprise any attempt to run counter to those "fixed instincts or principles" that form the matrix of one's identity—a tragic enterprise that Trollope not infrequently sidesteps, as I began this chapter by observing, by simply suspending his own deterministic assumptions and setting before us characters like Ayala Dormer, who, unlike Adolphus Crosbie, can change course with all the grace and buoyancy of Elizabeth Bennet herself.

But no number of brief quotations plucked in this way from novels can convey the pervasiveness of the sense of fixity in Trollopian drama; for, although this sense crystallizes occasionally into the kind of explicit statements that I have cited, what is really involved is less a detachable idea than an entire vision of the dynamics of normal human life. This vision is the essence, I think, of Trollope's realism, which too often in criticism has been reduced to a matter of surface, a mere photographer's precision of detail. I shall try to do fuller justice to our theme by commenting now in somewhat greater detail upon three of his most significant novels, spanning almost two decades of his career: *Orley Farm* (1862), *He Knew He Was Right* (1869), and *The Duke's Children* (1880). At first glance these works may not appear to have much in common, but on closer inspection they take on the aspect of a kind of trilogy, of which the constant preoccupation is the essentially tragic fixity of the self. At the center of all three lies the same vital paradigm, in which the dominant image of fixity is contrasted with that of youth ripening into maturity. Out of this counterpointed pattern arises a new mode of comedy all Trollope's own.

"ORLEY FARM": THE ORDEAL OF VIRTUE

Orley Farm is built around one central irony, which gradually sharpens as the action unfolds. Trollope's noble protagonist, Sir Peregrine Orme, is presented against a background of pervasive social, moral, and legal flux (for example, a lawyers' convention in Birmingham is imagined to be holding up to question the basic tenets of British legal ethics): in this context Sir Peregrine embodies a fixed and lofty moral standard. His rule of life is a virtually feudal code of rectitude and noblesse oblige. "It had been everything to him to be spoken of by the world as a man free from reproach, —who had lived with clean hands and with clean people around him" (chap. 59). *Orley Farm* is among other things a complex moral parable centering on the problematic relations of law, justice, and compassion, and it is part of Trollope's purpose to evaluate the ultimate adequacy of Sir Peregrine's almost prideful moral stance—as opposed, say, to the undemanding natural sweetness and magnanimity of Lady Staveley, the judge's rather daffy wife. More fundamentally, Sir Peregrine exhibits the stringencies of human personality itself. The irony is that his moral integrity, his absolutely unswerving adherence to a high ideal of conduct, is discovered to be merely one of those "fixed instincts or principles" to which one is helplessly bound even when they make no sense and when one's life is being devastated by them.

Having led a long life of austerity and isolation, Sir Peregrine one day recklessly alters the whole emotional economy of his existence by falling in love with a neighboring widow, Lady Mason, whose name is under a cloud. At first he argues with himself that his new course amounts to nothing more than protecting an innocent lady in distress, and thus involves no departure from his lifelong habits of chivalry. This view of things is soon undone by Lady Mason's confession that she is guilty as charged of forging a will, a crime from which the pure-minded old man recoils in instinctive horror. Trollope blamed himself for having defused suspense in this novel by revealing the "secret" of Lady Mason's guilt at an early point in the story (*Autobiography*, 167), but by doing so he artfully throws the full, sustained weight of narrative interest where it belongs: on Sir Peregrine's inward struggle with a situation that, as he now recognizes all too clearly, has torn him away from his usual moorings and seems to require of him that he renew himself in some essential way.

The implicit question in the remainder of the book is whether Sir Peregrine will ever forgive Lady Mason for her criminal act and return to her at last; and the story is carefully woven so as to encourage the most optimistic expectations. Moral revulsion against Lady Mason, for one thing, is dispelled as we (and Sir Peregrine) come to understand the true nobility and generosity of her character, as well as all the mitigating circumstances surrounding her great misdeed. "It was the manner of Sir Peregrine," Trollope has assured us long since, in another context, "to forgive altogether when he did forgive; and to commence his forgiveness in all its integrity from the first moment of the pardon" (chap. 4). He is a byword for "sheer goodness of heart" (chap. 59) and unstinting generosity. More weighty still is the great fact, gradually disclosed to the reader—this kind of gradualness being Trollope's artistic specialty—that Sir Peregrine has never stopped loving her. Given the usual workings of plot in popular novels and the absence of any external impediments, the reunion of Sir Peregrine and Lady Mason seems a foregone conclusion—but then, to the reader's surprise, never takes place after all. The decisive obstacle, as Trollope's design seeks to emphasize, is a wholly impalpable and invisible one, so subtle that it can scarcely be identified. It consists simply in Sir Peregrine's inability to act in opposition to his lifelong bias of character by seeming to excuse wrongdoing, even though he longs to do so, even though it seems morally the right thing, even though his inaction dooms him and the woman he loves to bitter pain, and even though he more than once seems a hair's breadth from taking the plunge after all. What Trollope devotes all his narrative skill to dramatizing in *Orley Farm*, in other words, is that the blockage of will lies far deeper in Sir Peregrine's nature than the level of conscious motives. Just as "there was that within her which could not do it" when the miserly Mrs. Mason of Groby Park strives for once to serve her guests a proper meal (chap. 23), just as Lady Staveley's nature "demanded of her that she should ask a guest to stay" (chap. 21), so Sir Peregrine's nature inexorably demands of him that he hold himself aloof from impropriety. He finds himself helplessly trapped, in effect, by his own rectitude, and it is this idea that governs the progress of the whole drama.

One result of these psychological dilemmas is that essential moral terms become loaded with ambiguity, and chief among these is "forgiveness." The continuing exegesis of this word in *Orley Farm* comes to a head in the memorable scene in chapter 79 where Sir Peregrine reaches his final decision, or, rather, realizes that no decision really is possible for him. "I think that we may forgive her now," soothingly says Mrs. Orme, Sir Peregrine's widowed daughter-in-law, and Sir Peregrine responds, "I have forgiven her altogether. To me she is the same as though she had never done that deed. Are we not all sinners?" But then he avows his wish to act upon this forgiveness by renewing his engagement, and Mrs. Orme recoils. The hypocrisy of her pious good will is so subtle that she can scarcely be held to account for it. "We may forgive her," she says, "but others will not do so on that account"; and Sir Peregrine, whose regard for social respectability is so deeply fixed in him as to have fused with his personality, at once gives up his wish forever. The truth is that "forgiveness" in such circumstances turns out to be a meaningless abstraction and little more. "It would be so sweet to forgive her," Sir Peregrine yearningly muses, giving the word a subtly different meaning, and still not realizing the insuperable nature of his impediments. It is Mrs. Orme who grasps the basic truth: "What could she say to him? In truth, it was all over,— such love at least as that of which his old heart was dreaming in its dotage. There is no Medea's caldron from which our limbs can come out young and fresh; and it were well that the heart should grow old as does the body." The allegory of Medea's cauldron articulates the deterministic idea that has turned out to govern *Orley Farm*: that in real life human nature cannot change, that rejuvenation is a fairy tale. Ruth apRoberts sees *Orley Farm* as centered on the edifying process of Sir Peregrine's attaining new "moral perception," finding that his absolutist ideas of right and wrong need to be modified to do justice to Lady Mason (p. 45); but this misstates, I think, the story's main emphasis, which falls ever more heavily on Sir Peregrine's tragic discovery that he is barred from *acting* upon any new perception he may have gained. Morally it is a chilling lesson, for it says that hard-earned moral knowledge even in the best of men is likely to be rendered useless by the same "fixed instincts or principles" that have governed him all along.

Running parallel to Sir Peregrine's story is that of his grandson Perry, who enters the novel in the guise of that archetypal figure of comedy that we have often encountered, the "wild extravagant fellow of the times," the young prodigal recklessly devoting himself to pleasure. Like Charles Surface in *The School For Scandal*, Perry is a "wild spark" with a "benevolent heart" whose destined role is to corroborate Sheridan's lesson (the distilled wisdom of comic literature) that "folly and dissipation" are not fatal to character and may even be good for it (*School for Scandal*, 1.2.43–44, 3.1.20). Joseph Surface and Lucius Mason, to extend the parallel between Sheridan's comedy and Trollope's novel, illustrate in much the same terms the deformities of character that go along with puritanical virtue and respectability. The practiced reader of comedy will not be surprised, then, by Trollope's strong implication that Perry's lawless early career—his expulsion from Oxford for various pranks, his long list of debts, his betting and brawling in low-life London dives—in some way reflects an essential soundness of character that the sober, hard-working, respectable Lucius cannot match. But Trollope lays a stress all his own on one aspect of young Perry: his capacity for a kind of change that seems beyond the grasp of the story's other protagonists. Lady Mason realizes long before Sir Peregrine comes to the same realization about himself that "no change was possible for her" (chap. 45), but Perry is all potential for change and growth. "The chief fault in the character of young Peregrine Orme was that he was so young," observes the narrator, seeing in Perry's undeveloped state cause not for regret but for optimism. "Fruit that grows ripe the quickest is not the sweetest," he declares, invoking Trollope's usual metaphor for this theme; "nor when housed and garnered will it keep the longest" (chap. 3).

Having thus promised the reader a story of sweetening maturation, however, the novel treats Perry's growing up quite differently. In effect his development is seen as the tragic loss of that delicious potential for ripening that he originally possesses, and the paradox is thus underlined that the capacity for change with which the young are endowed is nullified the moment the change occurs. Perry does grow up as the novel unfolds, gradually shedding his boyish inarticulateness and displaying more and more manly character in his painful dealings first with Lady Mason and then with Madeline Staveley, who refuses his offer of marriage. But the emphasis is far less on the improvement in his character than on the swift rigidification of his previously supple, fluid, and open personality. The sobering experiences that he undergoes in the course of the story, we are made to see, will shape his life ever afterward, permanently foreclosing any return to the world of unconditional pleasure that belongs only to the young. This awareness comes home to Perry himself at the memorable moment in chapter 50 when he revisits the fateful field and wood where Felix Graham had his hunting accident and where Perry's heart was broken by his discovery that Madeline was in love with his rival. "That field and that wood Peregrine Orme would never forget." In *Orley Farm*, to mature is to become subject to the stern law of fixity; prospective sweetness becomes full of bitterness, and comedy evaporates.

"He Knew He Was Right": Fixity as Madness

In *He Knew He Was Right* Louis Trevelyan begins by doubting his wife's faithfulness, eventually goes half-insane, and dies at the end a miserable death. Outwardly his story reflects a shocking human change, from urbane London gentleman to unkempt lunatic, but its inner logic is quite the reverse. Trevelyan is not so much a man undergoing change as one whose innermost qualities are seen coming irresistibly to the surface and riveting him ever more rigidly in a posture from which there is no escape. Trollope points to these qualities with a cluster of recurring synonyms like "obstinacy," "self-will," "stubbornness," and so on, but such terms are not finally commensurate with his theme, for they seem to suggest that Trevelyan's excesses spring merely from some defect or disorder of conscious will. In fact, the issue in *He Knew He Was Right* lies in a deeper stratum of human psychology than this. The idea of fixity in Trollope is inseparable from the idea, dramatized more fully perhaps by him than by any earlier English novelist, that people are ultimately ruled not by reason but by unconscious and therefore irresistible drives; and such is the particular focus of this novel. "I fancy sometimes," the fatuous clergyman Mr. Gibson observes at one point in *He Knew He Was Right*, "that some mysterious agency interferes with the affairs of a man and drives him on,—and on,—and on,—almost,—till he doesn't know where it drives him" (chap. 65). Louis Trevelyan's drift into deepening madness as he breaks with his wife, plots feverishly with the ex-policeman and comic Iago, Bozzle, and flees at last with his child to Italy, gives Mr. Gibson's notion a serious meaning and brings into relief Trollope's central thesis: that the mysterious agency is nothing more mysterious after all than the bent of one's innermost character. The development of this thesis in *He Knew He Was Right* is closely bound up with a critique of the Victorian ideology of marriage, but here we need only note the perverse self-division of Trevelyan's mental state itself. "Like the naughty child who knew that he was naughty," says Trollope of his tormented protagonist, "he was trying to be good. But he could not do it. The fiend was too strong within him" (chap. 3). These phrases echo many from other novels and suggest that Trevelyan's predicament, rather than being, as critics have assumed, an aberrant, isolated case of morbid psychology, is just an extreme instance of the recurrent Trollope story of individuals finding themselves at odds with permanent things in their own natures.

The prevalence of this theme yields again in *He Knew He Was Right* the distinctive configurations of one kind of Trollope plot, that in which the solution of some serious problem appears perpetually just around the corner, then fails to materialize after all. The Trevelyans have "every blessing that the world could give within their reach" (chap. 92), and their marital difficulties, based as they are on a sheer misunderstanding, are made to seem readily soluble. Despite their bitter resentment of each other the love between them, as Trollope is careful to stress, remains strong. They long to patch up their differences, and they are aided by various faithful friends and relatives who spend the entire novel devising one encouraging plan of reconciliation after another. As a result the story line of *He Knew He Was Right*, in a novelistic conceit that only fairly sophisticated readers are likely to appreciate, becomes ever looser and more inconclusive, a long succession of false starts, temporary expedients, short-lived renewals of hope; and at last we come to realize that this disconcerting pattern, given the properties of human nature, is inescapable. Trevelyan himself at one point of unusual lucidity defines the central issue very precisely and illustrates the classic Trollope dilemma:

> "You want change of climate, old fellow," said [Hugh]
> Stanbury.
> "Change of everything,—I want change of everything,"
> [Trevelyan] said. "If I could have a new body and a new
> mind, and a new soul!"
>
> (Chap. 93)

But again there is no Medea's cauldron to effect any such change: "We must go after our nature." Rarely does Trollope pursue the fact of human fixity to such grim consequences as Trevelyan's or to so extreme a point of existential self-awareness as the quotation above reveals. He is too committed as an artist to the domain of everyday life to allow himself much drama of such intensity, and yet, if I may repeat the major point here, Louis Trevelyan's anguished cry echoes in a heightened tone motifs that ramify throughout this novelist's work. It is the most striking illustration that one could have of the way Trollope's realism leads him to disavow at one and the same time the Victorian ethic of redemptive change and the neatly hinged plot design that that ethic implies.

Change and restoration are foreclosed for Louis Trevelyan, but the main comic subplot of *He Knew He Was Right*, the one centered on Dorothy Stanbury, subtly intersects the tragic plot in such a way as to point to another conception. Dorothy arrives as a visitor at her aunt's house in Exeter as "one of those yielding, hesitating, submissive young women" (chap. 34) whom everyone dominates; but as the novel goes on she seems to undergo a change and to acquire new strength of character. "The faded, wildered, washed-out look, the uncertain, purposeless bearing which had come from her secluded life and subjection to her sister had vanished from her," observes Trollope at last (chap. 58). In such a bleak novel this process of growth is especially poignant, and it carries a specific philosophical implication as well, for it seems designed to contradict the terrible lesson of Louis Trevelyan's story that human character is unchangeably fixed. This issue is pointedly raised in an exchange of dialogue where Trollope, significantly, has Dorothy's wise older sister Priscilla deny what seems so apparent. "Don't you think [Dorothy] is very much changed?" asks Mrs. Stanbury; and Priscilla's reply reminds us that in Trollope's world this very possibility is a vexed question. "Not changed in the least, mother," she says, "but the sun has opened the bud, and now we see the fruit" (chap. 58). When Trollope comes to consider the question closely he apparently cannot help dismissing or severely qualifying the idea of genuine human change. What may appear to be change becomes again merely the emergence of hitherto concealed but permanent, inevitable features of personality. Even so, the figure of the adolescent as sweetly ripening fruit takes on here the outline of a comic myth of a new kind, a myth of supple transformation and of the discovery of pleasure (particularly, in Dorothy's case, erotic pleasure), unlike what we saw in *Orley Farm*, where maturation means rigidity and the permanent extinction of youthful enjoyments. Dorothy, we shall see, is the harbinger of Trollope's most distinctive comic pattern.

Perhaps the question of the reality of change in Dorothy's case is moot, but raising it at least helps to make clear that, instead of having two wholly disparate plot lines, one tragic and the other "good humored," *He Knew He Was Right* has after all a strong underlying unity of thought, and a close relationship too to such a novel as *Orley Farm*. The tragic and comic stories cling together because they bear upon one fundamental issue. Still, the clash of tones in this novel is its most obvious feature; it reveals an imagination straining in two opposite directions at once, unable to reconcile (Priscilla's interpretation notwithstanding) tragic and comic answers to the crucial question. It is obvious too that Dorothy Stanbury's role in this dialectic does not begin to make a true counterweight to Trevelyan's. It is the spectacle of insane fixity that rivets Trollope's imagination here, not that of supple growth, and it is this first hypothesis that irresistibly carries the argument of the novel.

"THE DUKE'S CHILDREN": COMEDY RESTORED

In *The Duke's Children*, the last work of the Palliser series, the same complex of themes again calls forth two plots that argue in a subtle way against each other, one envisaging a sort of personal evolution that in the other seems to be inherently impossible. This bipolar arrangement is an almost ubiquitous device of structure in Trollope's fiction, but in *The Duke's Children* these antithetical strains for once are brought into a kind of final harmony.

The most basic subject of the Palliser series as a whole, if I may back up a step or two, is simply the persistence of character over time. This is the great underlying, unstated theme that encompasses all the overt ones (politics, marriage, duty, and so on), as Trollope himself suggests in the *Autobiography*, where the Palliser cycle is described first and foremost as experimental attempt at rendering in fiction the slow alteration—that is, the continuity—of a set of personalities over a span of many years (pp. 184, 318–20). The six novels taken together embody an immense imaginative essay, in other words, on the nature and extent of human change. The central figure in this project is Plantagenet Palliser, ultimately the Duke of Omnium and prime minister of England; and the main strand of Palliser's career is in turn the story of his ill-begun marriage to Lady Glencora MacCluskie. Trollope's handling of this grand story illustrates as forcefully as anything in his work how inextricably his mode of realism is tied to skepticism about the possibility of personal change and to a fundamental perception of how lives are shaped and governed by facts of personality.

The central issue in the Pallisers' marriage is simply that "Planty Pall" and Glencora find it hard to feel perfectly in sympathy with each other—a goal they both desire and seem intermittently to attain, only to find their closeness melting away anew each time it occurs. They form, in fact, just the latest incarnation of Trollope's perennial motif of couples struggling to achieve union against the subtlest, least palpable of obstacles. Over thousands of pages Trollope inspects the elusive incompleteness of this relationship, which in its eternal inconclusiveness presents an epitome of his view of human experience at

large. Glencora for her part learns at last to admire deeply her husband's "truth," "honour," and "chivalry." But mere admiration can
never enable her, as she finds to her own surprise, to forgive his great
and incurable fault: that "in manner he is as dry as a stick" (*The Prime
Minister*, chap. 56). As for Palliser himself, he strives to provide the
warmth and spontaneity that Glencora longs for (and was once drawn
to in Burgo Fitzgerald), but it is gradually borne in upon him and
upon the reader that his dignified, austere manner, which in a less
stringently realistic kind of fiction would be sure to evaporate before
long, cannot possibly be altered. "The nature of the Duke's character,"
we are told in *The Prime Minister*, "was such that, with a most loving
heart, he was hardly capable of that opening out of himself to another
which is necessary for positive friendship. There was a stiff reserve
about him, of which he was himself only too conscious, which almost
prohibited friendship" (chap. 42). The discovery that habits of stiff reserve may be, not merely surface features that a loving heart or a determined will can finally overcome, but fixed, massively permanent
barriers to happiness amounts to a major discovery about human nature; and the thoroughness, the astringency, with which this principle is driven home in the Palliser novels as an aspect of prosaic daily
life (though the protagonist *is* a duke and prime minister of England)
amounts to a signal extension of the scope of realism in the novel.
There is nothing else like it in Victorian fiction.

In *The Duke's Children*, which treats Palliser's life in the years after
Glencora's death, Trollope continues his study of the seemingly im-
mutable stiffness of his hero's character and its chilling effect upon his
relations with those he loves. Now it is his children from whom he
feels separated in spite of himself, although they do both love and
venerate their redoubtable parent—"the veneration perhaps being
stronger than the love" (chap. 2). Again Trollope's drama turns on precisely calibrated gradations and complexities of feeling, the irony of
this plot being that the escapades of the Duke's three children (especially along matrimonial lines) force him perpetually into the role of
mentor and even tyrant and thus bring out in high relief those uncomfortable traits of his character that have plagued him throughout his
life. At one point he wishes to deter his daughter Lady Mary from her
engagement by exercise of gentle persuasion rather than overbearing
authority. "But he was conscious," says Trollope, defining the eternal
Trollopian predicament all over again, "of his own hardness of manner, and was aware that he had never succeeded in establishing confidence between himself and his daughter. It was a thing for which
he had longed,—as a plain girl might long to possess the charms
of an acknowledged beauty. . . . But he knew of himself that he would
not know how to begin to be tender and forgiving. He knew that

he would not know how not to be stern and hard" (chap. 8). In episodes like this, Hardy's maxim "Character is Fate"[6] takes on fully
dramatized form.

Thus the story of the Duke's estrangement from his children simply
reenacts the difficulties he always had with Glencora: a man's life, as
Trollope's great cycle seeks to dramatize, never changes very much. Yet
in this last novel of the series there *is* a change after all, for the mood
of incurable sorrow and disappointment that pervaded the story of
the Palliser marriage is here progressively modulated into something
new, a mood of affectionate comedy. As the story unfolds, we find
that the asperities of the Duke's character can be, if not eliminated, at
least rendered harmless by the rich reserves of good feeling, charm,
resiliency, and wholesomeness that emerge in the younger generation, especially in the person of the Duke's elder son, Lord Silverbridge. To see this occurring is to discover that the Duke's intimidating
nobility of character is ultimately not sterile but is able, for all its pon-
derous gravity, to foster healthy growth in those around him: the
charm and warmth of Lord Silverbridge represent Trollope's final testimony to the excellence of the Duke himself and of the code of severe
integrity that he embodies.

In this new context the Duke's near-tragic flaw of pomposity comes
to seem more like a lovable foible. A major shift of feeling is implicit,
in other words, in the humor of various scenes where the Duke's solemn, admonitory streak is made most apparent: improving the occasion of a breakfast with his two somewhat feckless sons (chap. 25);
betraying his susceptibility to the vivacious Isabel Boncassen by "explaining to her matters political and social, till he persuaded her
to promise to read his pamphlet upon decimal coinage" (chap. 53);
making mental memoranda, as he reads a letter from Lord Silverbridge, as to grammatical and other principles to be inculcated at the
next opportunity (chap. 56); or lecturing his younger son Gerald on
the perils of gambling:

> "Facilis descensus Averni!" said the Duke, shaking his
> head. "Noctes atque dies patet atri janua Ditis." No
> doubt, he thought, that as his son was at Oxford,
> admonitions in Latin would serve him better than in his
> native tongue. But Gerald, when he heard the grand
> hexameter rolled out in his father's grandest tone,
> entertained a comfortable feeling that the worst of the
> interview was over.
>
> (Chap. 65)

This comfortable feeling more and more informs the story as a whole,
and ultimately the Duke is able to relax his severity enough to change

his mind and countenance the socially dubious marriages of both Silverbridge and Lady Mary. John H. Hagan has upset the book's carefully regulated tone by describing the Duke's surrender as a joyous transfiguration (p. 20). As some of the original reviewers of the novel observed, the Duke's chronic melancholy is never quite exorcised (Smalley, 469, 471), and there is no reason to think that his difficult character has fundamentally changed; such events "do not occur more frequently than other miracles" in Trollope. Still, at the end of *The Duke's Children* the stress does fall less upon the permanent liabilities of the Duke's character than upon the adjustments that this supposedly inflexible man is able to make to enable life to go on and that spare him finally the fate of characters like Sir Peregrine Orme and Louis Trevelyan.

The story of Lord Silverbridge in the same novel is intimately connected with those of Perry Orme and Dorothy Stanbury: for, if the Duke presents an image, albeit a softened one, of the pernicious fixity of human character, Silverbridge, the opposite element of Trollope's perennial dialectic, is made to embody a capacity for supple growth and change. An important vehicle for this story is yet another major borrowing from early drama. In the tale of the scapegrace Silverbridge, heir to one of the greatest dukedoms of the land and son of the head of state, who falls under the influence of the roguish ex-military man of very dubious battlefield credentials, Major Tifto, frequenting disreputable companions and becoming implicated in felonious schemes before eventually repudiating Tifto to take up the high political duties urged upon him by his father, we see plainly the outline of one of the central points of reference of English comedy, the story of Prince Hal, Falstaff, and the King. The Boar's Head becomes Trollope's Beargarden; Bardolph, Nym, and Pistol become Glasslough, Nidderdale, and Dolly Longstaff;[7] the exposure of Falstaff's lies about the robbery at Gadshill becomes the exposure of Tifto's "enormous lie" about his intimacy with the opera singer Mlle Stuffa (chap. 6). Tifto has all the effrontery of his great original, is a compulsive, self-destructive boaster like him, and is "broken-hearted" (chap. 58) as Falstaff's heart "is fracted" (*Henry V* 2.1.121) when his highborn young comrade at last disavows him. The invocation of Shakespearean comedy could hardly be more methodical.

Trollope exploits the Falstaff story so intensively because the fable of the prince turning away from debauchery and belatedly taking up his proper duties throws such a strong light on the myth of the change of heart. In Shakespeare's version this myth is severely qualified by signs that Hal's life of dissipation is from the first just a Machiavellian stratagem designed to heighten his glory afterwards, and that behind the mask of youthful exuberance, Hal is already a shrewdly calculating politician. Silverbridge's is an entirely different nature, and Trollope's recapitulation of Shakespeare's story has a logic all its own. Silverbridge is deliberately juxtaposed with strong, articulate figures like the Duke, Frank Tregear, and Lady Mabel Grex, and in the early parts of the novel he reveals his immaturity with his every turn of phrase. Lady Mab in one of her hyperlucid meditations puts her finger on Trollope's theme. "How was it that she"—actually Silverbridge's junior—"was so old a woman, while he was so little more than a child?" But Trollope again wants to evoke a subtler state than mere immaturity, namely, an immaturity that somehow conveys a strong promise of growth. "How fair he was, how far removed from conceit, how capable of being made into a man—in the process of time! . . . Though he was but a boy, there was a certain boyish manliness about him" (chap. 16). The capacity for change is, so to speak, his distinctive feature. And so, in the course of the novel, his amphibious in-between state evolves progressively toward full manliness, and we see him, as he gets expelled (like Perry Orme) from Oxford, dallies dangerously with Lady Mab, goes into Parliament, and is smitten by Isabel, ever so gradually acquiring a new bearing, speaking with a new inflection from one scene to the next. "All [his] little troubles," Trollope observes at one point, defining the special pace and texture of this unusual story, where outward plot is minimal, "were giving him by degrees age and flavour" (chap. 42). The essential action of this novel, Trollope is hinting, is nearly as imperceptible as the aging of wine: and to grasp Trollope's intent in this respect is to recognize another notable departure, in the name of fictional realism, from conventional patterns of plot, with their emphasis on tension, climax, and surprise.

To show how Trollope renders Silverbridge's acquisition of "age and flavour" page by page—how the young man's slangy inarticulateness gradually evaporates, for example—would require masses of long quotation, for the whole effect lies in fine nuances. Suffice it to say that he at last becomes manly enough to win the wonderful Isabel, one of Trollope's shrewdest, wittiest, most Shakespearean heroines, Rosalind transported into the world of *Henry IV*. This story is a fable that works to qualify the many Trollopian images of individuals finding themselves straitjacketed in personalities that cannot possibly be made to "give," however extreme the emergency. Lady Mab Grex here voices the theory in explicit terms: "A jackal is born a jackal, and not a lion, and cannot help himself," she fatalistically proclaims, alluding to herself (chap. 73). But Silverbridge, in defiance of this supposed law of fixity, gradually metamorphoses himself into a lion—a social lion, at least. The process is enlivened by few dramatic "effects," but it generates for careful readers aware of Trollope's large structure of themes a mood of growing expectation and delight; and this time the expectation is not cheated at the end.

Trollope's novel makes therefore a twofold commentary on its Shakespearean model. In glorifying Silverbridge's radiant, boyish sweetness, which he seems miraculously to retain while moving into fullfledged manhood, Trollope underlines the chilling and sinister side of Shakespeare's image of the ideal young prince. He stresses in this way (as his marginalia to old plays constantly do, noting the drastic shifts of taste from one literary period to another) the deep division separating his own Victorian bourgeois sensibility from the sensibility of the Elizabethan and Jacobean culture to which he was so indebted. More broadly, he dramatizes the potentialities of his own native literary medium, for the representation of such gradual change as Silverbridge undergoes requires the extended space and time, and the opportunity for densely textured detail, that only a full-scale novel affords. The discovery of gradualness as a literary subject—indeed, the discovery of the gradualness of "the process of time" itself—coincides with the development of the modern novel. Thus the tale of Silverbridge's imperceptibly slow maturation revises its Shakespearean model in such a way as to highlight the decisive alteration in the image of human experience implied by the transposition from stage play to the greatly expanded temporal scene of a 500-page novel. It remains as always a moot point whether Silverbridge's development represents a true change of character or just the progressive revelation of "constant traits." We do not need to resolve this puzzle, however, to appreciate the originality of Trollope's fusion of extreme psychological verisimilitude with the comic fable of the young prodigal whose "folly and dissipation" lead not to retribution, but only to prosperity and union with a captivating heroine. This myth of ripening adolescence, in which the comic principle of euphoric fluidity and the principle of fixity that is the basis of Trollopian realism seem somehow to have been reconciled, is one of Trollope's most powerful inventions, and wherever it recurs in his fiction it generates memorable stories.

6

Comic Imperfection

"Culture . . . is the study of perfection."
Matthew Arnold, *Culture and Anarchy*

IDEALIZATION AND THE VICTORIAN NOVEL

This book has argued that Trollope, portraying himself all the time as the "apotheosis of normality," habitually used the methods of comedy to generate a critique of central norms of the public for which he wrote. The presiding theme of pleasure is thus strongly identified in Trollope, as we have been seeing, with comedy's usual scheme of emancipation from these norms—with the vindication of worldly amusement, the dethroning of puritanical moral "seriousness" by impertinent charm, the freeing of impacted erotic life. These lines of emancipatory force in Trollope's work go beyond the specific field of the comic, however, when they converge on the central artistic problem for any Victorian novelist: that of the idealization of character in fiction.

From the time that modern realistic fiction became conscious of itself as something distinct from romance, it defined its own charter largely in terms of its rejection of idealized heroic and romantic stereotypes. The official basis of this charter was the conviction that mixed, unheroic characters are truer to life than flawless heroes and heroines, and therefore inherently of higher artistic worth. This principle had, however, a corollary that in practice was the key element in the program of nineteenth-century realism: the assumption that unidealized characters promote in the reader a higher degree of identification and sympathy than do the exemplary heroes and heroines of romance, and thus generate more intense, as well as more morally beneficial, involvement in fictional stories. This capacity for arousing emotional identification with imaginary characters has always (at least until Joyce) been the crucial, defining function of the novel, a fact that goes far to explain the rise of the novel as the chief popular literary form from the eighteenth century onward, when the cult of feeling

became a basic element of culture and the stimulation of feeling became the main goal of imaginative writing.

Thus, while one is inclined to think of romance as the fictional form
preeminently defined by the concentrated stimulation of feeling, perceptive theorists from the early days of the novel onward *equate sympathetic feeling with realism itself*, as though realism, rather than being the
antagonist of romance, as its self-publicity would lead one to believe,
were in fact only a new form of it after all. Some latter-day critics influenced by Michel Foucault have attempted to identify literary realism with "the incriminating techniques of policing and surveillance"
(Seltzer, 48), but such an account is exactly contrary to the declared
theory of this mode. In classic accounts the sense of "reality" in fiction is treated as identical with the function not of policing but of exciting sympathetic emotion, that is, of giving the reader the sensation
of actually entering into the story. Ford Madox Ford puts the proposition concisely, for example, in speaking of Defoe as "relying on the
verisimilitude of the details that he invented to confirm the reader in
the belief that his characters had really existed and so to awaken the
sympathy that makes books readable" (p. 89).[1] This equation of verisimilitude and sympathy, and the presumption that fiction without
sympathy would not be "readable," echoes Clara Reeve's well-known
definition of the novel in *The Progress of Romance* (1785). The "perfection" of the novel, according to her, "is to represent every scene, in so
easy and natural a manner, as to make them appear so probable . . .
that all is real, until we are affected by the joys or distresses, of the
persons in the story, as if they were our own" (Stang, 140). This close
linking of realistic verisimilitude and the arousal of sympathy was particularly important to Victorian novelists, given the transcendent
value they attached to emotional life. Clara Reeve's formula is again
echoed, for example, by George Eliot in her theoretical excursus in
chapter 17 of *Adam Bede*, where the realist's refusal to traffic in images
of idealized beauty is specifically seen as the key to the all-important
function of the release of sympathetic emotion. "Human feeling," she
says, "is like the mighty rivers that bless the earth: it does not wait for
beauty—it flows with resistless force and brings beauty with it." Accordingly, the "precious quality of truthfulness" in Dutch painting is
"a source of delicious sympathy" with the ordinary lives it evokes,
and it is the arousal of just such sympathy that she declares to be the
basis of her own fiction (p. 152). Henry Mayhew, working at the
boundary line between scientific sociology and imaginative literature,
sets up just the same rhetorical schema as he repeatedly assures the
readers of his *Morning Chronicle* essays of the rigorous truth to life of
his portraits of the poor, declaring that this is the only method able to

achieve what he seeks, "close communion" with his subjects and thus, aroused pity for "the mass of misery that festers beneath the affluence of London." "The truth will be given in stark nakedness," he warns his readers (1.41, 52).

The difference between Clara Reeve's statement and those of George Eliot and Mayhew lies in the troubled awareness of the latter two that this primordial function of the realist, the awakening of "fellow-feeling" for characters represented in an unglorified lifelike way, is not obvious and spontaneous, but rather a faculty needing cultivation, and one that contemporary readers are likely to find extremely difficult, even repellent. Both assume that their public needs to be earnestly admonished to interest itself in unheroic, unglamorous, unidealized materials, and that the primary job of the writer is to inculcate this faculty: Mayhew feels obliged to issue a specific rejection of the "morbid sympathy" (1.41) that is able to be activated only by images of unblemished virtue. Other writers of the period recognized no less clearly that the universally accepted criterion of "truth to life" (Skilton, p. 60) involved them in an almost insoluble predicament. Thus we find, throughout the heyday of realism, that writers' proclamations of the realist code are almost invariably couched in this same assumption that purging fiction of romantic idealization may, after all, impede readers' sympathy rather than enhance it. In the preamble to *The Heart of Midlothian*, for example, Scott vigorously but defensively asserts his determination to be "impartial" in describing his historical personages, and to present them in strictly unromanticized terms, even though he knows that many of his readers, who "love to hear but half the truth," will find this approach offensive (pp. 10–11). In *Père Goriot* Balzac invokes the same sanctification of sympathetic feeling that George Eliot does—"Are not our finer feelings the poems of the human will?" (p. 133)—and declares his own determination to confine himself to the most stringent realism. "This drama is not an invention," he goes so far as to announce in his opening chapter; "it is not a novel." And then he scornfully imagines his reader sitting down with a good appetite to his dinner, having been wholly unmoved by the story, whose supposedly unremitting realism has failed entirely to produce that flow of sympathy that Balzac declares to be the goal of his story (p. 8). This same unmoved reader entirely out of sympathy with what we may call the moral discipline of realism reappears, now named Jones, in the first chapter of *Vanity Fair*. Jones, says Thackeray, "admires the great and heroic in life and novels," and is bound to feel only aversion for the humdrum realism of this novel (p. 15). Over and over in the early sections of *Vanity Fair* Thackeray professes to apologize to his readers for his unidealized treatment of contemporary life, but declares that "one is bound to speak the truth as far as one knows it" (p. 80), even though this means alienating his public. At the end of the century Gissing, as we have seen, is still declaring that any genuine realism, any fiction, that is, really cleansed of idealization, especially in the portrayal of character, would be "unutterably tedious" to readers—would not be "readable."[2]

Evidently the idealized hero, who was condemned by such an impressive string of writers for more than a century and declared by Mario Praz to be "in eclipse" in the Victorian novel, proved extremely hard to banish from fiction after all. All the rhetoric directed against him proves his longevity. Could there have been a flaw in the whole ideology of realism in the first place? If so, it lies in supposing that mixed unidealized characters are necessarily more effective vehicles for sympathy than the paragons of romance. Clearly for many readers, at least, the very reverse has always been the case, as is proved by the immense popular success of characters like Clarissa Harlowe or Little Nell, not to mention various best-sellers on a different literary plane such as Charlotte Yonge's *The Heir of Redclyffe* (1853), Mrs. Craik's *John Halifax, Gentleman* (1857), or Mrs. Humphry Ward's *Robert Elsmere* (1888), each professing realism but centered on the portrayal of heroes and heroines of flawless, exemplary character, of courage, unselfishness, absolute probity and moral refinement. Plainly the capacity to achieve imaginative bonding with less idealized characters than these did not come easily to the reading public, even after decades of earnest lecturing on this theme by realistic novelists. When Trollope, therefore, declares in *The Eustace Diamonds* that "the reading world [has] taught itself to like best the characters of all but divine men and women" (chap. 35), he was not overstating the case.

Given the pervasive influence of Evangelical earnestness in nineteenth-century England, it could hardly have been otherwise. Roman Catholicism in its wisdom extends considerable tolerance to the frailties of human nature, treating small sins leniently and forgiving even great ones, and thus generates only a diminished insistence on the need to achieve perfection; and it is significant that in French novelists of our general period like Stendhal, Balzac, Flaubert, and Proust, the impulse to idealized heroism or moral perfection is usually absent (not that it doesn't emerge occasionally in characters like Eugénie Grandet). In England, the puritan moral imagination, driven by the anxious awareness that even trivial-seeming transgressions like wearing gilt earrings or buying riding breeches on credit can lead straight to perdition, the pressure to achieve perfection, especially in the form of moral immaculateness, was inescapable. Anything less than Arnold's "idea of perfection as an *inward* condition of the mind and spirit," any standard other than a "spiritual standard of perfection" (*Culture and Anarchy*, 49, 51), seemed dangerously flawed.

The "standard of perfection" exerted such powerful force over the nineteenth-century mentality that even the most rigorously realistic British novelists, those most committed ideologically to the dismantling of artificial images of heroism, found themselves hard pressed to live up to their own credo. The fact is that nineteenth-century British fiction is hostage first and last to the idealizing instinct, even though novelists strove to repress it as a danger to their art—or at least to wrap it in elaborate disguises. This disparity of theory and practice with regard to idealization is essential to serious nineteenth-century fiction, and is the source of many of the Victorian imagination's most impressive creations. The grand tragic heroine of flawless virtue in the style of Rousseau's Julie or Richardson's Clarissa gives way in the Victorian novel to characters whose ideal spirituality is surrounded by disablements of various kinds or is presented in some way in the guise of commonplace humanity—yet is emphatically insisted upon none the less. Scott's Jeanie Deans, Dickens's Mr. Pickwick, Amy Dorrit, and Arthur Clennam, Thackeray's Dobbin, George Eliot's Dorothea Brooke, endow this paradigm with particularly deep interest. There is no need to extend the inventory through characters like Jane Eyre, Meredith's Beauchamp, even Hardy's Tess, to make the point that throughout the nineteenth century the practice of "realism" and the insistence upon moral idealization were inseparably allied in British fiction. In this respect, the rhetoric of the Victorian novel is a deeply duplicitous one. The sympathetic imagination evidently could not energize itself, could not make itself legible, without the catalyst of some image of "all but divine men and women," whatever ironies might then be invoked to make this image appear consonant with the doctrine of the realistic representation of human nature.

This, then, is the ambiguous context within which Trollope launches his own attempt to practice realism purified of heroic fantasy. He bases his theory of novel-writing squarely upon the traditional idea of the equivalence of verisimilitude and sympathy. A novelist's first goal, he says, is to portray "men and women with flesh and blood, creatures with whom we can sympathize"; for "no novel is anything . . . unless the reader can sympathize with the characters whose names he finds upon the page" (*Autobiography*, 228–29). In practice, this theory led Trollope to some sharp contradictions, since he practiced it more rigorously than many of his contemporaries, as though to force the inherent contradictions of the theory itself into the open. Such in any case is the result, as we can see in the vein of disgusted commentary running through reviews of his novels as they appeared, complaining of his famous "photographic" realism: how dull, they frequently exclaim, exactly corroborating Gissing's Mr. Biffen, to read fiction so barren of ideal images! At best, according to these reviews, Trollope limits himself to portraying "vulgar" characters—the word "vulgar" recurs obsessively through his reviews, as I have said, charged as we can now see it to be with that demand for idealization that was central to Victorian taste—and at worst he shows a perverse pleasure in displaying images of moral turpitude and personal repulsiveness.[3] His fiction, complains one writer, is "designedly not made attractive" (Smalley, 440); indeed, says another, putting the issue plainly, he is devoted to "the delineation of moral malaria" and of "endless varieties of what we might almost term middle-class squalor" that "oppresses almost to nightmare the little moral ideality left to our age" (ibid., 446). Henry James himself, representing enlightened, cosmopolitan late-Victorian taste, launches one of the fiercest diatribes against Trollope's failure to give inspirational images of virtue. He "wantonly detract[s]" from "the glory of human nature," says James, by dwelling without relief on "vulgarity." "Miss Mackenzie is an utterly commonplace person, and her lover is almost a fool. He is apparently unsusceptible of the smallest inspiration from the events of his life. Why should we follow the fortunes of such people? They vulgarize experience and all the other heavenly gifts" (ibid., 235, 237). Trollope could have had this review specifically in mind, but in any case had the type of review it embodies in mind, in asking rhetorically in *The Eustace Diamonds* four years later, "Why should one tell the story of creatures so base [as to be unfaithful in love]? One does not willingly grovel in gutters, or breathe fetid atmospheres, or live upon garbage" (chap. 35). His parody of critical hyperbole and moral outrage in this passage scarcely exceeds the reality of the comments his fiction received.

The result of Trollope's stubborn devotion to "pictures of human nature distorted by vulgarity" (Smalley, 231), declare numbers of reviewers, is directly opposed to George Eliot's formula: it is the annihilation of sympathy. In *The Way We Live Now* the characters are said by one reviewer, in a phrase that cogently sums up the issue we are considering, to be "too commonplace to awaken any pleasurable glow of affection or of sympathy" (ibid., 412). Similarly, a review of *The Prime Minister* attacks Trollope for his "disposition to attribute to the majority of mankind an inherent vulgarity of thought," which, in the case of Lopez, for instance, means that "we feel no sympathy with him even when he dies" (ibid., 419, 420). A thought-provoking commentary on *Miss Mackenzie* in the *Saturday Review* shows with particular clarity how severe this problem of reconciling verisimilitude and sympathy was for contemporary readers—and thus for a novelist with

the audacity to fly in the face of current taste. Trollope's cast of characters, says this reviewer, is decidedly unsavory: "most of the persons
who figure in it are intensely mean, dull, and generally disagreeable
and uninteresting." It would seem, the reviewer says, shrewdly analyzing Trollope's fictional method, that there could be "no room for
sympathy" for the heroine and her unprepossessing lover—but Trollope generates it, somehow, after all. This seems like the model of an
insightful, appreciative review—but it turns out that even this reader
cannot quell his distaste. Why, the reviewer wonders, is it "worth
while to expend so much labour" on "the needlessly ugly and disagreeable people who are so prominent in this monstrously prosaic
[novel]"? Trollope's fixation on "odiously vulgar and stupid" characters is such, he concludes, that even "the staunchest champions of realism" are obliged to reject his fiction "in disgust" (ibid., 219, 221,
216). One recalls the disgusted response of the reviewer to the closing
scene of *The Belton Estate*, where Clara Amedroz reflects, as we saw,
on the red nose and advanced age of Captain Aylmer's bride. This
portrayal of the heroine as an ordinary mischievous girl, "without so
much as a hair of the creature's head idealized," strikes the reviewer
not as charmingly human but, "admirable as the principle of realism
in art may be," as "vulgar," "dull," and "sordid" (ibid., 263). The
schizophrenic response that both of these last-quoted reviews display
had earlier been very lucidly diagnosed by a writer in the *Cornhill*
who pointed out that readers demand "truth to nature" but then, with
complete illogic, "pettishly declare that Trollope has 'forfeited their
sympathies'" whenever his favored characters fail to embody standards of ideal moral perfection. The kind of idealization and worship
of perfection so insisted upon by "a widespread prejudice," says this
commentator, echoing George Eliot, only "directs our sympathies
away from reality" (ibid., 158–59).

Despite his luck in finding an occasional reviewer like this one, Trollope thus regularly set himself in opposition to the moral sensibility
of much of his original public, and inspired in many readers the same
violent revulsion that the scandalous morality of Fletcher's or Jonson's
comedy inspired in him: and if his novels seem innocuous to a fault
today, it is only a measure of the power exerted by the idealizing impulse in his day. I shall try in the rest of this chapter to spell out Trollope's relations to the "widespread prejudice" in the particular context
of his comedy, but we should notice how systematically he carries out
the undermining of idealized stereotypes of (quoting the *Cornhill* reviewer) "faultless human beings" (ibid., 158) in noncomic terms as
well. One of his chief story patterns, for example, involves constructing a fiction around some exemplar of rectitude, even of saintliness,

and then elaborately anatomizing the built-in contradictions of perfection of character. Abnormal devotion to virtue is almost always
assessed in Trollope as problematic, as it is in characters like Sir Peregrine Orme, Plantagenet Palliser, Mr. Harding in *The Warden*, Josiah
Crawley, or Roger Carbury, all of them endowed with a heroic purity
of heart that proves as much a liability as an asset. The central lesson
of all these essentially tragic stories has to do with the insufficiency of
virtue to enable a man to run his life well, without gravely damaging
himself and those he loves most. This fable, with its strong implications of moral skepticism, is peculiarly Trollope's among the novelists
of his time. Let us look now at its comic dimension.

THE COMIC FLAW

Comedy, with its traditional attachment to pleasure, worldliness, and
egoistic self-glorification, has a native antipathy toward any kind of
moral idealization (particularly those that stress self-denial), and indeed falls almost automatically, as we have seen, into connivance with
rascals. The pattern of explicit moral subversiveness is so strongly
etched in comedy that we scarcely can imagine a full-scale career in
comedy without it. Yet in Trollope this pattern appears only in occasional and very attenuated form. He is too much a man of his time to
allow scorners of virtue to take on that aura of irresistible charm that
comedy typically endows them with;[4] but the distinctive logic of comedy expresses itself clearly nonetheless in Trollope's conception of the
personal flaw that paradoxically becomes recognizable as the sign and
guarantee of wholesomeness and virtue. Imperfection in this inside-
out sense can range from innocent foolishness to flaws of character of
far more potentially damaging kinds that scarcely can be contained
within a comic perspective; in all its forms it defines a main axis of
his fiction.

A relatively benign instance of this pattern is met, for example, in
chapter 11 of *The Warden* (a work that otherwise could scarcely be
classed as comedy), where Eleanor Harding decides to appeal to her
all-but-declared lover John Bold to abandon his persecution of her father. In her desire to help the old man, "self-sacrifice was decided on
as the means to be adopted": she will preface her appeal to Bold, she
decides, by first banishing all thought of love between them. But how
unmixed are her motives after all? The narrator, while assuring us of
Eleanor's altruism, pointedly asks whether she is not at least half-
deliberately planning a scene sure to provoke Bold into openly declaring his passion at last. Many readers, he comments, "will declare . . .
that young women on their knees before their lovers are sure to get
kissed, and that they would not put themselves in such a position did

they not expect it." His denial of the cynical interpretation does not dispel the thought, so heavily insisted upon, that there is something equivocal in Eleanor's "self-sacrifice." And so we get the picture of her preparations for the imminent interview with Bold:

> Eleanor was certainly thinking more of her father than herself, as she arranged her hair before the glass, and removed the traces of sorrow from her face, and yet I should be untrue if I said that she was not anxious to appear well before her lover: why else was she so sed- ulous with that stubborn curl that would rebel against her hand, and smooth so eagerly her ruffled ribands? why else did she damp her eyes to dispel the redness, and bite her pretty lips to bring back the colour? Of course she was anxious to look her best, for she was but a mortal angel after all.

The warmly affectionate tone of this passage and its insistence that Eleanor's feminine cunning in no way devalues her altruism invites us, evidently, to see her vanity almost as a virtue, as though "mortal angels," though severe moralists might judge them in their rich state of imperfection too "sordid" for art, were the only kind worth having after all.

A reticent passage like the one above is a good example of the rheto- ric of this novelist who described himself as "a preacher of sermons" (*Autobiography*, 146) but indulges in virtually none of the overt ser- monizing that contemporary fictional standards authorized. The pas- sage also points to the moral principle that is central to Trollope's work, a principle rarely if ever fully stated by him, yet forming, I be- lieve, the deepest root of all his fiction. Since he shied away from ar- ticulating it except in implicit form, a critic's reconstruction can be only approximate at best, but it has to do with preserving unimpaired the wholeness of what he repeatedly says that serious novelists must strive to portray with utmost fidelity: "human nature." In this work of preservation, comedy performs such a major role that we can think of Trollope's morality as inseparably linked to the comic point of view. The key premise of this morality is that perfection is not a human state, and that admiration of the perfect is therefore a dangerous delu- sion, especially when (as in Victorian England) this implies activating harsh moral machinery for rooting out flaws of character. There is an important connection here with the theme of the previous chapter, for if it is true, as Trollope took it to be, that "we cannot alter our natures" (*Four Lectures*, 70), then morals designed to coerce improvement are essentially futile and only likely to result in more or less violent defor- mations. We need to see how sharply Trollope's moral assumptions cut across those of much of his contemporary world to understand his impulse to extend the principle of preserving "human nature" from moralistic coercion—that is, from the cult of "spiritual perfection"—to a view that actively, if never in quite so many words, glorifies personal flaws. For it is one thing to declare, in the spirit of George Eliot's tragic realism, that we must reconcile ourselves to human imperfection because the world, regrettably, offers nothing better, but it is another to honor it as the indispensable sign of humanity. "For all [Trollope's] common sense," W. P. Ker cryptically but very pertinently remarks, "there may be something paradoxical in his morality. There generally is, in comedy" ("Trollope," 141). Only comedy, indeed, with its mischievous disregard for propriety, could hope to make plausible the illogical proposition that men and women are enhanced by their worst qualities.

As I have said, one looks almost in vain in Trollope for plain statements of this doctrine that seems, nonetheless, continually implied in his stories. Maybe the closest he comes is in an *Autobiography* passage in which he defends himself against those who condemn his frankly mercenary view of his profession, declaring that artists should be above such base motives as the love of money. These moralists, snorts Trollope, "require the practice of a so-called virtue which is contrary to nature, and which, in my eyes, would be no virtue if it were practiced." In fact, he goes on, "the love of money is so distinctive a characteristic of humanity that [sermons against it] are mere platitudes called for by customary but unintelligent piety" (p. 105). He then adduces classic utilitarian arguments to vindicate the profit motive, but these are subsidiary to the argument that this great vice of loving money (and by extension other vices) is "so distinctive a characteristic of humanity" that for this reason alone no humanist can afford to despise it and that, indeed, anyone who is so foolish as to uproot it from his or her heart has to some degree violated his or her integrity as a human being. If we substitute, for example, "erotic pleasure" for "money" in the phrases above, we see the underlying logic of the (troubled) Trollopian defense of sex that we surveyed in chapter 3.

Never satisfied with any hard-and-fast dictum, however, Trollope in his fiction steadily exerts pressure on his own principle, testing just how far the acknowledgment of ordinary imperfection is consonant with "humanity" after all, and in some cases, extending his principle to the breaking point. A good example would be the case of Johnny Eames, one of the most problematic of Trollope's tribe of erratic goodhearted young men. Johnny's behavior is in many respects genuinely deplorable, particularly with reference to the girl he jilts, Amelia Roper, yet Trollope persuades us to see his reprehensible conduct as just a sign of "hobbledehoyhood" and thus as an augury of future maturation. The comic dispensation breaks down altogether, however, for similar characters whose imperfections go slightly too far and nullify the effect of their personal attractiveness: Harry Clavering or Ralph Newton, for example. It may well be impossible to determine the precise point at which imperfection in Trollope shades from a virtue into a vice, but it is easy to recognize that infallibility has no role to play in his fictional world, except as a false ideal that is perpetually discredited.

The key problem for Trollope—but also a powerful stimulant to fictional invention—is that of insisting on this doctrine of embracing flaws of character without falling into mere cynicism or moral anesthesia. The dilemma is only partly resolvable by stipulating certain qualities such as, say, kindheartedness, as absolutes, and certain others, such as vanity, as ambivalent. Trollope instinctively hated cynicism, and strongly objected to it, for example, in Thackeray, whom he accused of detecting his pet vice of snobbery wherever he looked (*Thackeray*, 80–81). One of his most elaborate explorations of this mentality, and of its perilous closeness to the tolerant morality he himself champions, is found in *The Eustace Diamonds*. As the particular representative of moral magnanimity in this novel, he sets up Lizzie's long-suffering brother-in-law John Eustace, "a thoroughly good-natured man of the world"—a phrase full of specifically comic reverberations—"who could forgive many faults, not expecting people to be perfect." No amoralist, he finds many of Lizzie's seedy associates to be morally distasteful, but he is willing to go to heroic lengths not to give way to moral indignation, particularly toward a member of his family (chap. 37). Trollope reaffirms this philosophy in his long excursus on the fictional portrayal of heroes in chapter 35, entitled, significantly, "Too Bad for Sympathy," where he appeals to the potentially recalcitrant reader to extend to characters in fiction the same sympathetic toleration of faults that we extend to our friends in real life, "not without a consciousness of imperfection on our own part." But this sweeping assumption that we are all imperfect and that to imagine real-life heroes is therefore absurd leads almost inescapably to moral cynicism, and this very condition is one of Trollope's leading themes in this novel. What he particularly satirizes in *The Eustace Diamonds* is not active vice but a general worldly dulling of moral sensitivity. Even people of relatively good character in the world of this novel take for granted that strict moral principles are quaint anachronisms at best. Lady Linlithgow has a strong sense of family duty and in some ways is a pillar of rectitude, but "would cheat a butcher out of a mutton chop, or a cook out of a month's wages, if she could do so with some slant of legal wind in her favour" (chap. 1). Politics too, as in the furious parliamentary debates over the Sawab of Mygawb, is shown to be a wholly amoral charade, in which the various contestants cynically pretend to moral indignation (not expecting any sophisticated listeners to take them seriously) simply to maneuver for personal advancement. "It is thus the war is waged" (chap. 7). The selection of bishops, Mr. Legge Wilson, the secretary of state for India, mentions casually, is purely a matter of practical politics too (chap. 17).

Among numerous other instances of this kind of deterioration of moral sensibility, Frank Greystock, the novel's nominal hero, is an especially telling case. Trollope's characteristic plea that we should look favorably on Frank even though he falls "lamentably short in his heroism" (Ch. 35) suits Frank's own attitudes to a T. He is very far from being a disciple of Matthew Arnold's cult of spiritual perfection.

> He had never declared to himself that deceit or hypocrisy
> in a woman was especially abominable. As a rule he
> looked for it in a woman, and would say that some
> amount of affectation was necessary to a woman's
> character. He knew that his cousin Lizzie was a little
> liar—that she was, as Lucy had said, a pretty animal that
> would turn and bite; and yet he liked his cousin Lizzie.
> He did not want women to be perfect, so he would say.
>   (Chap. 13)

Frank's easygoing cynicism, his preference for more or less disreputable people with no pretensions to being "perfect," his urbane assumption that deceit and hypocrisy are nothing to object to very strongly, all register a subtle parody of Trollope's own doctrine of moral tolerance. The reader is meant to see how fine a nuance distinguishes the two—and to see at the same time how vital this nuance is. One sign of this implication is the malicious irony to which Frank is subjected. "I don't like cunning women," he declares grandly, getting on his high horse when John Eustace suggests that he consider marrying Lizzie; two paragraphs later we learn that he is preparing a very complicated legal case "in order that he might present it to a jury enveloped in increased mystery" (chap. 13): being "cunning" is the way Frank earns his bread.

Trollope is keenly aware, in other words, that his moral system is prone to take a degraded form that he intensely dislikes; his problem is to preserve comic sympathy with human failings, to find them amusing and to discover in them evidence of vitality and charm—of humanity itself—but without falling into moral callousness or into what is termed at one point in *The Eustace Diamonds*, in a phrase that I

have quoted earlier, "that worst of all diseases, a low idea of humanity" (chap. 28). This precarious, paradoxical morality scarcely lends
itself to codification, but needs to be devised all over again in each
new novel to suit the particular circumstances of each case. In a sense
it can never be perfectly attained, and attempts at it must always leave
us uneasy. Trollope almost compulsively devises exhibits of just this
uneasiness. If Crosbie's desertion of Lily in *The Small House at Allington* is severely blamable (as it seems even to Crosbie's worldly pal
Fowler Pratt), how can we justify excusing Johnny Eames's desertion
of Amelia Roper as nothing more serious than a trifling misadventure
of a basically good-hearted hobbledehoy? If Mr. Arabin's interest in
Eleanor Bold's wealth is more than exonerated as a sign of his wholesome ordinary humanity (as we shall see in a moment), why is Mr.
Slope's interest in her wealth seen as sordid? If Captain Aylmer's coldly
tyrannical pomposity is sinister and repellent, why is Plantagenet Palliser's finally seen as a comic foible? Trollope sets up difficult conundrums like these, we can only suppose, to dramatize that the moral
system driving his fiction is reducible to no rigid calculus, but always
remains fluid and problematical, always requires assessing almost infinitely fine nuances and seeking to reconcile contrary principles. It is
a world designed craftily, in accordance with the basic tendency of
comedy, to make single-minded moralists uncomfortable.[5]

Laughter

One element above all in Trollope's work serves to guide us in making
these subtle moral discriminations and to render his fiction, where
sympathy is almost always equivocal, "readable": laughter. Laughter,
that is, has the specific function in Trollope of resolving the crucial
disparity between "truth to life" and sympathetic response. Yet critics
rarely mention Trollope's humor, no doubt because it is hard to square
with the assumption that he is uniformly "realistic." In Trollope's
fiction, laughter always marks a locus of artistic tension. (As a connoisseur of artistic tension, Trollope is all the more drawn to such moments.) This is because literary laughter seems inescapably to be a
function of certain conventionalized formulas, and any use of comic
"business" infringes therefore on the illusion of naturalness that is the
basis of Trollope's method. Consider, for example, the scene of the
Proudies' reception in *Barchester Towers* (chaps. 10–11), a scene presided over by the absurd Bertie Stanhope and climaxed by the devastation of Mrs. Proudie's dress by the runaway sofa (which seems, as
objects often do in the animistic world of Dickens, impelled by a mischievous intent of its own). "Gathers were heard to go," says the nar-

rator, "stitches to crack, plaits to fly open, flounces were seen to fall, and breadths to expose themselves." Bertie, the culprit, hastens to try to disengage what remains of the dress from the castor of the sofa, but is checked by Mrs. Proudie's furious rebuke: "Unhand it, sir!" We laugh at Mrs. Proudie's mishap not because there is anything inherently funny in seeing a lady's clothing, even an overbearingly pompous lady's clothing, ripped off: but because the hyperbolic comic style of the passage cues the reader unmistakably that this is a formal occasion, a ritual moment of the punishment of pride, and that, in effect, we are *supposed* to laugh. The realistic effect of witnessing naturally occurring events from a disinterested perspective is displaced by the awareness that the events before us are specifically comic events, encoded according to the protocols of the comic mode; and this awareness is the precondition of responding properly to a scene like the one that I have cited. The same effect obliquely makes us aware of the illusion of natural life as just this, an illusion that the skillful artist can heighten or diminish at will, meting out the pleasure of comedy by subtle nuances of style.

There is in Trollope's fiction a certain amount of broad buffo humor like the example above. He carries out numbers of exercises in what he terms, in his notes to Jacobean plays, "fooling": comical stories of "low" clowns who are supposed to entertain a sophisticated audience by their inarticulateness and absurd manners: John Crumb and Joe Mixet in *The Way We Live Now*, Farmer Cheesacre in *Can You Forgive Her?*, Mr. and Mrs. Lupex in *The Small House at Allington*. There are occasional "humor" characters like Mr. Prosper in *The Claverings*, and occasional brilliant grotesques like Sophie Gordeloup in the same novel. Taken all together, these instances of overt comicality in Trollope add up to an impressive array, and they have an important function to play in controlling the mood of his fiction at large. They define the set of effects that underlies other stories in tacit form only; they convey the hint that serious-seeming materials may turn out to be subliminally funny, if we look at them closely enough. This impression that the serious is full of amusing undercurrents is a key to Trollope.

Still, for a writer whose whole practice is deeply and directly influenced by stage comedy, it is the relative paucity of overt fooling that strikes us in Trollope. Especially notable by his absence is the figure of the vivacious joker, the prankster master or mistress of ceremonies who looms so large in traditional comedy: Falstaff, Rosalind, Mosca, Subtle, Horner, Millamant, Quilp, Pecksniff, and all the other comic stars whose genius for humorous improvisation is the animating spirit of the works they appear in. Trollope gives glimpses of this figure in characters like Glencora, Miss Dunstable, Mary Thorne, or Brooke

Burgess, but only in the most attenuated form. Instead, his humor focuses strongly on the chastisement of folly and the ironical exposure of pretension—for the conception of the redemptive comic flaw in no way prevents the making of keen moral judgments: in fact (as the scene of Eleanor at the mirror attests) it presupposes them. In the retributive bent of his humor, in any case, Trollope shows the strong influence of his much-admired Jane Austen; he is his own man, however, in his perfecting of a mode of comic playfulness that is feathered so delicately into the realistic setting that one can hardly notice the transition: a kind of effect designed to provoke an almost unconscious relish of comic amusement that never quite becomes outright laughter. The reader cannot help feeling at these moments that Trollope is not only displaying his very unobtrusive virtuosity, but conducting experiments in what we might call the chemical properties of literary styles, seeking to discover how far the comic and the realistic can be bonded together despite their intrinsic incompatibility. The sense of experimentation is heightened when we notice the same scenes being rehearsed over and over in differently inflected forms in successive novels.

Consider, for example, the following sequence of parallel scenes: the first meeting of the austere, dignified Josiah Crawley and the vulgar, breezy, good-hearted London lawyer, Mr. Toogood (*The Last Chronicle of Barset*, chap. 32); the scene, discussed above, of the snobbish Harry Clavering's first visit to the home of the unpretentious Burtons; and the scene of Plantagenet Palliser, armed with all his monumental dignity, paying a visit in *The Duke's Children* to his son's half-reputable club, where he finds himself obliged to chat politely with the disreputable racetrack character Major Tifto ("Well;—I can assure you,—your Grace, that is,—that since I've seen 'orses I've never seen a 'orse fitter than him" [chap. 27]). The three scenes are different in feeling, but they are all full of sophisticated humor and all are built on the same comic pattern, as exercises in an important class of comic effects that can be called the comedy of embarrassment. The mirthful quality of all three arises from the embarrassment that is inflicted upon the central character and that is rendered funny, again, because we are aware that each scene is a contrived (that is, essentially implausible) comic occasion, a ritualized moment carrying out comedy's traditional punishment of excess dignity. In this respect, these scenes are congruent with the scene of Mrs. Proudie's run-in with the sofa, the main difference being that in the three scenes mentioned— far more typical of Trollope than the one with Mrs. Proudie—the victim is a character toward whom we are meant to feel friendly rather than hostile. Trollope devises these three scenes with the barest minimum of comic cues and inserts them in novels that are far from being easily recognizable as comedies. Possibly excepting the Duke in the Beargarden, none of these scenes has that hyperbolic, outlandish quality by which comedy makes itself known—and in the Beargarden scene such outlandishness as the situation contains is only very subtly suggested. The result is that a reader not attuned to Trollope's finely nuanced play of style might well read over these scenes without discovering them to be funny—without realizing, that is, that Trollope has slyly drawn us just beyond the pale of realism and into the ritualistic realm of comedy, where to assume excessive dignity is infallibly to receive hilarious chastisement. Such scenes induce a slight feeling of aesthetic vertigo, as though the author were requiring us to keep a precarious balance just at the point of intersection of two incompatible modes.

It is a key to Trollope's sensibility, as all the discussion in this chapter should suggest, that most of his comic mockery is directed toward characters we are meant to like and to identify with, as in the first examples of the comedy of embarrassment cited above. Palliser's pompous air cannot escape unpunished, but at heart it is not a vice but just a comic flaw that renders him appealingly human and is felt by Trollope to magnify rather than to detract from sympathy for him; therefore the score can be settled (for the moment) by no chastisement more serious than the perfectly calibrated moment of discomfiture that he suffers at the Beargarden. A still milder form of comic mockery is exemplified in the charming scene in *The Small House at Allington* (chap. 22) where Johnny Eames and Dr. Crofts ride home together from Lord de Guest's and almost quarrel in comparing the charms of the two Dale girls, each praising the sister with whom he is secretly in love. Here the humor again is that of the mechanism identified by Freud, the spectacle of grown-ups acting like children. In this class of effects the comic pleasure seems to be exactly the inverse of what is involved, according to the usual explanation, in satiric laughter. In the latter we feel an exhilarating superiority to folly, but in the former we are allowed the delightful sensation of discovering the comic character to be as childlike as we ourselves are (at least while enjoying the playful entertainment of a comedy). The affectionate mocking of favored characters is such a characteristic event in Trollope, in any case, because it crystallizes the paradoxical comic morality in which imperfection is the basis of sympathy.

The fundamental reason that Trollope's laughter can operate so energetically without destroying sympathy was identified in an obituary essay by Trollope's most insightful nineteenth-century reader, Richard Holt Hutton. In Trollope, says Hutton, humor springs chiefly, and abundantly, from an "appreciation of the paradoxes of social life" and thus from "his keen perception of the oddity of human motives, pursuits, and purposes" (Smalley, 506). Given Trollope's analysis of Victorian England as a society in which paradoxically disjointed values are endemic, and where manners are thus full of contradictions, oddities can only be profuse. This state of affairs may easily take a tragic turn, as it does in *He Knew He Was Right,* where the collapse of the Trevelyans' marriage lays bare the anomalies of a marital code based on the principle of affectionate trust but also on that of unquestioned male authority. Trollope usually eyes paradoxes of this kind, however, with comic enjoyment. The death of the old Duke of Omnium in *Phineas Redux* provides a representative example. Throughout his life a disgraceful reprobate, he is widely praised as his end draws near. "It was acknowledged everywhere that he had played his part in a noble and even in a princely manner, that he had used with a becoming grace the rich things that had been given him, and that he had deserved well of his country." This, says the narrator, despite the fact that "perhaps, no man who had lived during the same period, or any portion of the period, had done less, or had devoted himself more entirely to the consumption of good things without the slightest idea of producing anything in return!" The point of this funny incongruity, we infer, is that dukes in these days are still spoken of as though they had some active role to play for the national welfare, whereas they are merely figureheads for a set of sham values that people find it reassuring to pay lip service to. Consequently it is enough for this man to have "looked like a duke" to be spoken of as a glorious benefactor of the country (chap. 24). The opposite and complementary image of this key paradox of social life is that of the subsequent duke, who strives to acknowledge a real bond with humanity at large, squirming with aristocratic embarrassment in his chat with Major Tifto.

The submerged joke running through much of Trollope's fiction is an implication of Hutton's principle and also the root joke of the whole tradition of comedies of manners: the one based upon the incongruity of dignified and polite ladies and gentlemen becoming involved in such inherently undignified activities as sex or politics. Wherever they do, they create situations rife with potential humor, even when tragedy threatens; and Trollopian drama creates subtle effects by drawing continually on this potential. It is present, for example, in the scene in *Phineas Redux* where the insanely jealous Scot Robert Kennedy, whose wife, Lady Laura, has just left him, confronts Phineas Finn in Macpherson's Hotel, furiously accuses him of being his wife's "paramour," as he quaintly phrases it, and attempts to murder him with a pistol (chap. 23). The scene could hardly be more full of grief and rage, and murder is not the stuff of comic amusement: Kennedy's madness is every bit as horrifying as that of his prototype Louis Trevelyan. Yet there is something irresistibly absurd about the scene none the less, thanks to the inherent absurdities of all the polite social conventions built up around the primal drives of the libido; and a keen eye may even detect the parallels between such a scene and all the endlessly varied elaborations of the theme of cuckoldry in comic drama. The figures of Pinchwife and Horner seem mischievously latent in those of the jealous husband Kennedy and the dapper ladies' man Phineas. As though to corroborate the implicit comic outlines of this scene, Trollope concludes it with a memorable joke. A moment after barely escaping alive from his unseemly encounter, Phineas, returning instantly to the world of conventional decorum, faces another problem. "Phineas was in great doubt as to what duty was required of him. His first difficulty consisted in this,—that his hat was still in Mr. Kennedy's room, and that Mrs. Macpherson altogether refused to go and fetch it." As far as I can see, it remains a riddle why such an image should arouse delighted laughter, but clearly it has to do with the fragility of dignity and with the tyranny of civilized proprieties, which, in the ultimate paradox of social life, imperiously demand respect even in the most inappropriate circumstances. Probably by laughing at such a joke we release anxieties about our own subjection to codes of propriety and the straitjacketing of our own instinctual life. Phineas, in any case, needs his tall hat, the sign of his standing as a gentleman, in order to step outside and call a cab; without it, evidently, he is reduced to helplesness. No gentleman (so runs the implicit logic of the scene) calls a cab or reports an attempted murder to the police without his hat on his head. Hats, Phineas intuitively knows and here consciously realizes, are absolutely vital to the functioning of civilized life. For the moment, therefore, his concern for his hat eclipses every other aspect of his situation, and even impels him, we notice, to plead with the landlady to go into the room with an armed homicidal maniac to get it back for him. The comic stagecraft compressed here into a single sentence yields quite a profound glimpse into "the paradoxes of social life," and gives a wonderful example of the structure of Trollope's humor. Then it is confirmed by a second joke almost funnier than the first. "The two [chambermaids] were now outside the bar shaking in their shoes, and evidently unwilling to face the danger. At last the door of the room above was opened, and our hero's hat was sent rolling down the stairs." Even a bloodthirsty maniac knows the sanctity of hats, and realizes that it is imperative to return a gentleman's hat when he leaves!

"Barchester Towers" and the Charms of Imperfection

The immediate context of the *Autobiography* passage about the love of money as a "distinctive . . . characteristic of humanity" is Trollope's discussion of the publication of *Barchester Towers*. "They who preach this doctrine [of the contempt of money] will be much offended by my theory, and by this book of mine" (p. 105), he declares. *Barchester Towers* is indeed the vehicle of Trollope's moral theory in the form most likely to offend the "widespread prejudice" in favor of idealization in fiction; it is also, not coincidentally, an express exercise in comedy, the first in Trollope's career and among the most significant in English in the half-century since Jane Austen. The artificiality and playfulness of comic style signal themselves continually in this novel: for example, in the interlarding of the story with allusions to and direct quotations from literary texts, particularly comic ones: *Tristram Shandy*, *The Comedy of Errors*, *The Rivals*, *Don Quixote*, *Tartuffe*, and *The Taming of the Shrew*, among others. In this way we are given continual notification of the mode to which the novel belongs—a mode distinctly skewed away from the melancholy realism of its predecessor, *The Warden*. No less explicit in its announcement of literary artifice is the dominant stylistic device of *Barchester Towers*, mock heroic ("As Achilles warmed at the sight of his armour, as Don Quixote's heart grew strong when he grasped his lance, so did Mrs. Proudie look forward to fresh laurels" [chap. 26]).[6] These auguries of comic entertainment are confirmed in every aspect of Trollope's story: in its assemblage of classic comic killjoys and eccentrics, its scenes of antic pandemonium like the episode of the runaway sofa, and in its narrator's remarkable assurance at an early point in the story that the dire marriages threatening Eleanor Bold are only, as the rule of comedy demands, mock dangers not to be taken seriously. "Let the gentle-hearted reader be under no apprehension whatsoever. It is not destined that Eleanor shall marry Mr. Slope or Bertie Stanhope" (chap. 15). Notice is almost too plainly served that we are not here in a world of potentially uncontrollable consequences like that of *The Warden*, but a regulated comic world where bad outcomes can be ruled out from the start—need to be, in fact, in order for the intended pleasures of the text to come through.

Barchester Towers embodies, too, as we briefly noticed in chapter 2, the central themes of comedy. Nominally the conflict between the clerical establishment of Barchester and the interlopers, the Proudies and Slope, has to do with issues of church doctrine and of liturgy— "opinions as regarded dissenters, church reform, the hebdomadal council, and such like" (chap. 5)—but in fact the two sides are deployed by Trollope as the classic polar opposites and eternal antagonists of comedy: the partisans and enemies of pleasure, the former led by Archdeacon Grantley, with his frank love of "the good things of this world" (chap. 4), the latter represented by the puritanical new-comers, the Proudies and Slope. As we noted, Trollope ties the personal and moral deformities of Slope and Mrs. Proudie closely to their unnatural suppression of their own cravings for pleasure. The same argument sheds light on the "diabolical" machinations of the voluptuous siren Madeline Vesey-Neroni, who fascinates men despite being "a poor invalid" paralyzed from the waist down and thus, as the narrator circumspectly phrases it, "debarred from the ordinary pleasures of life" (chap. 27). Her compulsive seduction of men clearly is a pathological compensation for the absence of all hope of erotic pleasure. To be cut off from pleasure in this world is to suffer almost necessarily a serious damaging of personality.

More than any other single factor, however, the comic argument in *Barchester Towers* revolves around an idea of character in which sympathy flows toward human imperfection rather than toward faultless idealization. The opening scene of the novel focuses attention on just this principle with enough emphasis to make its shocking, morally provocative aspect stand out sharply. The beloved old Bishop of Barchester is dying of a "long and lingering" illness, and his son, Archdeacon Grantly, who expects to be named the new bishop providing his father dies before the imminent fall of the Conservative government, is tormented by involuntary wishes that the old man die without waste of time, and thus not cost him his chance at this promotion. The archdeacon's worldly ambition could hardly be cast in a more troubling light, even though he at last is able to drive the horrid wish from his heart: "The proud, wishful, worldly man, sank on his knees by the bedside, and taking the bishop's hand within his own, prayed eagerly that his sins might be forgiven him." Such a scene is far removed from the gaiety of the comic. But then, in a virtuoso passage of Trollope's peculiarly unobtrusive kind, the story swiftly, subtly modulates into comedy, the basis of which is the tangled mixture of human motives.

The bishop dies; the archdeacon is moved by the solemnity of the occasion and yet is desperate to communicate the news to the government without the loss of a minute. At this vital juncture (not really vital, however, for the government, unknown to the archdeacon, has already fallen) he is trapped in a ludicrous predicament: Mr. Harding seizes his hand to console him—and won't let go. The archdeacon is wild to send a telegram. "But how was he to act while his father-in-law stood there holding his hand? how, without appearing unfeeling, was he to forget his father in the bishop—to overlook what he had

lost, and think only of what he might possibly gain?" We are surprised to find ourselves *laughing* at the ludicrous image, in which a
complex of comic effects fuse: moral anxiety is dispelled by laughter;
fit chastisement is meted out; and especially, by the establishment
of the comic view (in which a personal failing like the archdeacon's
almost heartless ambition is sufficiently punished by a moment of extreme embarrassment), it is intimated that even rather grievous imperfection of character is not to be condemned and not merely grudgingly forgiven, but comically enjoyed. Thanks to the alchemy of comic
laughter, his ambition renders the archdeacon more appealing rather
than less. The effect has a strong moral logic: the archdeacon's imperfection richly humanizes him and gives the virtues that coexist with
his vices deepened poignancy at the same time, a poignancy that "all
but divine men and women" can never possess. A man with no mixed
motives in such circumstances, the scene hints, would be a sheer unreality or an intolerable prig. These implications of the comic event
are distinctly spelled out, then, in the final paragraphs of the chapter,
where Trollope formulates the moral lesson of the episode we have
just witnessed. "If we look to our clergymen to be more than men," he
says, "we shall probably teach ourselves to think that they are less,
and can hardly hope to raise the character of the pastor by denying to
him the right to entertain the aspirations of a man." The standard of
flawless perfection can only be corrupt.[7]

This affirmation of imperfect character as the proper standard of
virtue, or rather of humanity, proves to be the central theme of *Barchester Towers*, and is subsequently restated more than once. "There is
nothing godlike about us," declares Mr. Arabin, referring again specifically to clergymen, though the broader reference is to his role as
hero in a novel (chap. 21); "Till we can become divine," says the narrator afterwards, referring here to men and women at large, "we must
be content to be human, lest in our hurry for a change we sink to something lower" (chap. 43). But more significant than these polemical
statements is Trollope's rich comic dramatization of his idea throughout the novel. The archdeacon is always central to this effect. He is
overbearing and crotchety, as in the subtly mock-heroic scene where
he rants about the evils of round dinner tables, which suggest to his
mind "something democratic and parvenue" (chap. 21); especially, he
stands as an almost culpably worldly and ambitious man, and as one
devoted to pleasure. The carefully designed story works, however, to
turn this great vice (for a man of the cloth at least) into a saving virtue,
and the hilarious effects surrounding this moral transposition express
the exhilarated liberation from the oppression of "customary but unintelligent piety" that forms one of comedy's chief functions. The

archdeacon's frankly worldly pleasure-loving nature is a virtue because it guarantees his immunity to the ranker kinds of intolerance,
cruelty, and hypocrisy that go (as so many examples in the novel
testify) with low-church fanaticism. Thus his presumed vice of worldliness is correlated throughout the novel with the fundamental goodness of character that he clearly possesses—the unmistakable sign of
this being his affectionate intimacy with his father-in-law Mr. Harding, the novel's touchstone of moral integrity. We see here, again, the
failure of the idea of comic laughter as necessarily destructive or humiliating: when we laugh at the archdeacon's egregious worship of
Mammon we are collaborating in comedy's moral legerdemain, sub-
scribing, that is, to the interpretation of his patent flaws as strengths
in disguise, as claims on our approval.

The same comic transvaluation operates still more fully in connection with the other outsider who comes to live in Barchester, the
ascetic scholar Mr. Arabin. Since he is as authentically a man of self-
denying virtue as the Proudies and Slope are not, his resemblance to
them as another quasi-fanatical ideologue and enemy of pleasure at
first goes unnoticed. But it is precisely the function of Trollope's comedy to bring it surprisingly, even shockingly, into view, and thus to
usurp ordinary moral patterns in fiction. Arabin has made for himself
a reputation as "a man always ready at a moment's notice to take up
the cudgels in opposition to anything that savoured of an evangelical
bearing" (chap. 20), and is imported to Barchester to play just this role
in its ecclesiastical wars. His partisan combat in the name of his sec-
tarian ideas of righteousness and his code of self-denial link him,
however, to his adversaries. Trollope never states this key irony in so
many words; rather, he disarms it by having the saintly Arabin undergo and succumb to the seductions of worldliness and pleasure. As
the image of flawless perfection dissolves into one of ordinary carnal
humanity, Arabin's standing in the novel, as the paradoxical logic of
comedy dictates, is not damaged but enhanced.

Thus, this paragon who is "always in earnest" (chap. 20) enters the
story bearing a guilty secret: he is sick of poverty and envies his fellow
clergymen who have encircled themselves with luxurious comfort.
"Surely Mr. Arabin was not a man to sigh after wealth! Of all men, his
friends would have unanimously declared he was the last to do so.
But how little our friends know us!" (chap. 20). Trollope is unusually
emphatic in his exoneration of Arabin: the code of asceticism and un-
worldliness, he declares, is "an outrage on human nature," which can
only be debased and distorted by attempting to suppress its longing
for "wealth and worldly comfort and happiness on earth" (chap. 20).
Just how provocative Trollope means his endorsement of the illicit val-

ues of materialism and selfishness to be is shown in his choosing the morally disreputable Signora to deliver, in the form of a catechism administered to the still-agonized Arabin (who has scandalized himself by admitting inwardly that his love of Eleanor is mixed with love of her fortune), the speech that sums up the novel's moral program. "The greatest mistake any man ever made is to suppose that the good things of the world are not worth the winning," she declares in a passage that ought to make clear why Trollope's fiction seemed morally dangerous to so many contemporaries. "Why are beautiful things given to us, and luxuries and pleasant enjoyments, if they be not intended to be used?" And especially, "Why were women made beautiful if men are not to regard them?" (chap. 38). The Signora is as close as Trollope comes to using in his own comedy the device, so central in comic literature, of the rascals or mockers of virtue endowed with such charm and vitality that we are obliged to share their own delight in rascality. Her exhortation to Arabin, in any case, is the liberating, magnanimous gospel of comedy, which assures us that "the ordinary pleasures of youth" (chap. 15) reproved by Mr. Slope—and the pleasures of middle age too—are not to be despised.

Arabin has to confess not only his craving for "the pleasures of the world" (chap. 3), but also his propensity for what earnest evangelicals would call lust. At the same time as he is falling in love with Eleanor, he is magnetized by the seductive Signora, a married woman. Considering the severe code of sexual morality current among Trollope's public in the mid-1850s, the striking thing is the more than indulgence extended to this signal straying from virtue in Arabin. His only punishment is the finely graduated one appropriate to comedy: he is made to look amusingly foolish in his wooing, as when he suspects that Eleanor prefers the loathsome Slope to him: "Poor Mr. Arabin!— untaught, illiterate, boorish, ignorant man! That at forty years of age you should know so little of the workings of a woman's heart!" (chap. 30). In his affectionate laughter at Arabin's expense, Trollope confirms our sense that the clergyman's various failings only humanize him and make him all the worthier of sympathy and esteem. Again, this transvaluation is the special prerogative and the hallmark of comedy, which by ingrained tendency mocks the heroic, the idealized, the perfect, and in this way works to restore cheerful sympathy with ordinary defective humanity.

Trollope confirms this tactic in the benediction in the final chapter of *Barchester Towers*, where he describes, for example, Eleanor's almost excessive tendency toward Catholic liturgy: "A few high church vagaries do not, [Mrs. Grantley] thinks, sit amiss on the shoulders of a young dean's wife." Once again a failing becomes, seen in the right light, a virtue. In a less whimsical tone Trollope closes the novel with an odd eulogy of Mr. Harding that goes out of its way to deny that this half-saintly figure is to be seen as "a perfect divine," "as a hero [or] as a man to be admired and talked of"; he is merely, says the narrator, "a good man without guile." In this final disavowing of the "standard of perfection," Trollope is reminding us of the serious moral argument that his comedy has implied throughout. To aim at perfection can only lead to a distortion of humanity. From the comic point of view and from Trollope's, this is not a melancholy or disillusioned conclusion but, rather, an invigorating one that makes possible a more authentic sympathy with one's fellow men and women, and thus forms the basis not only for moral optimism but for the practice of a genuinely humane realistic fiction.

7

The Way We Live Now: Puritanism, Laughter, Make-Believe

"How fond she is of finding morals in things!" Alice thought to herself.

Alice's Adventures in Wonderland

If the argument of this book has been convincing thus far, *The Way We Live Now* ought to seem a substantially different novel from the one usually evoked in criticism. Its heavy ironies and its air of bitter disenchantment make it possibly the Trollope novel most attuned to twentieth-century tastes, and it has accumulated as a result an amount of sophisticated critical commentary sufficient to mark it as one of the major literary works of its period. By and large this commentary might have been written by Trollope's saturnine country squire Roger Carbury, who stands at the center of the cast of characters, for its tone is solemn and its method of analysis strenuously moralistic. In this the book's critics are only following the lead of Trollope himself, who declares in the *Autobiography* that the motive of *The Way We Live Now* is to condemn all forms of modern-day "dishonesty" (pp. 354–55). Thus the world of the novel, we are told, is primarily one of moral standards in collapse. The artistic purpose is to indict modern decay of principle, and the mood is bleakly pessimistic. In "his horrifying vision of the nihilistic world of *The Way We Live Now*," says one writer, Trollope is denouncing modern life as corrupt to the core (Harvey, 71). His theme, says another, is "the desolate reality" of the nineteenth-century scene (Tanner, 271). This mode of criticism tends to extract from the novel a set of supposed moral judgments and then to treat these judgments as constituting the work itself, always a dubious procedure and especially misleading, perhaps, in the present case. That this novel, for example, is *entertaining*, unusually rich in humorous invention, especially in those areas supposed most to epitomize modern moral degeneracy, is an anomaly hard to square with the usual account. If the great financier Augustus Melmotte simply embodies "dishonesty"—to such an extent indeed that he is no true character at all, just a sheer "void" or "nothingness," as has been stated (Slakey, 253–54)—how is it that Trollope renders him not only fascinating but finally more than a little sympathetic? "Anyone who traffics [like Melmotte] in [mere words], rather than using [them] to express a reality to another, comes to nothing," declares one critic, summing up the stern and rather platitudinous moral that Trollope is supposed to be advocating (ibid., 257). Melmotte has come to nothing? His grandiose, eerily palpable image dominates a major novel, and a century later he continues to stimulate critical commentary. Melmotte flourishes brazenly in the very teeth of moral disapproval, and in so doing suggests a need to consider this novel from a different point of view.

Even in its own terms the moralizing criticism of *The Way We Live Now* goes astray in ways that seem as obvious as they are significant. This is particularly true in reference to the figure of the absolutist and relentless moralist Roger Carbury, taken by most critics as the novel's image of "the good man" (Tracy, 167), as "Trollope's moral norm" (Harvey, 138), "the one really admirable man of principle" in the novel (Polhemus, *The Changing World*, p. 195).[1] These terms may be open to question, but they are just the terms in which Roger views himself as he aggressively lays down the moral law to those about him, "making continual pronouncements of a ringing, Biblical sort" (Kincaid, 172) as to the corruption he sees on all sides. Undoubtedly he embodies a moral norm of rectitude and a fidelity to traditional country values that Trollope often in his fiction expects us to applaud. But Roger's claim to monopolize the novel's moral platform by sheer vehemence is, to say the least, a dubious one. The grating puritanical tone of his voice does tend at length to make him seem disturbingly like a mere "crank" or "malcontent," as Kincaid rightly notes (p. 172), and there is strong reason to doubt that his railings against "the degeneracy of the age" (chap. 55) need be taken at face value. They are, after all, gently rebuked by his friend the bishop, himself an ideal image of nondogmatic but genuine piety and unselfishness, who sees the age not as one of universal iniquity at all but of gradual enlightenment (chap. 16). Trollope himself pointedly rejects Roger's brand of Carlylean pessimism in his comments on this novel in the *Autobiography* (p. 354), scoffing at Carlyle's view that modern society is "going to the dogs"—the very phrase that Roger uses twice in his debate with the bishop. But we should not require external evidence of this kind to recognize that Roger is no judicious observer of contemporary life, but rather an almost monomaniacal scold. Worse, his own conduct in the tale is hardly above reproach.

His denunciation of the great financier Melmotte for his questionable antecedents, on the grounds that a man whose reputation is clouded even by unsubstantiated rumors should be ostracized by respectable people, proves justified, making Roger look for the time being prescient and admirable. His persecution of the cruelly abused and totally blameless American widow Winifred Hurtle, a campaign that absorbs an increasing amount of his energy, puts him in quite a different light. To her discredit, Mrs. Hurtle has a hot temper and is willing in casual conversation to praise Melmotte for the grand scale of his enterprises (critics severely chastise her for such unladylike talk: see Tracy, 173); otherwise she emerges as the novel's clearest standard of intelligence, bravery, refinement, kindness, and true feeling, not to mention dignity, urbanity, and witty charm. As John Crumb says, using one of Trollope's most unambiguous moral terms, Mrs. Hurtle "is a lady as is a lady" (chap. 87). Roger, however, having heard certain malicious rumors that her enemies have conspired to put in circulation, brands her on the spot and forever "a wicked, intriguing, bad woman" (chap. 87)—which obviously, even taking the dimmest possible view of her, she is not—and interferes implacably in her engagement to Paul Montague, with results that are devastating to her. His virulent distaste for her arises naturally from the fact that he is "prejudiced against all Americans," especially American women, whom he pictures to himself "as being loud, masculine, and atheistical" (chap. 87), though he seems never to have met one before accidentally running into (the ravishingly feminine) Mrs. Hurtle. His ignorant aversion to Americans is in turn just one facet of the strongly pronounced snobbery of this man who dislikes houses and people who savor "of trade" or are otherwise deficient in what he most values, "that thoroughly established look of old county position which belonged to Carbury" (chap. 14). Impelled by the deeply ingrained bigotry that Trollope so strongly underscores, Roger does not scruple to insist that Paul break his formal engagement of marriage to Mrs. Hurtle on the grounds that he was "entrapped" into it (chap. 46)—knowing full well as he makes this argument that the engagement was in fact all Paul's idea and that Mrs. Hurtle, though "she did love [Paul] with all her heart" (chap. 27), long opposed it. This is not a minor issue in the novel, and it makes even Kincaid's divided judgment that Roger is "a good-hearted gentleman but an untrustworthy spokesman" (p. 173) seem far too generous to Roger. Such a formulation obscures, too, the destructive effect and the audacity of the irony that Trollope has brought to bear on this character who masquerades so convincingly as a "moral norm." Roger may be naturally goodhearted, but this does not alleviate the novel's emerging negative judgment of him: quite the contrary, it only stresses the deforming effects of his absolutist puritan morality, which has made him harsh, intol-

erant, self-righteous, and actively cruel. Mrs. Hurtle is scarcely overstating the case when she sums up her perceptions of English life in
an eloquent, restrained statement that implicitly links Roger with
Melmotte, Mr. Longestaffe, and all the novel's other boorish bullies.
"It seems to me that everybody here is either too humble or too overbearing," she says. "Nobody seems content to stand firm on his own
footing and interfere with nobody else" (chap. 71).[2]

I have belabored this question to set the novel as distinctly as possible in the context of the problem of legibility incurred by a comic
writer in the age of "the fatal shift toward over-seriousness." By beginning to disrupt the pattern of stern moralistic commentary on *The Way
We Live Now*, I hope at the same time to highlight some of its other
values, especially comic ones, basically antagonistic as these are to
the kind of grim moral temper, sure of its own exclusive authority and
obsessed with the war against other people's moral backsliding, that
Roger embodies and that modern readers find so congenial. Yet this
novel is plainly no comedy according to the fairly strict definition that
I have been using. Instead of the artificially geometrical plot that is the
hallmark of comic form, in *The Way We Live Now* Trollope pushes the
loose and baggy Thackerayan form to an extreme, interweaving four
or five main stories, and several secondary ones besides, into a sprawl-
ing megatale with no clear shape or focus at all (see Tanner, 263–64).
In the second half there are some plainly comic couplings, notably
between Ruby Ruggles and John Crumb and Marie Melmotte and
Hamilton K. Fisker, yet the comic mood of these subplots is submerged in the moods of mental anguish that dominate more important story lines centered on Melmotte, Mrs. Hurtle, and Roger
Carbury. The love stories of Paul and Hetta and Lady Carbury and
Mr. Broune end in happy matrimony but lack altogether that quality
of gaiety and delighted surprise that identifies the comic. Comic
charm—the mischievous kind that renders rogues irresistibly appealing—is confined in *The Way We Live Now* to the jaunty Fisker, who
puts in only brief appearances. And the novel's general ambience is
dominated, to an extent that would seem to rule out the possibility of
comedy, by violence and fear.

The story is punctuated by outbursts of physical violence and threats
of it: Ruby Ruggles being dragged about by the hair by her grand-
father; Marie Melmotte being cruelly beaten by her father; Sir Felix
being beaten to a pulp by John Crumb; Mrs. Hurtle's tales of violent
assaults and homicide in the United States and her repeated threats
(never acted on, of course) to flog Paul Montague with a horsewhip.
But the most pervasive and frightening species of violence in *The Way
We Live Now* are not physical after all. Often they are subtle and

oblique, and typically they mask themselves with the appearance of respectability or even friendliness: none the less do nearly all forms of social relations—family, sexual, marital, financial, professional, or class relations—turn out here to be violent at the core. Hence the novel's ubiquitous metaphorical imagery of tearing, devouring, flaying, crushing. Thus Lady Carbury's friend the newspaper editor Mr. Alf, who, like Roger Carbury, thinks of himself as a figure of high-minded rectitude in a world of mendacity, sets "one of his most sharp-nailed subordinates" on the review of her new book and has it "pulled . . . to pieces with almost rabid malignity" (chap. 11). Along with his professed goal of dispensing "Aristidean justice," remarks the narrator, Mr. Alf is moved by "the second purpose of enticing readers by crushing authors,—as crowds used to be enticed to see men hanged when executions were done in public" (chap. 89). This massing of imagery of violent physical assault should make readers uncomfortable at the spectacle of the meting out of strict "justice." In her relations with her son Sir Felix, Lady Carbury, already metaphorically dismembered by Mr. Alf's reviewer, is like a mother pelican allowing "the blood to be torn from her own breast to satisfy the greed of her young" (chap. 23). Marie Melmotte thinks with justice that her father will "cut [her] into bits" if she doesn't obey him (chap. 29). To Paul, Mrs. Hurtle seems like a woman with "wild cat's claws" (Ch. 38), and her instinct is to avenge herself on him by tearing him "limb from limb" (chap. 51) or by giving him "a violent seizing by the neck" (chap. 90). The violent Melmotte, after all his maneuvering, at last has "his back . . . so utterly crushed" that recovery is impossible (chap. 88); Mrs. Hurtle, already abused and robbed by her drunken scoundrel of a husband, is "ground to pieces" by Paul's abandonment of her (chap. 97). This complex of figurative language, basic to the fabric of the novel, illuminates the essential violence of a wide range of other transactions in *The Way We Live Now*: the urbanely disguised violence with which Melmotte humiliates and subjugates Lord Alfred Grendall by calling him "Alfred" and asking him just to pull the bellrope or run an errand; the violence of speculative capitalism; the violence of the snobbery that ostracizes the gentlemanly Mr. Breghert for being a Jew and causes Georgiana Longestaffe to be "trampled upon" (chap. 65) for her loss of caste in visiting the Melmottes; the emotional violence of mercenary marriage-brokering or of casual seductions.

This world of perpetual, many-faceted violence, full of treacherous friends and implacable enemies, breeds one emotional state above all: *fear*; and more than anything else it is the prevalence and the intensity of fear in *The Way We Live Now* that eclipses the mood of comedy, where almost by definition fear is suspended. In this novel fear is the keynote, the word "fear" and its close analogues occurring scores of times throughout the text (I count fifty or so significant instances). Thus Mr. Longestaffe, though he tyrannizes over his daughter Georgiana, is "also to some extent afraid of her" (chap. 21). In his finances he is utterly short-circuited by fear. "Fearing his son, especially fearing [the lawyer] Squercum," he decides to press Melmotte for payment of his debt—but finds himself "to be afraid even to give a hint to Mr. Melmotte about ready money" (chap. 45). Even the great Melmotte, whom so many fear, lives in such dread of exposure that he is stricken at times with an actual "palsy of fear" (Ch. 62). "That a man so vexed with affairs of money, so laden with cares, encompassed by such dangers, should be free of suspicion and fear it is impossible to imagine. . . . Surely his whole life must have been a life of terrors!" (chap. 59). And so on. Fear is the essence and catalyst of social life in this world. Trollope analyzes an intense reciprocal relationship between fear and violence: people are made fearful by the pervading violence of their environment, and fear makes them violent in their turn.

Yet this novel, though its mood seems so far from the normal mood of comedy, tantalizes the reader with glimpses of the comic, as though the story were built around almost subliminal comic patterns and references (indeed, there is a grotesquely humorous side to this vision of a society in which everyone quakes in fear of everyone else). For one thing, Trollope's story yields a small galaxy of allusions to comic drama. Roger Carbury, for example, springs from classic comic prototypes including Marston's malcontent Malevole and, especially, Molière's Alceste, another somber railer at the iniquities of the world (Roger, observes Lady Carbury, is "becoming an old misanthrope" [chap. 16]).[3] The novel is also tied by a network of parallels to *The Way of the World*, not only by general themes of sexual predation and manipulation, but more particularly by the shared tale of plots to marry a girl whose inheritance may be cut off by a disapproving parent or guardian, by variations on the motif of blackmail, and by the device, important in both plots, of a previously executed deed making an unexpected person the trustee of property in dispute. The very name of Trollope's novel, indeed, plainly echoes that of Congreve's comedy.

The dominating figure of Melmotte, too, is a vortex of comic analogues. As is well known, Melmotte has his origins in some famous contemporary cases; and he has an unmistakable literary antecedent in Mr. Merdle of Dickens's *Little Dorrit*. At the same time he embodies a classic figure of comedy, and readers of early English comedies will recognize some striking parallels. One recognizes a precursor of Melmotte, for example, in the great capitalist Goswin of Fletcher's comedy *The Beggars' Bush*, who, like Melmotte, spends most of the play striving desperately to fend off imminent ruin. Both works reflect on the mysterious nature of "credit" in financial transactions. "Gentlemen who don't know the nature of credit," declaims Melmotte, "how strong it is,—as the air,—to buoy you up; how slight it is,—as a mere vapour,—when roughly touched, can do an amount of mischief" (chap. 40). In such a speech we hear echoes of Goswin soliloquizing on his own impending collapse: "Why, then, 'tis destined, that I fall, fall miserably, / My credit I was built on, sinking with me!" (3.2). But chiefly Melmotte testifies to the close relationship between this novel and Massinger's comedy *A New Way to Pay Old Debts*, another title that Trollope's echoes. The center of this connection is the congruence of the figure of Melmotte with that of Sir Giles Overreach, the enormously wealthy financier and "cruel extortioner" of Massinger's play, and a character that Trollope particularly admired.[4] But in *A New Way to Pay Old Debts* we find not only the figure of the thieving financier, but the plot of the whole Melmotte family prefigured as well. Sir Giles Overreach is obsessed with his scheme of marrying his daughter to a lord, as is Melmotte, but the previously obedient daughter, like Marie Melmotte, at last defies him to marry the man of her own choice. Betrayed like Melmotte by his sycophantic business associates, Overreach is ruined financially in machinations involving (as in *The Way We Live Now*) false signatures on deeds, goes out of his mind, and topples to the ground before a crowd of onlookers, as the ruined Melmotte, drunk and going insane himself, does in the House of Commons. Massinger's comedy contains, moreover, characters who seem very like precursors of Lady Carbury (Lady Allworth), of Sir Felix (the dissipated and penniless prodigal Wellborn), and of Melmotte's surly flunky Miles Grendall (Marrall: another echoing). The point here is perhaps less that *The Way We Live Now* is directly indebted to Massinger, though it undoubtedly is, than that it evokes a whole literature of cruelly satirical and largely humorless Jacobean "city comedies" in which character types like these are well-established conventions.

Other areas of Trollope's novel point to other comic models. Roger Carbury's efforts to reform his dissolute nephew Sir Felix, for example, are unmistakably reminiscent of the plot of Jonson's comedy *Every Man in His Humour*, where Knowell and the country squire Downright strive to reform their son and young half-brother respectively, two young ne'er-do-wells who spend each night carousing with a band of dimwitted "rakehells" who very much resemble the habitués of Trollope's haven for young scoundrels, the Beargarden. The play's protracted theme of the degeneracy of the present age compared to a more wholesome past comes out notably in Jonson's play in a long speech by Knowell (2.5.1–66) from which Roger often seems to be quoting directly in his diatribe on the same theme in chapter 55 of *The Way We Live Now*, where he declares that England is "going to the dogs." "Now we are all fallen," says Knowell. "Look, how we live!" he cries, in a phrase that again echoes Trollope's title (2.5.12, 32). Massinger's *The City Madam*, a play much admired by Trollope,[5] also seems to have contributed to the gestation of this novel. In the comedy one finds in prominent form the theme of the contrast between the wholesome country gentry and the embarrassed city aristocracy, a theme that pervades *The Way We Live Now*; more particularly, in Sir John Frugal's struggles to restrain the spendthrift ways of his wife and two daughters in this play, one sees an apparent prefiguring of Trollope's Adolphus Longestaffe, his wife and two daughters: the two situations, at any rate, are closely similar.

A later comedy, Farquhar's *The Beaux' Stratagem*, affords a vivid preview of yet another sector of Trollope's novel. Lady Bountiful in the play is, as the *dramatis personae* puts it, "foolishly fond of her son Sullen," a brutally dissipated young man who staggers home blind drunk at all hours and is indifferent to his love-starved wife, who was made to marry him for the sake of her dowry; Lady Bountiful also has a virtuous but rather pallid daughter, who is the center of one of the play's love plots. In all this, Farquhar seems to provide Trollope with the detailed blueprint of the Carbury family (except that in Trollope's version the son's mercenary marriage never quite comes off). Moreover, in the figure of the indignant, eloquently acerbic, but witty and kindhearted Mrs. Sullen (one of the most striking heroines of comic drama), married by compulsion to a violent drunkard who has apparently stolen her dowry, denouncing the subservience of women in a male-dominated world, Farquhar distinctly prefigures Mrs. Hurtle herself, whose traumatic near-rape in Oregon, in the course of which she killed her attacker, has its parallel in the chilling scene where Mrs. Sullen barely escapes being raped by Archer. As in Trollope's novel, the blandness of the nominal heroine as contrasted with the more vivid personality of the "other" woman is explicitly commented upon and made a significant theme in Farquhar's play. Given this system of correspondences, we can hardly doubt that Trollope had *The Beaux' Stratagem*, too, in mind in conceiving his novel. Wherever we look in *The Way We Live Now*, in other words, we discover deeply embedded comic prototypes; no doubt there are even more than I have mentioned. My intent is not to tie every detail of Trollope's story to comic models, but simply to bring into view the organizing conceit of this novel, which, like *Mr. Scarborough's Family*, incorporates masses of comic materials, is actuated everywhere by comic potential—yet steadily refuses to turn into a full-fledged comedy.

Even so, the sense of embryonic or suppressed comic patterns is rarely absent for long in *The Way We Live Now*, and a main reason for this is the importance in the novel of the perpetual comic dispute concerning pleasure. This theme is embedded more deeply here than in, say, *Barchester Towers* or *Rachel Ray*, and its treatment seems far more ambiguous and unstable than in such novels as those, but it has in the last analysis a no less powerful organizing function. Its axis lies between the polar opposites of Roger Carbury and the young members of that disreputable gentleman's club the Beargarden.

Behind Roger stretches the whole lineage of comic puritans, quashers of pleasure: he wars on pleasure in all forms, seeing in it only moral laxity. "He pronounced the word 'brandy' in a tone which implied that it was a wicked, dissipated beverage," says the narrator, with a telltale hint of irony at Roger's expense (chap. 17). Roger spends his life denouncing extravagance and worldly frivolities, from London parties to keeping hunting horses to falling in love with socially unsuitable women. "I have my duties plainly marked out for me," he says at the end, in his typically priggish, self-congratulatory tone; "I should never allow myself to be withdrawn from them by pleasure" (chap. 100). As though to confirm Roger's values, the novel metes out generally deflationary treatment to such advocates of pleasure as Sir Felix, Dolly Longestaffe, Lord Nidderdale, Miles Grendall, and others. Roger's view of pleasure as morally deleterious certainly seems borne out at the Beargarden, where the raffish young men gamble recklessly, drink themselves into a stupor night after night, and generally lead idle, cynical, parasitical lives. This all-absorbing devotion to pleasure seems to have undermined pleasure itself, causing life at the Beargarden to be charged with ennui, with the strain of occupying one's time when one has nothing whatever to do and amusement itself fails to amuse. Sir Felix's life is being ruined by the expense of keeping a string of hunting horses that fills Roger with indignation, but in the course of the novel he goes hunting only once and never mentions his outing afterward. The exhilaration of hunting and the bliss of talking about it later can momentarily revivify even so inauthentic a person as Lizzie Eustace, but Sir Felix is too far gone in vice even to respond to this, the most exquisite of Trollopian pleasures. At the Beargarden the sole form of entertainment, in fact, is gambling, and as a result the club is likely to seem not an outpost of pleasure but, rather, as Trollope stresses and as various critics have underlined, just a miniature version of the world of strife, capitalistic speculation, and anxiety that predominates in society at large. The relations that prevail among the club members, consequently, are tainted by rancor, suspicion, and dislike.

This motif of perverted or self-undermining pleasure stands out with particular vividness at the Beargarden but is ubiquitous in the novel, which portrays what seems superficially like a world of energetic pleasure-seeking, but where the incessant social festivities are almost always spoiled by the intrusion of the pressures, conflicts, and anxieties of life in general. Social occasions in *The Way We Live Now* are just so many arenas for maneuvering where everything, as is said of the Melmottes' ostentatious ball, is "done for a purpose" (chap. 4) and thus is rendered barren of real pleasure. At Lady Pomona Longestaffe's dinner party in chapter 20, where the "purpose" is to try to stave off bankruptcy by forming an alliance with Melmotte, the presence of several normally lively conversationalists is all to no avail: "nobody [can] utter a word" and painful boredom prevails. As Sir Felix concisely puts it in reference to various parties whose real "purpose" is matrimonial prospecting, worldly amusement in this environment is "weary work" (chap. 5). "It isn't for pleasure that I want to go up," says Georgiana to her father, pleading for permission to visit the Melmottes in London for the social season. "There isn't so very much pleasure in it." "I am so tired of it!" she exclaims later. "Pleasure, indeed!" (chap. 21). Her father could hardly sympathize with the pleasure motive, for he too, like Roger Carbury, though for quite different reasons, is a man wholly anesthetized to it. "He had not any very lively interest in life. He did not read much; he did not talk much; he was not specially fond of eating and drinking; he did not gamble, and he did not care for the farm" (chap. 21). In such an image of crippling ennui the other side of Trollope's argument comes into focus: pleasure is crushed on the one hand by Roger Carbury's puritanical earnestness, while on the other its deterioration is almost the prime symptom of the general human deterioration so apparent in the world of *The Way We Live Now*, where listlessness, apathy, imbecilic stupidity, and boredom are endemic. Roger's severe analysis notwithstanding, the reader comes to see that it is perhaps not dishonesty that is most lethal in this world, still less the supposed wanton devotion to pleasure, but rather the near extinction of it. Sir Felix displays this condition, as he displays every unhealthy condition, in its most advanced form. The profligate baronet, says the narrator at one point,

> was chiefly tormented in these days by the want of amusement. He had so spent his life that he did not know how to get through a day in which no excitement was

> provided for him. He never read. Thinking was altogether
> beyond him. And he had never done a day's work in his
> life. He could lie in bed. He could eat and drink. He could
> smoke and sit idle. He could play cards; and could amuse
> himself with women. . . . Beyond these things the world
> had nothing for him.
>
> (Chap. 67)

In Trollope's analysis, then, real, vivid pleasure is everywhere drastically on the wane, signaling in turn a broad waning of human faculties themselves, libidinal, intellectual, and aesthetic. The consequences of this condition are suggested in the unemphatic but real hint of almost suicidal alienation and despair in the last phrase of the passage just cited. The hint is picked up repeatedly in the novel. There is a lethal pun in the comment quoted above about Mr. Longestaffe, who, lacking amusements, "had not any very lively interest in life." "Melmotte's [suicide] was rather awful," observes Nidderdale one day amid the disintegration of the Beargarden. "Not half so awful as having nothing to amuse one," replies Dolly Longestaffe (chap. 96). Of the scores of characters in *The Way We Live Now*, precisely two relatively minor ones retain something like a full-bodied taste for pleasure: Ruby Ruggles, who adores (too much) beautiful young men and is intoxicated like Rachel Ray and Polly Neefit with the pleasure of dancing (chap. 43), and Sir Damask Monogram, an amiable young man who devotes his existence to hunting, yachting, shooting pheasants and pigeons, and attending horse races (chap. 32). These two, not coincidentally, though hardly paragons of character, rank with the sanest and most appealing figures in the novel. In any case they provide clear points of reference for measuring the atrophy of libido that afflicts the rest of the novel's population.

To present the novel's configuration of themes in this way is to see it gravitating strongly back toward the mentality of the comic after all— toward the mentality, that is, that places pleasure at the center of human needs and instinctively finds authoritarian moral policemen like Roger Carbury repellent. This gravitation makes itself felt even more distinctly on the level of dramatic pattern and effect: for Trollope's dire, "horrifying" picture of a world where playfulness seems extinct is itself extravagantly playful and full of delectable jokes, though no critic appears to notice them. Perhaps the hugest joke of all is the introduction of the Chinese emperor, "the Brother of the Sun," as the guest of honor at Melmotte's valedictory dinner party. The full humor of this device eludes explication, but it has much to do with the double perspective in which the emperor is seen. On the one hand he is a grotesque, a preposterously inflated image of grandeur who mimics such a figure as Melmotte himself, whom society deifies for his aura of omnipotence. When Nidderdale jokes about the emperor ("the grandest old duffer out," in his opinion) as a mechanical puppet stuffed with hay "made up fresh every morning at a shop in the Haymarket" (chap. 62), his joke implicates a whole social system based on the veneration of grand public figures of dubious substance. At the same time the emperor, "awful, solid, solemn, and silent," highlights the wild and unseemly ludicrousness of this social ceremony focused upon himself, a scene where all civility is lost in frantic petty maneuvering, where the host is rigidly debarred from having the slightest contact with the guest of honor, and where invited guests feel obliged to visit the premises ahead of time to see who else is attending before deciding whether to bring their wives. From this visitor's point of view, the narrator reflects, the cream of English high society must look like "some far-distant outlandish people" (chap. 59)—a perspective that we are invited to share, and to enjoy.

R. H. Hutton's analysis of Trollope's humor as a highly-cultivated "appreciation of the paradoxes of social life" illuminates much of the comic structure of *The Way We Live Now*, where laughter, whether overt or only latent, is inseparable from concerted social analysis. The paradoxes upon which Trollope throws his comic limelight are always significant, and always point to a vision of modern social life as a strenuous, never-ending attempt to reconcile irreconcilable values and motives. Thus the root joke of this novel centers on the paradoxes generated at every moment by a society both enamored of money and the ethic of commerce *and* tied to traditional, albeit half-vestigial, ideas of gentility. (Trollope's fable makes them seem traditional, at least: historically they were of recent growth. But this is another issue.) Social life in such a world can hardly fail to be a series of ludicrous contortions. Melmotte's dinners, where "society" flocks with almost rabid eagerness to the house of a man it despises, embody the fundamental paradox that runs through virtually every transaction in this world, as it runs, for example, through Lady Carbury's affectionate reception of Mr. Alf, whose paper has just savaged her new book, or Mr. Longestaffe's finding himself imperceptibly drawn into pleasant business and then social relations with Mr. Breghert, whom he has very recently vilified as a repulsively unworthy aspirant to his daughter's hand. What underlies the overt or subliminal humor of these and a score of equally incongruous social circumstances in *The Way We Live Now* is Trollope's fundamental insight that the structural logic of society at large imprints its pattern upon even the most private or instinctual-seeming transactions that take place within that society:

which means that in a structurally incoherent social world, personal experience is bound to be dominated, as it everywhere is in *The Way We Live Now*, by unresolvable ambivalence. A very shrewd reviewer of *Miss Mackenzie* made Trollope seem like a prototypical structural anthropologist: "Mr. Trollope," he said, "is always strongest when painting individuals through the customary manners of a class, and even of classes he paints those manners best which are almost an artificial language in themselves" (Smalley, 223). The kind of humor that pervades this story arises from an insistent analysis of those points where the syntax of such languages has broken down.

What we see particularly in *The Way We Live Now* is a pervasive contradictoriness in emotional life, and especially in love. This theme takes its overtly humorous form, for example, in the relations of Dolly Longestaffe and his mother, Lady Pomona, who perpetually writes notes to him, begging him to spend some time with his family. "He would open them, thrust them into some pocket, and then forget them. Consequently his mother worshipped him; and even his sisters, who were at any rate superior to him in intellect, treated him with a certain deference" (chap. 13). All the humor compressed into Trollope's "consequently" stems from his analysis of how personal feelings are dictated by current institutions of familial and sexual relations (the absurdity of the Longestaffe ladies' worshiping Dolly because he ignores them is at bottom the many-leveled absurdity of a whole social system based among other things on male dominance, on a cult of maternal love, and on the retrieving of family fortunes by marrying heiresses, which only sons can perform). In an array of similar cases Trollope plays out Lady Pomona's paradoxical emotional life in less overtly humorous forms, but where the glint of potential laughter is none the less ever-present. We see the same predicament, for example, in Paul's deeply divided feelings toward Mrs. Hurtle. "He liked the warmth of her close vicinity, and the softness of her arm, and the perfume from her hair,—though he would have given all that he possessed that she had been removed from him by some impassable gulf" (chap. 46). Analogous states of affairs: Roger's stubborn determination to leave Carbury Manor, which he cherishes, to the person he most despises, Sir Felix, who is sure to destroy it overnight; or Lady Carbury's helpless devotion to this same Sir Felix, or Mrs. Hurtle's love for the feeble "overcivilized" Paul, whom in her heart she almost holds in contempt. "She loved Paul Montague with all her heart, and she despised herself for loving him. How weak he was;— how inefficient . . . !" (chap. 97). Or the seemingly absurd comfort that Melmotte derives from his wholly simulated friendship with Nidderdale. "It had been pleasant to him to talk as though he were talking to a young friend whom he trusted" (chap. 74). The members of the Beargarden feel this way even toward the treacherous Herr Vossner, who has been found to be a thief. "But then as a thief he had been so comfortable that his absence was regretted with a tenderness almost amounting to love even by those who had suffered most severely from his rapacity" (chap. 96). Much of the drama of this novel, in other words, is built on the ever-recurring joke, full of poignancy, of love as a preposterously contradictory state in a world of contradictions.

There are jokes of many other varieties in *The Way We Live Now*: jokes of satiric portraiture, as in the picture of Dolly Longestaffe's transcendent indolence, or absurdist jokes enacting the encounter of the rational mind with a wholly lunatic reality, as in the Alice-in-Wonderland scenes of Paul Montague at the railway board (chap. 37). Given the satiric bent of this novel, however, maybe the broadest class of its jokes are those in a retributive mode, centering, as in *Barchester Towers*, on humor of embarrassment and discomfiture. As the epitome of a type of event that occurs often in *The Way We Live Now*, one might take the encounter of Father Barham with Melmotte in London in chapter 56. Father Barham, received courteously by Roger Carbury, has made a growing nuisance of himself by his rudeness in praising his own religion and openly disparaging that of his friends, but Roger's gentlemanly code of manners prevents him from rebuking this boor as he deserves. In comedy boors are doomed inescapably to suffer chastisement, and it is a sign of the comic basis of *The Way We Live Now* that this predestined scene at last occurs just as it ought. The insufferable priest brings it upon himself by unwisely placing his dignity at the mercy of someone even ruder than he is himself, Melmotte, who looks at him as the emperor of China looks at the English, as simply a ridiculous annoyance:

> "I am a poor servant of the Cross, who is anxious to know from the lips of Mr. Melmotte himself that his heart is inclined to the true Faith" [said Father Barham].
> "Some lunatic," said Mr. Melmotte. "See that there ain't any knives about, Alfred."

The comeuppance scene is felt as a ritual moment of comedy, and it is a ritual often enacted in *The Way We Live Now*: for instance, in the urbane runaround that the pompous, arrogant Mr. Longestaffe receives in Melmotte's offices, where he is kept waiting for so many hours that he misses his lunch, whereupon Melmotte suddenly appears and seeks to hurry him off to a meeting of the railway board. "It was cruel," says the narrator in mock sympathy, "that a man so hungry should be asked to go to a Board by a chairman who had just lunched at his club" (chap. 53). But the specially designated victim of comic mortification in *The Way We Live Now* is Sir Felix, who is punished so often and so painfully that the reader soon recognizes him to play the role not so much of an image of moral delinquency (he is too extreme an example of worthlessness to take very seriously in this way) as that of a kind of comic lightning rod, an occasion for the perpetual meting out of comic justice and for the crucial comic function of displacing indignation by laughter. With every step Sir Felix takes, he encounters some new and even more excruciating mortification. As in the meeting of Father Barham and Melmotte, for example, Sir Felix meets one of his many Nemeses in the form of Miles Grendall, the only man in London even more insolent and devoid of principle than Sir Felix himself. This is the essential joke of the hilarious scene in chapter 24 where poor Sir Felix tries to force Miles to give him advice about dealing with the wily Melmotte, while Miles evasively envelops himself "from head to foot in smoke" like some elusive creature, again, from *Alice in Wonderland*. The attempted elopement with Marie collapses in such farcical incompetence that Sir Felix is ashamed to show his face at the club afterwards. His multiplied mortifications culminate in his pulverizing by John Crumb, which leaves the beautiful baronet a frightful sight; he is so humiliated by his misfortune that he lets himself be sent off meekly at last to exile in Germany under the care of a chaperone. As such episodes show, comic laws operate throughout *The Way We Live Now*, efficiently enacting comic justice and very copiously bestowing comic pleasure; and it is chiefly this effect, I believe, that accounts for the impression voiced by more than one critic that the supposedly "horrifying" world of this novel is not all that horrifying after all.[6]

I have stressed the close tie between the exhilarated mood of traditional comedy and its themes of playacting and masquerade. Determined as he is to remain within the idiom of a stringent realism, Trollope generally leaves this fundamental resource of comedy untouched. But in *The Way We Live Now* it enters his fiction on a large scale, as indeed it had two years earlier in *The Eustace Diamonds*, and fills the novel with hyperbolic comic effects—though these are so cunningly assimilated into the prevailing mode of realism that the reader may well fail to recognize them for what they are. That Trollope's imagined world here is one of rampant illusionism, where semblances and fakery everywhere overwhelm truth, is well recognized. Critics, we have seen, have treated this theme simply as signifying a decay of moral values; but Trollope's whole effect is more complicated. In a slack, lackadaisical world, where indolence and ennui have become widespread and where young gentlemen of pleasure scarcely possess enough energy to go hunting, intrepid though morally defective rogues like Fisker and Melmotte inevitably seem to embody certain positive qualities. More than once Trollope underlines the quasi-heroic scale of their impostures, which involve nothing less than conjuring make-believe railroads out of thin air and persuading the world at large that their brazen inventions really exist. Whatever their failings, such scoundrels at least rise above the general state of being petty, sordid, and vindictive: their vocation is indeed robbery, but robbery "by magnificently false representations" (chap. 92). The great Vera Cruz railway scheme and all the financial legerdemain surrounding it represent in fact the one locus in this novel of that "play-element" that Huizinga studies and that I take to be central, in particular, to comedy. Swindling in *The Way We Live Now* takes on the aspect of an audacious game not for the faint of heart, and its rewards, Trollope makes clear enough, are only in the first instance financial; mainly these players are addicted to the sheer euphoria of the game.

For the "gorgeous and florid" Fisker (chap. 9), a brash comic swindler of a familiar type,[7] but who otherwise, as the narrator significantly stresses, is scrupulously honest, devising fabulous swindles is not just a way to make money: it is, rather, "the delight and the ambition of his life" (chap. 92). That nearly extinct factor of "delight" is less visible but possibly just as real in the case of the more somber Melmotte, who in effect is engaged in the task of creating *himself* out of thin air. The play-element, Huizinga stresses, is by no means incompatible with conflict. In the potlatch ritual, for example, "the opposed groups do not contend for wealth or power but simply for the pleasure of parading their superiority—in a word, for glory" (*Homo Ludens*, 59). It is precisely Melmotte's fatal flaw that instead of confining himself to a mere struggle for wealth and power he becomes intoxicated with "the pleasure of parading [his] superiority," snubbing dukes, making a public spectacle of his arrogance, and thus mortally weakening his position by alienating all his political and financial associates (chap. 81). He becomes so swept up in the game and in the masquerade self he has invented, in other words, that he forgets the crucial dividing line between play and reality. "Perhaps the most remarkable circumstance in the career of this remarkable man," observes the narrator, "was the fact that he came almost to believe in himself" (chap. 56). This self-delusion is the recipe for just what in fact occurs in the second half of *The Way We Live Now*, the transmutation of the potentially, one may perhaps say fundamentally, comic into a kind of tragedy.

However, until that happens, Melmotte performs the part of a great

joker whose career on the public stage lies in concocting ever more flagrant and preposterous pretenses, that society swallows whole. His
role is just that of Horner in *The Country Wife*, the notorious woman-
izer pretending in defiance of obvious truth to be impotent. Melmotte
is a recognized swindler pretending to be a pillar of security and even
going beyond this to assert (his crowning audacity) that transactions
involving mere money are beneath his notice. "As for many years past
we have exchanged paper instead of actual money for our commodi-
ties, so now it seemed that, under the new Melmotte régime, an exchange of words was to suffice" (chap. 45). This "consummation of a
new era in money matters" (chap. 45) is a new way to pay old debts
indeed. The spice of this outrageous joke is in the foolishness, gulli-
bility, and greed that it reveals in the social world that furnishes his
victims. Like Horner, Falstaff, Volpone, Becky Sharp, and other comic
swindlers, Melmotte in his playacting is driven largely (we can surmise) by his loathing of the hypocrisies of his society; in this respect
he has much in common, as we may be surprised to perceive, with his
great adversary Roger Carbury. Forced to conceal his Jewishness in a
rankly anti-Semitic country, excluded like the honorable Mr. Breghert
from real social acceptance by a caste system that venerates "old
county position" above all else, how could Melmotte fail to despise
his contemporaries *en masse*? His hatred of them, indeed, forms his
most obvious drive, as witnessed in his belittling treatment of Lord
Alfred Grendall and Mr. Longestaffe. And his chastisement of this
world takes the distinctively comic form of an outlandish masquerade
that only a pack of fools, rascals, and hypocrites could be deceived
by—as everybody save Roger more or less is.

So we should not be surprised by the sympathy and admiration increasingly extended to Melmotte, in spite of the novel's nominal moral
scheme, which makes him the scapegoat for all the moral failings of
modern society. This sympathy begins as something only involuntary
and unspoken, but finally it is plainly declared. The narrator finds
himself constrained to admit, for example, that there was "a certain
manliness" about Melmotte (chap. 81). The fact is that the kind of duplicity practiced deliberately and with agile virtuosity by Melmotte
and Fisker throws its own satirical light on the more demeaning kinds
of moral duplicity that other characters in the novel widely practice
upon themselves. Some relevant instances would be, for example,
the racial bigotry that enables anti-Semitic snobs like Mr. Longestaffe
and Lady Monogram to imagine themselves superior to Mr. Breghert;
the genteel code that authorizes Paul and Roger to take a high, self-
flattering moral tone as they plan the shabby betrayal of Mrs. Hurtle;
or the moral obtuseness that causes Marie Melmotte to worship the

worthless Sir Felix. These and other cases ought to arouse contempt, and that, at least, is one feeling that we are never allowed to have toward Fisker and Melmotte.

Something of the same surprising moral immunity for rogues—one of the unmistakable hallmarks of comedy—is extended even to the Beargarden, supposedly the novel's main exhibit of modern-day dissoluteness and corruption, but in fact (as a clear-eyed reading of the novel ought easily to discover) treated with a sneaking friendliness by Trollope. It is significant that at least two of the Beargarden's "odious swarm of . . . parasites" (Polhemus, *The Changing World*, 193), Nidderdale and Dolly, are by no means devoid of principles of honor, even though they apply them erratically at best. In fact, Nidderdale's refusal to spurn the disgraced Melmotte in public counts as one of the novel's signal moments of moral refinement (contrasting notably with Roger Carbury's self-righteousness), though Trollope treats it as unemphatically as he often does treat the most important events in his stories (chap. 83). But the crux of whatever is appealing in the Beargarden world is its entire devotion to the cause of play and frivolity. We have seen how hard it is to attain anything like the full spirit of play in the violent, fear-infested world of *The Way We Live Now*, but the habitués of the Beargarden persevere. Their goal has been to establish amid inclement circumstances an oasis of holiday and pleasure, a world like Falstaff's Boar's Head tavern (a parallel that becomes explicit, as we have noticed, in *The Duke's Children*), based on the principle of the relaxation of rules. Trollope's narrator takes a censorious tone, but the relaxation seems for the most part innocent enough, involving mainly staying open all night and serving suppers at all hours (chap. 3). The one amusement actively indulged in at the Beargarden is gambling at cards, and in order to safeguard this cherished pastime, their sole escape from boredom, the members have tacitly agreed to suspend reality itself by pretending to play for gain in deadly earnest while in fact merely exchanging worthless IOUs which it is considered a gross breach of manners to attempt to cash in. If real cash were in question these very impecunious young men would have to cease playing at once; rather than face that prospect, they deal in make-believe. In this blithe setting of stern reality at defiance for the sake of pleasure, the Beargarden embodies the paradigm of comedy itself. It expresses, too, the heart of comic doctrine: that pleasure does not (as puritans like Roger think) threaten social order, but rather creates and guarantees it. Against the backdrop of the fragmented, incoherent social scene portrayed in *The Way We Live Now*, the Beargarden, for all its frivolous character, stands out very strikingly as the sole image of something like an authentic, self-sustaining community in which it is possible to achieve equilibrium between egoistic drives and the welfare of the group.

The money transactions in this community strongly parallel those of Melmotte in the world of finance, where "it was a part of the charm of all dealings with this great man that no ready money seemed ever to be necessary for anything" (chap. 45). The "charm" of investing in Melmotte is of course delusive and very dangerous, but that of playing cards at the Beargarden is real. Thus it doesn't matter that Miles Grendall fails to pay his debts and then even turns to cheating; Sir Felix's futile attempt to persuade the other club members to ostracize Miles only thrusts Sir Felix himself into the ignominious position of the comic spoilsport rightly detested by his fellows (chap. 28). Unfortunately for the club, it eventually betrays its own *raison d'être* by seeking to bring itself back into alignment with reality, resolving that henceforth "the play shall be somewhat lower, but the payments punctual" (chap. 49). From a moralistic point of view this attack on the spirit of extravagance and of "play" may be commendable, but its effect within the subtly comic perspective of the novel is wholly melancholy. Once the bonding power of pleasure is thus dispelled, the club slides rapidly downhill toward its smashup in the last chapters. Melmotte, in a speech quoted above, speaks of the great damage that can be done in the world of finance by "gentlemen who don't know the nature of credit, how strong it is,—as the air,—to buoy you up; how slight it is,—as a mere vapour,—when roughly touched" (chap. 40). Melmotte directs attention to the root sense of "credit": belief. If belief is shaken, the great, buoyant, mysterious force of credit evaporates, and this is just what happens to the spirit of play at the Beargarden. It seems a very nice point at last, though the novel's critics have never seen it this way, whether gambling with worthless IOUs at the Beargarden is to be seen as evidence of "the degeneracy of the age" or as a delightful respite from it. The whole novel balances on the edge of this ambiguity.

Thus *The Way We Live Now* emerges as a key example of a mode of Trollope's later fiction that we have studied already in the case of *Mr. Scarborough's Family*, a mode defined by the quite elaborate deployment of comic patterns and values within an imaginative world that would seem so dark and "realistic" as to prohibit comedy entirely. Both novels read finally like allegories of the fate of comic imagination in social and literary contexts where comedy's defense of play and pleasure seems not only a futile enterprise but a morally untenable one as well. The deepening of modern anxieties, the fragmented, equivocal quality of modern social life, and the reign of puritanical earnestness, Trollope seems to have concluded, had by the 1870s made traditional comedy all but impracticable. Hence the continual impression, which I have tried to analyze, of modal tension and incoherence in this perplexing novel—though this is an effect that, far from disabling *The Way We Live Now*, energizes it and gives its various strains of humorous invention their special vividness. Hence, too, the special poignancy of a late novel or two in which Trollope flies in the face of his own diagnosis and produces some of his richest and sweetest comedy, as though the oppressive burden of working out the fate of comedy had at last been lifted from him. These books are *The Duke's Children* and the one with which we shall close, *Ayala's Angel*.

8

Ayala's Angel: Folly and Scarce Resources

I think I may fairly make two postulata.
First, that food is necessary to the existence of man.
Secondly, that the passion between the sexes is necessary and
will remain nearly in its present state.

Malthus, *On Population*

If the keynote of comedy is the sensation of being propelled into a world of artificially heightened enjoyment, the opening of *Ayala's Angel* is deceptive. The world of this novel seems a densely realistic one, consisting as it does chiefly of a complex structure of family and socio-economic relationships that the narrator anatomizes in far too methodical a way to allow for the swift peripeties of comic plots. The mood, too, is the reverse of the gay effervescence that prevails in comedies. Egbert Dormer has died of grief after the death of his wife, and, thanks to his improvident ways, has left his two daughters Lucy and Ayala "utterly penniless upon the world" (chap. 1). The story's first movement focuses on the painful adjustment that Lucy, the elder daughter, has to undergo when she is taken in by her impoverished aunt and uncle, the Dosetts. Aunt Dosett wants to be kind, and Lucy wants to show due gratitude, but the older woman's stern, censorious manner only deepens her niece's mood of resentment and despair. To all appearances, this is a world of relentless material and psychological pressures that would seem to leave no room for the buoyant ease of comedy. But then, with a gradualness that is central to the novel's whole effect, this realistic drama is infiltrated by the kinds of phenomena that belong to the gaudy world of the comic; verisimilitude unravels so subtly that we are hardly aware it is happening.

First there are the patterns of the plot, which increasingly take on the stylized and outlandish aspects that identify comic action. The two sisters, one confided to the rich relations and one to the poor, both encounter difficulties in their new homes—and before long, with much ado, switch places. Nor is it long after that, more difficulties

having been encountered, that the attempt is made to switch once
again. This is a lot of switching back and forth for one novel. Then
there is the series of Ayala's various admirers, who pop up on all sides
with a frequency and a pertinacity that strike all bystanders in the
story as excessive: Tom Tringle, then Colonel Stubbs, then Captain
Batsby, each of whom she refuses over and over. To her exasperated
uncle Sir Thomas Tringle, she seems to have "as many suitors as Pene-
lope" (chap. 43). Her cousin Gertrude has a still more vexed career, in
which she swings back and forth between her two suitors like the Dormer girls between the Dosetts and the Tringles: courted and finally
abandoned by the fortune hunter Frank Houston, who refuses to
elope with her to Ostend, she elopes a month later to the same place
with Ayala's ex-suitor Captain Batsby, is brought home unmarried by
her father, makes a new play for Frank, and marries Captain Batsby
at last. The playful hyperbolic quality of all these story lines is the
essence of comic effect, and it is more than confirmed in the way
Trollope ends his tale not with the one requisite marriage, but with
four of them, an abundance that even the narrator exclaims about in
the last chapter.

At the level of individual scenes, plot in *Ayala's Angel* is increasingly
controlled by a device central to the drollery of this novel and, indeed,
of Trollope's fiction at large: that of conceiving action as a series of encounters between pairs of incongruous personalities. A Trollope novel
has exactly the dynamic principle, one could say, of an astrological
cosmos, in which planets of strongly marked individuality enter into
conjunction in one pairing after another, each new alignment setting
off new reverberations of energy. For the reader attuned to the comic
pulsation that this formula generates, plot suspense is almost entirely
subordinated to the skillfully fostered anticipation of witnessing one
unlikely encounter after another. The ultimate example of this paradigmatic unit of action in Trollope may be the shatteringly funny interview between Bertie Stanhope and the new bishop of Barchester,
who come into conjunction behind the sofa at Mrs. Proudie's reception in *Barchester Towers* (chap. 11), but the meeting of Father Barham
and Melmotte in *The Way We Live Now* or of Palliser and Major Tifto in
The Duke's Children, or scores of similar occasions, illustrate the principle just as well.

Ayala's Angel signals its unusually strong comic impulse by being
unusually profuse in such scenes. One thinks, among many other examples, of the scene of the worldly, witty Lady Albury winning over
the melancholy Admiralty clerk Mr. Dosett (chap. 22); of the delivery
of Tom Tringle's challenge to the urbane Colonel Stubbs by Samuel
Faddle (chap. 35); or of the unlikely visitors who make a comic pro-
cession through Sir Thomas Tringle's office in a series of chapters

whose titles highlight the sense of a recurring, stylized occasion rife with ludicrous possibilities: "Isadore Hamel in Lombard Street" (chap. 33); "Captain Batsby in Lombard Street" (chap. 57); "Mr. Traffick in Lombard Street" (chap. 58). The mere title of such a chapter—especially when it contains the name of a character as stupendously funny as Septimus Traffick, the incarnation of pomposity and bland effrontery—is a promise that Trollope's characteristic comic event, the essence of which is the vivid exhibition of personality, is about to occur all over again. No other Trollope novel, perhaps, surpasses this one in sheer exuberance of comic imagination.

The deeply traditional nature of this imagination is suggested by the intimate relations between *Ayala's Angel* and *Twelfth Night*, the play from which Trollope evidently derived much of his novel's atmosphere and dramatic detail. Rather than transposing materials more or less directly from his source into a modern setting, as sometimes is the case in his borrowings from early drama, Trollope seems here half-unconscious of his allusions to a play that he dissolves in his imagination in order to redistribute it over a very different dramatic field, splitting characters in two, merging two into one, transposing plot lines. The sublimely pompous Malvolio, for example, is easy to recognize in the form of Septimus Traffick (another outsider living like Malvolio in someone else's house), but the comic business of his yellow stockings cross-gartered is transferred to Tom Tringle decked out in his own bizarre courting regalia, chains and rings and a fantastic waistcoat that make him, in the narrator's words, "a thing disgusting to be looked at by any well-trained female" (chap. 31). Tom also absorbs the role of Orsino, the plaintive lover whose lady refuses to see him. Cesario's comic challenge to Sir Andrew Aguecheek becomes Tom's absurd challenge to Stubbs; the episode of Orsino sending Cesario, who (as Viola) secretly loves him, to plead his cause with Olivia becomes in *Ayala's Angel* the episode of Tom asking Stubbs to compose a love letter for him to Ayala, not knowing that Stubbs loves her himself (chap. 31). More at the center of the dramatic structure, the story of Olivia refusing her three suitors (Orsino, Sir Andrew, Malvolio) and loving instead Cesario, who in a sense is a sheer illusion (being a woman in disguise), is transposed by Trollope into the story of Ayala's refusal of her own three suitors in the name of her own devotion to a nonexistent lover. Few if any of Trollope's other novels are so profoundly anchored in a single source, though he ultimately uses this connection, as we shall see, as his point of departure into modernist lines of thought all his own. Before this, he uses *Twelfth Night* as the foundation and constant point of reference for what he seems to have designed as a virtual synopsis of comic thinking.

To see *Ayala's Angel* as having the structure of a kind of treatise on

the fundamental principles of comedy should help to sum up the argument of this study and also, perhaps, help to redeem this superlative novel from the dismissive treatment it has received from critics
with little or no sympathy for the special dialectics of comedy.[1] The
main terms of the dialectic are very distinctly set out at the beginning
in a passage that may look like the idle garrulousness for which Trollope has often been blamed, but that has, after all, an important symbolic function.

> How little do we know how other people live in the
> houses close to us! We see the houses looking like our
> own, and we see the people come out of them looking like
> ourselves. But a Chinaman is not more different from the
> English John Bull than is No. 10 from No. 11. Here there
> are books, paintings, music, wine, a little dilettanti
> getting-up of subjects of the day, a little dilettanti thinking
> on great affairs, perhaps a little dilettanti religion; few
> domestic laws, and those easily broken; few domestic
> duties, and those easily evaded; breakfast when you will,
> with dinner almost as little binding, with much company
> and acknowledged aptitude for idle luxury. That is life at
> No. 10. At No. 11 everything is cased in iron. There shall
> be equal plenty, but at No. 11 even plenty is a bondage.
> Duty rules everything, and it has come to be acknowl-
> edged that duty is to be hard. So many hours of needle-
> work, so many hours of books, so many hours of prayer!
> . . . To be comfortable is a sin; to laugh is almost equal to
> bad language. Such and so various is life at No. 10 and at
> No. 11.
>
>   (Chap. 2)

The two mentalities allegorized here are of course nothing other than,
at No. 10, the comic ideal of a world of unconfined pleasure, where
laws are relaxed or abolished to allow delightful freedom of movement and where seriousness is mocked by a studied devotion to frivolity, and, at No. 11, the anticomic, "cased in iron," dedicated to
eliminating the two possibilities (essentially identical, according to
comedy) of limberness and of enjoyment. Like all significant comedies, *Ayala's Angel* will complicate the apparently clear-cut antinomy
of the two polar attitudes; but it sets them before us in nearly pure
form here at the outset in order to delineate the questions at issue in
what follows.

The comic ideal is elaborated most fully in the two main characters,
Ayala Dormer and her lover Jonathan Stubbs, two of Trollope's most
intriguing creations. Ayala, with her fixation on an imaginary lover, is
a comic monomaniac of a deeply traditional kind, though her kinship

with the likes of Jonson's Morose and Molière's Orgon is obscured by her "poetic charm" (chap. 1). Trollope conceives her, in fact, as embodying the concentrated essence of the appeal of comedy: she is charm personified, the ideal specimen through which to study this attribute that has fascinated him throughout his career. Of the intensely erotic nature of this charm there is no doubt; nineteen-year-old Ayala with her "peculiar look of childhood" (chap. 8) is the sexiest of all Trollope's heroines, and no doubt the sexiest one in Victorian fiction. To numerous bystanders in the novel, however, Ayala's manifest charm seems a puzzle. The narrator returns again and again to try to analyze her secret, and continually he strikes the same note. Her predominant trait, which expresses itself in one form after another, is what we have been calling "limberness" and treating as the cardinal virtue of comedy. *Ayala's Angel* is an extended dissertation on this property—and on its antitheses.

Even as a little girl, Ayala possesses the gift of effortless ease and fluency to an almost preternatural degree, learning to sing, for example, "as though Nature had intended her to be a singing-bird,—requiring no education, no labour," picking up French in a three-months' stay in Paris with the same effortless facility (chap. 1), then, in a visit to Rome, learning Italian "so readily that she could talk it almost at once" (chap. 15). "For running up and down stairs at the bijou," says the narrator, "Ayala had been proverbial," flying around the house "as though she were a tricksy Ariel" (chap. 5). It is this mercurial, birdlike, Ariel-like nimbleness that has ripened into her riveting sexual appeal as a young woman, seen here, for example, through the love-struck eyes of Tom Tringle:

> The black locks which would be shaken here and there, the bright glancing eyes which could be so joyous and could be so indignant, the colour of her face which had nothing in it of pink, which was brown rather, but over which the tell-tale blood would rush with a quickness which was marvelous to him, the lithe quick figure which had in it nothing of the weight of earth, the little foot which in itself was a perfect joy, the step with all the elasticity of a fawn,—these charms together had mastered him.
>
> (Chap. 7)

Everything about her is quickness, suppleness, and mobility, to such a degree that she seems (at least to the men, including Trollope, who are fascinated by her) almost supernatural. In the culminating instance of the series of figurative images that observers use to attempt to fix her tantalizingly elusive nature, she is said as a girl to have been "up and about the house everywhere, glancing about like a ray of the sun reflected from a mirror as you move it in your hand" (chap. 53). Here, limberness goes so far as to become totally disembodied, and the hint is clearly registered that her erotic charm and her ability to suggest elusive intangibility may be virtually identical. Trollope carries this point further, as we shall see.

In comedy, we have noticed all along, the faculty of magical nimbleness is not so much a moral quality as the sign of a heightened aptitude for pleasure, and this linkage is fully dramatized in Ayala. Affronting with her usual impertinence the Victorian ideal of demure, self-denying, libidinally repressed fictional heroines (the very ideal that Trollope incarnates, for purposes of comparison, in Lucy), Ayala scarcely tries to conceal her intense appetite for carnal and worldly enjoyments—despite her devotion to an ideal otherworldly lover, whose role we shall discuss in a moment. I have quoted in an earlier chapter passages describing Ayala's bliss amid the "ecstatic pleasures" (chap. 25) of her stay at the Alburys' country house at Stalham, a deeply traditional comic image of "a world of joy" where "everybody was at his ease, where everybody was good-natured, where everybody seemed to acknowledge that pleasure was the one object of life!" (chap. 23). The words *ease* and *easy*, we shall see, are central to the comic lexicon of this novel. Of all the hedonistic pleasures of Stalham, in any case, the keenest for Ayala is her first day of hunting, a pastime whose whole appeal lies in a euphoric freedom of movement that exactly suits this "tricksy Ariel" of a heroine and fills her with "delight and glory." For all the shameless worldliness of these amusements, they steadily evoke in this novel a quasi-religious (some would say sacrilegious) vocabulary. "The other side of the brook [that Ayala is about to leap on horseback] was heaven." Full of exhilaration, she cries out to her friend Nina that hunting is "divine," and Nina casts "up her eyes to Heaven," making a gesture with her whip "intended to be expressive of her perfect joy" (chap. 24). The salvational movement of most Victorian novels, as *Ayala's Angel* seems intended to remind us, is purgatorial, corresponding as it does to an experience of trial, resignation, and self-denial, but in this comic one with its persistent mock-theological overtones, salvation is paradisal, intimately associated with the fantasy of a world of perfected pleasure. After the bohemian luxury of her father's house and the lavish opulence of her uncle's, in any case, Ayala is no stranger to worldly pleasure, but her entry into the "world of joy" at Stalham gives her the feeling that she is embarking on "a new phase of life" (chap. 24).

The qualities in Ayala that arouse such interest and desire are the qualities that she herself instinctively is drawn to. Isadore Hamel, though young, handsome, and intelligent, falls short of her standard of a potential lover, because, as she reflects, he is "too bashful to talk easily to the girl he admired" (chap. 5). Fluency and nimbleness are all. Much of the cast of characters surrounding Ayala is designed therefore to set off these vital qualities by contrast. Sir Thomas and Mr. Traffick, each "a disciple of business, not of pleasure" (chap. 5), are two paunchy, heavy men whose want of birdlike (or, rather, "angelic") limberness is pointedly stressed—though in a telling scene in Rome that has its own aura of paradisal imagery, Mr. Traffick, momentarily under Ayala's rejuvenating charm, actually is able to "[trot] after her with admiring breathless industry" all the way to the top of St. Peter's while she "[skips] up the interminable stairs" ahead of him, airily defying gravity as usual (chap. 6). Traffick's fiancée Augusta Tringle remains resentfully on the ground, for, as has been said of her in another context, "a young lady who is already half a bride is not supposed to run up and down stairs as readily as a mere girl" (chap. 5). Young Tom Tringle, Ayala's hapless suitor, has many virtues, but he too embodies earthbound heaviness. "There was the heavy face, and there were the big chains and the odious rings, and the great hands and the clumsy feet" (chap. 7). The imagery of heavy encumbering paraphernalia, of chains and manacles, recurs in Colonel Stubbs's make-believe ideal of "a nice prim little woman," full of conventional bourgeois virtues, whose "cuffs and collars are always as stiff as steel" (chap. 23). As in the image of life at No. 11, where "everything is cased in iron," metallic stiffness is the antithesis of the energizing values of this book, which in its single-minded glorification of the ideal of "quickness" and "elasticity" sums up the deepest implication of all of Trollope's comedy, and of comedy itself.

Like Ayala, Jonathan Stubbs is a distillation of comic mythology as well as a vividly idiosyncratic character in his own right. His dominant qualities are precisely in harmony with Ayala's. Said to be "one of the most rising officers in the British service"—again the imagery of mercurial ascent—he is very much "a man of pleasure" (chap. 16), and all his personal characteristics express his own forms of amazing agility. He is a wonderful dancer and horseman (though he tumbles into the brook), but chiefly he is a wonderfully fluent user of words, a man blessed with "free and easy speech," an "easy mode of talking" (chap. 16). Unlike many heroes of stage comedy, Stubbs is of impeccable moral character, but this does not prevent him from being a mischievous joker or from declaring, in the midst of one of his elaborate pranks, "I must be a rogue" (chap. 16). He has, says the narrator, "a certain aptitude for drollery which pervaded him" (chap. 31). When Ayala at their first meeting makes a saucy remark about his common-sounding name, Stubbs tells her a cautionary tall tale about the girl who jilted him to marry "Mr. Montgomery Talbot de Montpellier," much to her eventual sorrow. Throughout his career as a novelist Trollope makes comic charm one of his greatest specialties, but Stubbs, one is tempted to say, is almost his supreme illustration of this ideal.

Ayala is fixated on her dream-image of the perfect male, the Angel of Light, whose details are "terribly vague" (chap. 12), but who embodies "a concentration of poetic perfection" (chap. 6), "the extreme point of perfection" (chap. 10). She sees him as another Ariel-like creature like herself, borne on wings that give off a magical azure light. We know how dubious the ideal of perfection is to Trollope, and this novel, accordingly, is designed as a fable of the replacement of Ayala's "ideas of some transcendental, more than human, hero" (chap. 6) by the real-life figure of Colonel Stubbs, who, among other things, happens to be as physically ugly as Ayala is beautiful, and has far more "fun" and "good humour" in his makeup (chap. 16) than is compatible with romantic heroism. This at least is the putative program of the book. To a large extent it is undermined by the main premise of the story, which is that Stubbs is virtually perfect after all. Like Frank Gresham with his "joyous, genial lustre," Stubbs turns out even to have his own halo of light, although Ayala, expecting it to be azure, cannot see it at first.

> "I declare," said Nina, "sometimes, when he is talking,
> I think him perfectly lovely. The fire comes out of his eyes,
> and he rubs his old red hairs about till they sparkle. Then
> he shines all over like a carbuncle, and every word he says
> makes me die of laughter."
>
> (Chap. 16)

This vision of Stubbs shooting fire from his eyes, sparkling and shining all over with a benign radioactive incandescence, emitting an occult laughter-inducing energy, tells us that this is no ordinary military officer but some kind of divinity in mortal form, an epiphanic figure. He is an Angel of Light after all, even though he is the antithesis of the suavely beautiful hero of Ayala's fantasy. Then Trollope names this radiant deity very precisely: he is "the Genius of Comedy" (chap. 16). This is not a passing figure of speech, but a literal statement, and one that takes its reverberating significance from Trollope's whole career as a student and a practitioner of comedy. His late works seem often to declare that comedy can no longer survive except in drastically impaired shapes; but in *Ayala's Angel* he means to give us a vision of comedy in its pristine form, with all its potency—its genius—restored.

Pristine, however, does not mean unproblematic; in fact, the novel goes deeply into several bedeviling problems in the value system of comedy. Foremost among these is the near impossibility of disentangling the pleasure ethic from its crassest financial implications. That pleasure forms a strongly positive value in this novel is never at issue. But Trollope relentlessly juxtaposes comedy's argument "that pleasure [is] the one object of life" with reminders that pleasure in this world is a function of material resources that have fixed limits, that "straitened circumstances" (chaps. 20, 33) to one degree or another are the human lot, and that only the affluent few, as a matter of practical fact, are able therefore to devote themselves carelessly to pleasure. For everyone else, pleasure is at best a compromised ideal. This is a killjoy's point of view, but one that is dwelt upon throughout the novel, as though to test whether the comic ethic can survive in the face of this awareness.

In the second paragraph of the novel we meet the fabulously rich Sir Thomas, "who was said to have told [his wife] that money was a matter of no consideration." This prodigious exception is set up to spotlight the rule of pinched resources, of "continued care as to small pecuniary needs" (chap. 22), that governs nearly every other character in the novel. It especially governs the Tringles' relatives the Dosetts, whose financial affairs Trollope audits in detail, using them as a parable of conditions in general. Having been incautious in their early expenditures, the Dosetts contracted a debt the servicing of which (in the form of life-insurance premiums of 175 pounds per annum) dooms them to permanent poverty. This state has had deeply deleterious personal consequences. "The cares of the world, the looking after shillings and their results, had given [Mrs. Dosett] that look of commonplace insignificance which is so frequent and so unattractive among middle-aged women upon whom the world leans heavily" (chap. 10). Stubbs himself conjures up much this same dismal picture in his discussion with Isadore Hamel on the pleasures and pains of matrimony for a man of not unlimited income. Such a man "is generally thinking whether he shall endeavour to extend his credit with the butcher, or resolve that the supply of meat may be again curtailed without injury to the health of his five daughters." "The seriousness of life has pressed the smiles out of him." Worst of all, a man in these circumstances, subject to the tyranny of material needs, can hardly fail before long to have "an altered heart" toward his careworn wife (chap. 20). Both Lucy and Ayala, for all their moral refinement, are "disgusted" (chap. 3), upon their introduction to the Dosetts, who must endure real privation to receive them, at what seems to them the "mean and vulgar" (chap. 21) calculations their aunt must make to be sure the week's income will suffice to cover the necessary provisions of bread, mutton, tea, and sugar. Stubbs, Isadore, and Frank Houston all find themselves making just the same anxious calculations to decide whether their intended marriages will allow them to maintain a suitably comfortable style of life. The alternative to such unpleasant calculations has been seen in the casual extravagance practiced by Egbert Dormer at the bijou, enabling himself and his family to lead a life of elegant luxury—but leaving his children destitute at his death. Wherever we turn in *Ayala's Angel*, in other words, we encounter chilling reminders that the predominant fact in this world is the limitation of resources, and that this fact has genuinely frightening moral consequences.

In forcing this issue so obsessively throughout the novel, Trollope creates a moral dilemma that implicates nearly every significant character in the story, but especially Ayala. In her romantic idealism, the central tenet of which is the exalting of aesthetic and intellectual pleasures above base material concerns, Ayala is particularly committed to the scorn of money. "No one despises money so much as I do," she declares repeatedly (chap. 3). But can this high-minded attitude coexist, after all, with that keen responsiveness to pleasure that this novel, in accordance with the doctrine of comedy, tells us is vital to moral health? It turns out that Ayala's attempt to embrace the two principles simultaneously involves her in treacherous self-deceptions, of which she herself is well aware. From the point of view of high romantic ideals the gravitation to a world of pleasure seems morally blameworthy. "It is bad to like pretty things and money, and to hate poor things," she says, angry at her own dismay at going to live in the dingy poverty of the Dosetts' house in Kingsbury Crescent. "Or, rather," she continues, letting her real feelings spill over, "I do not believe it is bad at all, because it is so natural. I believe it is all a lie as to its being wicked to love riches. I love them, whether it is wicked or not" (chap. 10). This is the liberating gospel of comedy much as it was preached by the Signora Neroni in *Barchester Towers*, but in this more rigorously analytical novel the problems it entails are more tenacious. Loving riches is not at all the same thing as loving pleasure, but does not the latter commit us to the former even against our will? "Don't let us be hypocritical," Ayala declares to Lucy (chap. 10), but hypocrisy is terribly hard to avoid when contradictory ideals are so closely intertwined. Thus Ayala, having rejected Stubbs's offer of marriage, finds herself yearning for the "Elysium" of luxury that such a marriage would lift her into. "As to his income she thought nothing and cared nothing," but she thinks very precisely about the horses, carriages, beautiful clothing, and "pleasurable pursuits" that life in his aristocratic milieu would bestow on her (chap. 26). She is "devoted to the society of rich and gay people" (chap. 27) and even, we are told—what an admission for a Victorian heroine!—has "a pretty taste for diamonds" (chap. 32). Is it not a moral obtuseness close to hypocrisy to declare oneself indifferent to a potential husband's income when one is in love with sybaritic luxury?

Ayala in a sense eludes this dilemma, since, fortunately for her, the man she finally learns to love purely for himself is also able to provide her the life of luxurious pleasure she craves. But the novel more than entitles us to wonder, What if he couldn't? Would it in that case be morally incumbent upon her to doom herself, in the name of an amorous infatuation at age nineteen, to a lifetime of the kind of debilitating poverty endured by the Dosetts? Would not this be an example of the kind of absurdly self-destructive "romanticism" that comedy has always had a special license to demolish? When Sir Thomas appears in Kingsbury Crescent to plead with Ayala on behalf of his son, stressing Tom's excellent worldly position and countering Ayala's objections by remarking that "romance . . . won't buy bread and butter" (chap. 15), is this crass materialism or sound wisdom that Ayala would ignore at her peril except for the golden safety net provided by Stubbs? We enter this morass of vexing questions from the opposite direction by reflecting on the involuntary hypocrisy of Ayala's exalting of purely personal qualities in a lover above all considerations of worldly resources, but failing to see what Trollope sees with unflinching lucidity: that the kind of refined, gaily lightfooted, gallant, cultivated, witty—in a word, aristocratic—lover that she requires could only originate in a social caste founded upon abundant surplus wealth soundly invested in land or the four per cents. It would be out of the question for a girl imbued with the ethic of the bijou ever to fall in love with the poor fellow (envisioned by Stubbs) "whose step is ever heavy and whose brow is always sad" from struggling to make ends meet (chap. 20). Lest we miss this point, Trollope at one point states it with acerbic emphasis. "The Angel of Light generally appeared 'in forma pauperis,' though there was always about him a tinge of bright azure which was hardly compatible with the draggle-tailed hue of everyday poverty" (chap. 11). This predicament, we can see, is everywhere thrust forward by *Ayala's Angel*; and it yields no stable solution.

On one level a story of material and other difficulties besetting the consummation of young love, *Ayala's Angel* needs to be read more deeply, I have been trying to suggest, as an extended meditation on the fate of comedy in an age where two antithetical moral principles converge. The first of these, graphically illustrated in the novel, is the impulse toward the otherworldly, the immaterial and the ideal, that is the connecting link between Romanticism and modern-day puritan-ism. Just as pervasively documented in *Ayala's Angel* is the modern Malthusian-democratic mentality obsessed with the awareness of the finite nature of material resources, of the damaging effects of short-ages, and of the unequal distribution of these finite resources in so-ciety. Maybe the clearest linguistic sign of the advent of this mentality is the way the word "economy" increasingly takes on the particular meaning of exercising frugality in expenditure; and this term in its modern sense reverberates throughout *Ayala's Angel*. Mrs. Dosett, for example, makes it her duty to initiate Ayala into "the unsavoury mys-teries of economy" (chap. 22), and Frank Houston "regarded it as an unkindness in Providence that he should not have been gifted with economy" (chap. 41). This fixation on the need for "economy in the use of pounds of butter and legs of mutton" (chap. 49) is particularly associated in the novel with the pressures of an explosively expanding population, although the Malthusian calculus is given no wider scope than that prospect of babies multiplying annually in the nursery that Frank, Stubbs, and Isadore Hamel all worry about at different times as they contemplate matrimony. Given the scantiness of Frank's re-sources, says the narrator in a startling phrase, "it was clear that he and Imogene ought not to marry and encounter the danger of all those embryo mouths" (chap. 41). The counterpart of this disturbing imagery is found in the novel's continual precise notations of food-stuffs, as at the moment when Ayala, having just delivered herself of an only half-joking denunciation of eating as base and vulgar, is seen returning from market "carrying a pound of butter, six eggs, and a small lump of bacon in a basket" (chap. 21). What this complex of im-agery adds up to is an extreme vision of fixity, a negation of comic buoyancy and expansiveness: life in this view is indeed "cased in iron" by the constraints of material existence.

When the "romantic" and "Malthusian" currents of thought com-bine, an indelible moral taint becomes associated with the idea of money, and thus, since it is futile to pretend (when the point is pressed) that everything needn't be paid for, with the idea of worldly pleasure of almost any kind. The "woodcock and champagne" that Frank feels are necessary to his happiness (chap. 41) seem inherently wicked when it is forced on our attention so insistently that the Dos-etts must scrimp and save to be able to afford a weekly joint of mut-ton. In this cultural environment, *Ayala's Angel* ever more plainly testifies, comedy can only seem fraught with insoluble moral contra-dictions. These may be treated humorously, as, for example, when Mrs. Dosett, one of that class of people "who look black at any allu-sions to pleasures" (chap. 15), none the less urges Ayala to "make hay while the sun shines" (chap. 27) by going to parties so as to find a wealthy suitor. But a moment's laughter cannot make these problems other than lethal, in the long run, for the comic spirit, and this perception lies dangerously near the heart of the novel.

In a sort of counterpoint to the argument just traced, *Ayala's Angel* pursues a more conventional comic argument centering on folly, a word that with its cognates recurs almost innumerable times in this novel, as it does, say, in *As You Like It*. We can distinguish several main categories of folly. The first includes comic monsters like Septimus Traffick, Tom Tringle, and Captain Batsby, among others, characters whose absurd behavior makes them into laughingstocks of a familiar sort—and imparts comic glory to them in the usual way. *Ayala's Angel* is full of another kind of "folly" too, that of worldly imprudence, the fear of which is constantly at odds with the dictates of feeling and loyalty. "Of course I think that you and Imogene are two fools," snorts Mudbury Docimer when his sister and Frank Houston renew their engagement despite their prospect of a life of relative poverty. Lord John Battledore, a cynical clubman, takes the same view of Stubbs's decision to marry Ayala. "He is such a fool!" says Sir John, "hor-rified,—nay, disgusted,—by the folly of the world" (chap. 63). This is the kind of folly that we are meant to look on with more than toler-ance, even though, as we have seen, in a world of such perilously short resources, prudent expediency is not to be scorned.

The novel's principal fool, Ayala herself, has a folly all her own, and it too proves to be at least partially a virtue in disguise. We may not quite agree with Sir Thomas's judgment that Ayala is "romantic and foolish" for caring so little about the wealth that Tom could bestow on her (chap. 15), but clearly the folly of her worship of her Angel of Light is a genuine aberration that needs to be corrected. It is aberrant because it goes along with the extravagant, foolish pride that causes her, for instance, to deem her cousin Tom to be "infinitely beneath her,—worlds beneath her,—a denizen of an altogether inferior race, such as the Beast was to the Beauty!" "Her assumed superiority," says the narrator, "existed in certain intellectual or rather artistic and aes-thetic gifts,—certain celestial gifts" (chap. 13). We need only think of the compulsive self-abnegation of heroines like Esther Summerson and Amy Dorrit to realize Trollope's daring in asking his readers to remain sympathetic to this conceited nineteen-year-old who imagines herself "celestial." Her romantic extravagance is foolish also, and pri-marily, because it cuts her off from a real flesh-and-blood man like Stubbs. Lady Albury tells her that refusing a man like this, especially considering that he will eventually come into two thousand pounds a year, because he doesn't fit an abstract ideal of perfection, is "sheer folly." "It is what I call romance," says this worldly lady. "Romance can never make you happy" (chap. 26). Plainly this phrase expresses the novel's doctrine. "Romance," for all its ordinary connotations of sensuous excess and dreamy luxury, is indicted by Trollope as an especially perverse form of asceticism and self-denial, and as a type of that state of fixity that comedy abhors.

But Trollope's argument really lies in the paradoxical twist that makes Ayala's foolish romanticism her most wonderful quality after all. It does, for one thing, give her a true high-mindedness that in a world rife with cynicism carries authentic value. More fundamentally, it is inseparable from the vitality that makes her a more richly variegated human being than, say, her rather solemn and dull sister Lucy. Her outrageousness is the basis of her charm. So the paradox is apparent only when Trollope, having just chastised and cured Ayala's tendency to live in a romantic dream-world, seems to turn the whole fable on its head. "That the dreams had been all idle she declared to herself,—not aware that the Ayala whom her lover had loved would not have been an Ayala to be loved by him, but for the dreams" (chap. 51). Much the same transvaluation of "folly" occurs in the case of Tom Tringle, Ayala's despised suitor, whom she abuses as a lout, an oaf, an idiot, and a Beast, and whom his father, exasperated at Tom's incurable infatuation, declares to be "the biggest fool that ever lived" (chap. 13). Trollope punishes Tom's lunacy by putting him in one absurd and humiliating position after another, but ultimately it is Tom's persistence in folly that earns him, too, a high standing in the novel's hierarchy. Tom, says the narrator at the end, "if the matter be looked at aright, should be regarded as the hero of this little history." This, because although handicapped fatally in his suit of the exquisite Ayala by being "foolish, vulgar, and ignorant," and knowing himself to be so, he has had the courage to fight his forlorn battle "to the last gasp" (chap. 61). Once again we are led in this comic world to the praise of folly. All the glory of such a world is in its fools: this is the comic principle *par excellence*.

Trollope's praise of folly is not so much contradicted as it is mediated and reinforced by his strong foregrounding of a set of characters who stand for beneficent authority and wisdom. The Dosetts are on the fringes of this group in *Ayala's Angel*, but its central members are two worldly ladies, the Marchesa Baldoni and Lady Albury, and especially the great magnate Sir Thomas, who seems at first merely to serve as the foil to the comic pandemonium swirling around him—"I don't suppose anybody ever had such a set of fools about him as I have," he exclaims (chap. 48)—but who, in his deepening sympathy with Tom's plight, emerges as a main embodiment of Trollope's belief in mature, steady judgment tempered by tolerance and generosity. The kind of wisdom represented by Sir Thomas is not, like Mrs. Dosett's or Roger Carbury's, or that of traditional comic scolds like Touchstone in *Eastward Ho* or Malevole in *The Malcontent*, the kind that seeks to suppress folly, hold it at arm's length, subject it to stringent dictates of prudence and respectability. Sir Thomas stands, rather, for an ethic that accepts living in proximity even to rather extreme misbehavior— though he does draw the line at allowing his insufferable son-in-law Mr. Traffick to freeload at his house forever. Like Mrs. Dosett, he understands that in a world of scarce resources a wise person must be extremely charitable in applying rules of conduct. "After all," he says, "fools must live in the world" (chap. 57). The moral interest of *Ayala's Angel* lies, then, in the delicate equilibrium that Trollope creates between the opposite charms of folly, the principle of extravagance, and of wisdom, the principle of flexibility and moderation. In effect the novel tries to reconcile the two, to portray folly that has in it the seeds of wisdom, and wisdom that knows better than to sever all its ties with folly. It is just this moral economy that is symbolized by the vexed courtship and final union of Ayala and Stubbs, the fool who is redeemed by wisdom and the wise man who falls head over heels in love with the charm and vitality of folly, "almost making a fool of himself," as he feels, in the process (chap. 46).

The axis along which all these themes coalesce in *Ayala's Angel* is the central one of comic drama, that of relations between the sexes. The view of sex set forth in this novel, however, is far from the world of insouciant lechery that is the usual sphere of comedy. Erotic attraction in *Ayala's Angel* is what it is in *Jude the Obscure*, "a compelling arm of extraordinary muscular power" (*Jude*, 48) that seizes men and women and drives them roughly toward some destined mate in defiance of reason, prudence, and wisdom. This is the pagan conception of love as brutal divine force, a conception that at bottom (if a Shakespearean pun is permissible) is antithetical to the comic glorification of pleasure. *A Midsummer-Night's Dream* stands out as the great comic exploration of this view of love, and Trollope's narrator makes a point of alluding to it in the midst of a discussion of Tom Tringle's passion for his ravishing young cousin. "It is not always like to like in love," he says. "Titania loved the weaver Bottom with the ass's head" (chap. 7). Love, as Titania found, is a compulsion likely to render the lover a grotesque and pitiable spectacle, and this is just the image of love that Trollope weaves throughout *Ayala's Angel*. He seems again to be working at the outer edges of comedy, experimenting to see how much disturbing material can be brought at last safely under the aegis of comic pleasure.

This focus of interest is announced right away in the brief synopsis of the careers of the two Dosett sisters, Adelaide and Emmeline, each, like their parents before them, "conspicuous for personal beauty." Beauty in this novel, we see, is not, as in the usual sentimental romance, simply conventional ornamentation for the heroine, but the very subject of the book. And already it is seen as an occult enslaving power that ravishes the wits of those who behold it.

> Adelaide had been the more attractive from expression
> and brilliancy. To her Lord Sizes had offered his hand and
> coronet, promising to abandon for her sake all the haunts
> of his matured life. To her Mr. Tringle had knelt before he
> had taken the elder sister. For her Mr. Progrum, the
> popular preacher of the day, for a time so totally lost
> himself that he was nearly minded to go over to Rome.
> She was said to have had offers from a widowed Lord
> Chancellor and from a Russian prince.
>
> (Chap. 1)

This great beauty then shows her own subjection to the folly of love by squandering her power and her brilliant prospects by giving her hand to the sweet-natured but luxurious, spineless, dilettantish Egbert Dormer, a benign Gilbert Osmond prototype. The folly of passion is displayed from another angle in the portrayal of the stunning Emmeline Dosett in her later incarnation as the middle-aged Lady Emmeline Tringle, a short-tempered, dimwitted woman whose husband can barely tolerate her presence.

This family history is thus a long exhibit of the force of beauty and the blind irrationality of sexual desire, and it continues into the younger generation once Tom Tringle has been, in his mother's eloquently mixed metaphor, "carried away by [Ayala's] baby face" (chap. 12). Trollope at one point analyzes the violence of love in explicitly pagan terminology that makes the frightening implications of his story stand out plainly. When a man feels that he is dealing with an ordinary woman, says the narrator, he can remain master of the situation. "But, when he feels the goddess, he cannot carry himself before her as though she were a mere woman, and, as such, inferior to himself in her attributes. Poor Tom had felt the touch of something divine, and had fallen immediately prostrate before the shrine with his face to the ground" (chap. 54). Subjugated as he is by what ancient writers called the force of Eros or of Aphrodite, Tom is an exhibit of that fixity that in

Trollope always has tragic overtones. Stubbs, using a more modern clinical vocabulary, believes him to have become "insane" in his pursuit of Ayala, and his diagnosis is confirmed in the episode of Tom's heartbroken wanderings in the rainy London night after his last rejection by his cousin, an episode that culminates in his demented, basically self-destructive assault on his rival and takes us into deep psychological waters far from the usual latitudes of comedy. "Beauty indeed!" cries Tom when Ayala suggests to him that he may find consolation in meeting "some beautiful young lady" on his travels. "Think what I have suffered from beauty! From the first moment in which you came down to Glenbogie I have been a victim to it. It has destroyed me,—destroyed me!" (chap. 61). Tom may survive after all, but the idea of physical beauty as a dangerous, destructive force pervades the novel. Beauty on the one hand breaks rejected lovers' hearts; on the other it raises the specter of those "embryo mouths" multiplying in the nursery and dooming husbands and wives to poverty, breaking hearts in another way. Tom's lament reminds us of how fine a line is followed in this novel between the comic and the tragic views.

The frame of reference finally most appropriate to Trollope's study of love in *Ayala's Angel* is not, however, that of pagan mythology, but a distinctly modern one that looks forward to Proust in particular, even though the comic idiom of *Ayala's Angel* may initially make such a connection hard to see. Again we have the sense of a concerted effort on Trollope's part to pierce to the heart of a lifelong theme and to understand why love, from the comic perspective, tends so strongly to appear as an absurd predicament of mistaken identities that only the imperious drive of the libido suffices to resolve. Conventional accounts of comedy that stress the role of "blocking characters" in separating young lovers do not tell us much about why comedies resort so often to tales of love embroiled in weirdly delusive situations: lovers falling in love with disguised members of their own sex, shifting their love from one twin to another, imagining a lover or spouse to be altogether unlike his or her real nature, imagining that one is utterly in love with A when one really loves B all along, falling in love with the object of a seduction scheme and then being unable to avow one's real identity, courting one's lover by means of abuse and sarcasm, writing a love letter to one's own love on the behalf of a rival—and on and on. In all the registers of comedy, from the realistic to the fantastic, we see love portrayed in the same terms as a pattern of crazily substitutive images—the pattern epitomized in the title of Shirley's comedy *Changes, or Love in a Maze*. These are the kinds of love predicaments (or rather, the variations on what we feel to be a single fundamental

predicament) that most keenly arouse the comic imagination, that especially arouse Shakespeare's in *Twelfth Night*, and that Trollope plays
upon throughout *Ayala's Angel*, using them to try to get to the heart of
love itself.

The intuition that informs the whole novel is that love is directed
not toward other people but toward one's own mental images, and that
desire, for all its appearance of almost brutal directness, is necessarily
oblique and reflexive. One implication of this principle is stated in the
scandalous axiom that Trollope, in the guise of a learned scientist of
love, lays down with regard to Lucy's love of Isadore Hamel. "A girl
loves most often because she is loved," he asserts, "—not from choice
on her part. She is won by the flattery of the man's desire" (chap. 17).
What they love, that is, is the idealized image of themselves reflected
back in their lover's eyes. This conception of love as essentially nar-
cissistic and thus as involving the lover in delusion, in desire for a
figment of one's own imagination, is carried much further in the main
theme of *Ayala's Angel*, the heroine's obsession with her make-believe
lover. That the main function of "the picture in [Ayala's] imagination"
(chap. 45) is self-"flattery," that it is a device, that is, for confirming her secret image of herself as "celestial," is too plain to need to be
said in so many words. In allowing her emotional life to become fixated upon "that image of manly perfection which her daily thoughts
had created for her" (chap. 27), Ayala falls into the classic predicament of comic lovers, and becomes the butt of the novel's extended
joke, even as she illustrates that distinctive nineteenth-century pathology that I have connected with the representative case of Thackeray's
Amelia Sedley.

It is true that the novel seems to resolve this state of affairs reas-
suringly enough. Ayala learns at last to recognize that the Angel is a
mere delusion, enabling her to fall in love at last with Stubbs's real virtues. On the level of explicit statement, in other words, Trollope seems
to deny his own constant implication that love is only a fascination
with "images" that flatter the person imagining them. There seems to
be nothing equivocal about Ayala's love for Stubbs, who is as substantial and unambiguous an embodiment of high masculine character as
Trollope ever portrayed. But Ayala's love for Stubbs does not turn out,
after all, to be the central story of the novel: this role is occupied by a
much subtler and more elaborate development, the story of Stubbs's
love for Ayala, a fable of a much more problematical kind. We get a
clue to its nature in the first words that allude to his dawning interest
in her. Isadore Hamel has just announced to Stubbs his engagement
to Lucy Dormer, but Stubbs can only pay partial attention, since, as
the narrator says, "during the whole of this conversation, and for

many days previous to it, his mind had been concerned with the image of Lucy's sister" (chap. 20). In another novel this turn of phrase—he is concerned not with Ayala exactly, but with his own "image" of her—would be without particular significance, but in this one, focused as it is from the first on the delusions that arise from creating images of lovers in one's mind, it resonates. The hint it carries is steadily magnified thereafter, and most of the novel's shrewdest comedy flows from it.

One of the novel's chief ironies, for example, is in the very uncharacteristic poverty of description of the heroine, whose beauty, after all, is the mainspring of the plot, and who is said on the last page to be setting up as "a professional beauty." As we know, Trollope is usually lavish and minute in describing his heroines' appearance. In *Orley Farm* he devotes four long paragraphs to the most detailed inventory of Madeline Staveley's beauty, considering in turn her height and weight, the shape of her face, her complexion, the color of her hair, her smile, her bodily movements. "Her nose was Grecian, but perhaps a little too wide at the nostril to be considered perfect in its chiselling" (chap. 19). Of Ayala, excepting that feverish vision of her through Tom Tringle's eyes quoted earlier, we have almost no description whatever. She is often called "little," especially in the phrase "little fool," and we hear that her hair is dark, but aside from this she is a blank. Instead of concrete description, what we get of her is that array of similes—especially striking in this novelist usually so sparing in figurative language—by which observers try to evoke the impression she makes on them. She is like a bird, like a fawn, like Ariel, like a ray of the sun reflected from a mirror one holds in one's hand. She is both magnified and diminished by this translation into an ever-shifting constellation of images, which confers on her a kind of mythic status and makes her a supreme icon of that limberness that comedy glorifies, but which also screens from view her true image. Of all her figurative semblances, the image of her as a ray of light reflected from a mirror is the most suggestive, implying that her beauty is something projected outward from her male admirers, and something that can only dazzle and blind if looked at directly.

An even more disturbing ambiguity than the one surrounding her physical appearance, however, is the one surrounding her intelligence. No novelist, as we have seen, is more enamored than Trollope of the ideal of witty, articulate feminine charm, and no one renders it more often or more convincingly than he does. Ayala is repeatedly declared to be witty and clever, but these declarations are sharply at odds with the evident reality. Especially if we think of her alongside such witty young ladies as Mary Thorne or Isabel Boncassen, we can only be struck by the unremittingly infantile speech that goes along with her "baby face."

> "I suppose you had not heard of [Mr. Traffick] before," [Augusta] said to Ayala.
> "I never did."
> "That's because you have not attended to the debates."
> "I never have. What are debates?"
> "Mr. Traffick is very much thought of in the House of Commons on all subjects affecting commerce."
> "Oh."
> "It is the most glorious study which the world affords."
> "The House of Commons. I don't think it can be equal to art."
>
> (Chap. 5)

Stubbs's sparkling wit makes Ayala's adolescent inarticulateness all the more unmistakable by contrast (she always takes his jokes literally, and people must explain them to her afterwards). Underlining the point, Trollope has numerous bystanders in the novel comment plainly on Ayala's mediocrity. In the stories of girls like Lucy Robarts in *Framley Parsonage* or Grace Crawley in *The Last Chronicle of Barset*, their detractors quickly discover, once they meet face to face, the sterling qualities that the girls possess. But Ayala so forcefully impresses good judges with her insignificance that one becomes aware that Trollope is building this novel around an especially audacious irony. Lady Tringle thinks of her as "a little chit of a girl of whom [Tom] would probably be tired in twelve months after he possessed her" (chap. 30). Aunt Dosett finds Ayala "little, and flighty, and like an elf," inferior in beauty to her sister (chap. 39). Sir Harry Albury, having had Ayala as a guest in his house more than once, admits her to be "a pretty girl enough," adding "but I doubt whether she is worth all the trouble" (chap. 55). The shrewdest judge of all in these matters is Lady Albury, and she repeatedly strikes this same note. At one point, for example, she "again considered how wonderful a thing it was such a girl as Ayala, so small, apparently so unimportant, so childish in her manner, with so little to say for herself, should become a person of such terrible importance" (chap. 46). Contemporary reviewers added their own strong objections to Ayala's thinness, apparently not seeing that Trollope deliberately creates this effect and goes out of his way to emphasize it, and unable to imagine that a novelist might play such a prank on his readers as to design a 600-page love story around a heroine who is not "worth all the trouble" (Smalley, 484, 486).

The focus of this irony that emerges in higher and higher relief is Stubbs, the exemplar of masculine force of character, who is punished for his pride in having been a scoffer at matrimony by being shown to be just as vulnerable to beauty's charm as Ayala's other suitors are. The ignominious position this places him in is pointed out by his friend Lady Albury, who rightly says that his infatuation with Ayala puts him on the same plane with the two most foolish of men, Tom Tringle and the preposterous Captain Batsby. He is too wise to feel himself to be humiliated by this circumstance: all men, he replies to her in effect, are equal before the power of Eros (chap. 46). But even he cannot command enough wisdom to see the joke involved in his worship of "the goddess" who presides over this novel.

> What was the use of independence if he could not allow himself to have the girl whom he really loved? Had any human being so perfectly lovely as Ayala ever flashed before his eyes before? Was there ever a sweeter voice heard from a woman's mouth? And then all her little ways and motions,—her very tricks,—how full of charm they were! When she would open her eyes and nod her head, and pout with her lips, he would declare to himself that he could no longer live without her.
>
> (Chap. 25)

If Ayala's hypnotic charm is made to appear rather trivial in this passage, and if the last sentence turns on a glaring non sequitur, these are by no means accidental effects, as we have seen. Dispassionately and objectively considered, she is far from being an adequate match for a man like Stubbs, but there is no way for him to get such a view of her. "She had caught by her instinct the very nature of the man," says the narrator, making the half-predatory quality of Ayala's charm apparent, "and knew how to witch him with her little charms" (chap. 64). Just as Ayala herself pursues a chimerical Angel, so too she seems, like Proust's Odette de Crécy, Albertine, and other intensely desired women, to have been endowed with the power of making men see in her a fascinating image that is scarcely real, a reflex somehow of their own erotic imaginations. Eros in this novel is a formidable force, but an inveterate prankster, mischievously leading his victims astray, subverting reason and judgment, driving eminently sensible men to upset their life's plans because of the facial mannerisms of a nineteen-year-old girl.

At its deepest level, then, *Ayala's Angel* embodies a dialectic between the consciousness of inhabiting a world of painfully limited material resources and this analysis of modern love as a delusion of the imagination. The recklessly inflationary devotion to beauty that afflicts the characters of the novel is just the mode of emotional life (we are meant to see) that is bound to arise in a world where all experience is so strongly conditioned by the sense of "straitened circumstances."[2] Or rather, it is one polar mode: at the other pole is the cynical, mercenary mode that Frank Houston tries to adopt and that he repeatedly proclaims to be universal in contemporary society (chaps. 18, 28). Trollope steadily views this state of affairs with a comic eye, treating the ludicrous excess of the commotion that Ayala unleashes wherever she sets her pretty foot as a sign of the delightful vitality of this world. To be immune to Stubbs's kind of folly would be to sacrifice one's very humanity, argues the comic spirit. The phenomena that the novel has described are susceptible of a much bleaker interpretation, however, as Proust's treatment of them testifies, and as Trollope hints in a striking passage. At the end, the story modulates for a moment into a rueful tone when Stubbs promises Ayala that his love for her will not be impaired by their having become man and wife, and the narrator replies, "Alas, no! There he had promised more than it is given to a man to perform" (chap. 64). Even the life of feeling, it seems, is subject to a cruel Malthusian law of "straitened circumstances," and must eventually pay for early reckless expenditures. Stubbs may not, like Proust's Swann after his marriage to Odette, become tired of Ayala "in twelve months after he possessed her"; he will, however, become more economical in his adoration of her in the years ahead. But Trollope's remark, rather than dispelling the novel's rich mood of gaiety, only testifies one more time to the distinctive limberness and resiliency of the comic imagination, which is able to see reality with a sharp eye and still, in spite of everything, in defiance of its own most disheartening perceptions, reaffirm the supremacy of pleasure.

Notes

INTRODUCTION   FICTIONAL DUPLICITY AND COMIC VOCATION

1. R. C. Terry likewise identifies Trollope as "the most representative author of the Victorian middle class" and of the "conventional thinking of his time," particularly with reference to the glorification of matrimony, which Terry sees as the crux of all Trollope's writing (pp. 198, 144). Bill Overton attacks Trollope as being at heart a mere publicist for "the ways of behaving, feeling and thinking that characterised the dominant social class to which he belonged," though he admits that some Trollope novels seem almost inadvertently to lend themselves to interpretations that conflict with upper-class ideology after all (p. 164). This pejorative view of Trollope was sometimes expressed by his original readers: for example, the sneering reviewer of *Orley Farm* who derided him for embodying in his fiction "the precise standard of English taste, sentiment, and conviction" (Smalley, 167; see also p. 385).

2. This judgment is repeated by Bradford A. Booth, who sees Trollope's "capitulation" to the stereotyped fiction demanded by his public as the "tragedy" of his career (p. 164).

3. Another reviewer of the same novel adds: "We do not know any other living writer of fiction who would have been so bold as to undertake . . . such a subject" (Smalley, 238). What usually most amazed reviewers was, as E. S. Dallas put it, Trollope's daring "sacrifice of the usual means of exciting interest" in fiction (ibid., 108). For comments similar to the ones quoted above, see Smalley, 198, 216, 229, 364, 383, 464, 466.

4. For reviewers' complaints about Trollope's vulgarity, see Smalley, 76, 178, 185, 212, 216, 231, 234, 249, 263, 325, 399, 419–23, 426, 444, 494.

5. See Qualls, *The Secular Pilgrims*, for a convincing account of the Carlylean and biblical strains in Victorian fiction. Kathleen Tillotson (*Novels of the Eighteen-Forties*, 150–56) also strongly emphasizes Carlyle's influence upon the novel. Robert Scholes and Robert Kellogg observe in *The Nature of Narrative* that in modern critical parlance, the words "tragic" and "realistic," mere neutral descriptive terms, "are normally applied to literary works as terms of praise" (p. 8); indeed, they commonly are used as synonyms.

6. A marginal exception to this statement would be the realistic comedies of T. W. Robertson, such as *Society* (1865) and *Caste* (1867). These dull plays are strongly influenced by Thackeray; *Caste*, especially, is full of close parallels to *Vanity Fair*, turning as it does on the story of a young widow named Amelia who has a baby son named Georgy and whose husband has (supposedly) been killed in battle.

7. Gamaliel Bradford inaugurated this topic in 1905 by noticing Trollope's use of the main premise of *The Old Law*, by Massinger and others, for his novel *The Fixed Period* (p. 458), and Bradford Booth and Robert Tracy have explored other such connections since then, as we shall see. The fullest discussion so far of Trollope and the drama, however, is that of Geoffrey Harvey, who lists six Trollope novels each of which he claims to be based directly on a single seventeenth-century model (in one case, on two models combined). His notion of the transaction between Trollope and his supposed sources is a simple one: he sees the novelist as simply seizing material for his own use when his imagination "faltered" (p. 29). At least three of the cases that Harvey cites seem to me highly doubtful. He identifies *Eastward Ho*, a comedy by Jonson, Chapman, and Marston, for example, as a source for *The Three Clerks* largely on the basis of the similar pairings in each work of earnest and dissipated young men, but, as Trollope himself comments in his manuscript notes on *Eastward Ho*, the fable of the diligent and the idle apprentices is one of the commonest traditional stories, one that Trollope could have encountered in scores of different works (*Marginalia*, PR 2691 H3, Copy 2, Vault 2, III.102). Moreover, *The Three Clerks* dates from 1858, and Trollope's notes, usually characterized by the fastidious accuracy of official Post Office memorandums, show that he read *Eastward Ho* on 7 June 1873. Even if Harvey has in part overstated his argument, however, he has contributed to our understanding of Trollope by alerting us to the possibility of a constant relationship between Trollope's fiction and old plays. As for the claim that Trollope turned to the old dramatists for help at moments when his imagination was failing him, if there is any evidence to bear this assumption out, Harvey does not refer to it. It is clear, on the contrary, that Trollope drew on this source uninterruptedly and no doubt often unconsciously, as a basic element of his creative process. See Harvey, 17–38.

8. Trollope greatly admired *A Fair Quarrel* and singled out for special praise the main plot involving the pugnacious Captain Ager, who spends much of the play burning to avenge aspersions cast on his mother's honor, only to be covered with shame when she finally confesses to him that the rumors against her are true: she was seduced as a young girl, before marrying Captain Ager's father (*Marginalia*, PR 2711 D8 As. Col., III.549). The congruence of the dramatic line and the personalities of this story with those of the story of Lucius Mason and his mother in *Orley Farm* is so close as to make a direct borrowing seem likely, even though the recorded date of Trollope's reading of the play (31 March 1878) is long after the writing of the novel.

9. The crux of the resemblance between the two texts lies in the characters of Vanbrugh's Sir John Brute and Trollope's "false and brutal" Lord Ongar (chap. 7), two violent drunkards who pathologically loathe and tyrannize over their unoffending wives. Sir John Brute, like Lord Ongar, dreams of divorcing his wife if he can only, as he says, "catch her adulterating" (3.1.103). Sir John correctly accuses his wife of marrying him solely "for money" (1.1.41), just as Lord Ongar accuses his own wife. "He told me," says Lady Ongar, "that I was staying with him for his money" (chap. 7). Not surprisingly, the two witty, mercenary wives, each in love with another man yet determined to preserve her "honour," inject strongly into their respective works the theme of matrimonial oppression, one of the staple subjects of comedy. When Lady Ongar complains of her "slavery" to Lord Ongar (chap. 7), she echoes Vanbrugh's extended theme of the "poor sordid slavery in marriage" (3.1.404–5). These

likenesses add up to a fairly safe presumption that Trollope modeled part of his novel upon *The Provoked Wife*; in any event, they tie the two works very closely together and go far to suggest the underlying comic structure of *The Claverings*.

10. There are many signs that Fletcher's play (read at least twice by Trollope, in 1851 and 1874) furnished Trollope with a model for the character of Lord Chiltern and for the story of his courtship of Violet Effingham in *Phineas Finn* (1869). Geoffrey Harvey states that there are no direct verbal echoes of early drama in Trollope, but here there are many. Fletcher's protagonist is the fierce, appallingly warlike Memnon, who is suddenly smitten with love for Calis, just as Chiltern, who has led a wild dissipated life, is famous for his reckless riding, and has lately killed a Newmarket ruffian with his fists, falls in love with Violet. Both court their ladies by inarticulately growling "I love thee" (in Chiltern's case, "you") over and over. Memnon seems to his friends "march-mad" (1.1), and Chiltern declares that if some rival were to win Violet's hand "I should be half mad": it would be, he says, as though this rival "wanted my own heart out of me" (chap. 24), and here he picks up the imagery of hearts being pulled from bodies that is the key one of *The Mad Lover*, where Memnon has the idea of committing suicide by sending Calis his own heart in a golden cup. Each of the two monomaniacal lovers has a close friend who becomes his rival (Polydore, Phineas) but with whom he is warmly reconciled before the end. Both lovers threaten to go lead desperate lives abroad if refused (*Phineas Finn*, chap. 52; *The Mad Lover* 5.4), and both ladies declare that they are frightened of their suitors. Memnon's counselors condemn his rough, abrupt proposal to Calis, and urge him to use more polite and courtly speech (1.1, 1.2), but he gruffly rejects their advice (1.2). In the same way, Chiltern's sister Lady Laura repeatedly urges him to speak to Violet more gently (chaps. 11, 24), but is rebuffed: "I can't make civil little speeches," he declares (chap. 24). And both lovers are successful at last. The correspondences between play and novel in this case are too elaborate to leave much doubt that a direct nexus, whether conscious or unconscious, exists between the two texts.

11. See below, chap. 7.

12. See below, chap. 4.

13. *Marginalia*, PR 2421 D8 1843, Copy 2, As. Col., vol. II, endleaf.

14. Trollope here makes a point of denying having borrowed story materials from other writers' works—but in terms that strongly invite us to look for such borrowings in his fiction. "How far I may unconsciously have adopted incidents from what I have read,—either from history or from works of imagination,—I do not know. It is beyond question that a man employed as I have been must do so. But when doing it I have not been aware that I have done it. I have never taken another man's work, and deliberately framed my work upon it. I am far from censuring this practice in others. Our greatest masters in works of imagination have obtained such aid for themselves. Shakespeare dug out of such quarries wherever he could find them. Ben Jonson . . . built up his structures on his studies of the classics" (pp. 115–16).

15. For the complaint that Trollope fails to make novels end tragically, see, for example, Smalley, 146, 175, 246–47, 252, 286; Booth, 56; Terry, 174. An especially clear instance of the hostility to comedy in fiction is found in George J. Becker's attack on Trollope as a mere "pseudorealist." Trollope, Becker sternly declares, "does resort to novelistic contrivance, he does soften the impact of human incapacity and deterministic erosion of strength and will." The world

depicted in his novels is unrealistically "narrow" and "protected." In a word, Becker concludes, summing up his indictment, Trollope's "approach [is] that of the comedy of manners" (p. 136). Becker implies throughout what Harold H. Watts makes explicit: that comedy is a literary type "likely to inhibit profound insight" (Watts, 193). See Kincaid, 10, for a lucid exposure of the "fallacy of arbitrary generic rankings."

16. Latter-day critics, just as subject to Trollope's devious strategies as Victorian ones were, persistently express discomfort and embarrassment in appraising him, speaking of him in equivocal, self-contradicting terms: damning him with faint praise, depicting him as a mediocrity whose work none the less shows incongruous signs of genius, calling him "one of the very best of the second-rate writers" (Skilton, 30), abruptly jumping back from extolling his brilliance to reminding us of his well-known limitations (McMaster, 218). Recent commentary, with which I associate myself, has increasingly drawn attention to the gap between his disingenuously simplistic self-portrayals and the complex reality of his fiction, or to the failure of the stated moral arguments of the novels to tally with the stories that these novels actually tell. Seen in this perspective, he becomes an "artist in hiding" (Terry), or even "two Trollopes" regularly advancing contradictory views within the same novel (Barickman, 196).

17. Several of Trollope's more thoughtful modern critics have preceded me in analyzing comic structures in his work. William A. West, in "Trollope's Comic Techniques," and Robert M. Polhemus, in The Changing World and Comic Faith, have made notable contributions to the study of comedy and of Trollope, but the usefulness of their work is limited, in my opinion, by their adoption of a sentimentalized and pietistic model of comedy that largely equates it with moral beauty, the overflow of benevolent emotion, and supernatural religion—a model with little relevance to traditional comic literature (particularly the harsh, scandalously indecent Jacobean comedy that Trollope was devoted to) and that obscures, as a result, the complexity of Trollope's negotiations with comedy. To some extent the same problem affects James R. Kincaid's Novels of Anthony Trollope, an excellent book which marks a real critical advance by attempting the first sustained analysis of Trollope's use of comic form. I am much indebted to Kincaid's work, and throughout this book I follow his main line of argument: that Trollope's career is shaped by his "exploration of the range of comedy" (p. 92), an enterprise that includes not only full-fledged comedies but also novels designed to "stand comedy on its head" (p. 146) or "to stretch the comic pattern so as to include the darkest and most unlikely processes" (p. 164).

If there is a weakness in Kincaid's astute study of these things, it is inherent in his definition of comedy itself, which follows Northrop Frye in assuming that "the establishment of community . . . is the basis of comedy" (p. 53) and follows such critics as West in its focusing upon "the comic virtues: understanding, tolerance, love" (p. 169). These premises, which take comedy to be a transmission of ideas of harmony and moral beauty, lead Kincaid to use the term "comedy" as indistinguishable at different times from "pastoral," "romance," "idyl," even "saints' lives" (p. 97), to identify the mild holy man Mr. Harding as Trollope's representative figure of comedy (p. 144)—though he doesn't go so far as to argue, as West does, that the episode of Mr. Harding's death in The Last Chronicle of Barset epitomizes the comic spirit (West, 127–28)—to speak of Paradise Regained and In Memoriam as comedies (p. 96), and

to describe the tradition of comedy of manners as though its sole representative were the decorous, severely moralistic Jane Austen. (To invoke names
like, say, Massinger, Jonson, Shirley, Fletcher, Wycherley, or Etherege sharply
alters the valences of the discussion and makes comedy seem far less morally
inspirational.) Kincaid's view of comic structure is by no means entirely erro-
neous, as his insightful analyses of particular Trollope novels testify. In this
book, however, I propose a different model of comedy, and my readings of
Trollope's novels, as a result, usually have little in common with Kincaid's.

CHAPTER 1   COMEDY: THE WORLD OF PLEASURE

1. Maggie Tulliver in *The Mill on the Floss* thus strikes a characteristic modern (and especially mid-Victorian) note when she rejects popular romance fiction like Scott's and Byron's on the grounds of its deficient seriousness. What
Maggie craves in literature, the narrator observes, is not entertainment but
"some explanation of this hard, real life" (p. 251).

2. Benjamin Lehmann reiterates the familiar point: "Though we laugh at actions and utterances in comedy, we do not laugh at the comedy as a whole.
For the comedy as a whole is a serious work" (p. 164). "The subject [of com-
edy] is serious," says R. M. Polhemus, who identifies comedy with religious
faith (*Comic Faith*, 22).

3. Terry Castle puts this point clearly, quoting Goethe: "the most lively and
exquisite delights are, like horses racing past, the experience of an instant
only, which leaves scarcely a trace on our soul" (Castle, 1).

4. A notable exception is Ian Donaldson's *World Upside-Down*, which focuses interestingly on comedy's imagery of inversion and disorder, seeing
these themes as productive of the pleasure of seeing feared authority figures
brought low. Donaldson's argument accords well with the view of comedy that
I am presenting in this book.

5. "The older members of almost any society," remarks Frye, "are apt to feel
that comedy has something subversive about it" (p. 164).

6. "Is not a comonty a Christmas gambold or a tumbling-trick?" asks Christopher Sly in the Induction of *The Taming of the Shrew*. "No, my good lord, it is
more pleasing stuff," replies the page (2.134–36). The epilogue of *The Tempest*
(classed as a comedy in the Folio of 1623) strikes the same note. Without your
applause, says Prospero to the audience, "my project fails, / Which was to
please" (12–13).

7. See, for example, Earl R. Wasserman, "The Pleasures of Tragedy," *ELH* 14
(1947):283–307; Eric Rothstein, "English Tragic Theory in the Late Seventeenth Century," *ELH* 29 (1962):306–23; W. P. Albrecht, "Hazlitt, Keats, and
the Sublime Pleasures of Tragedy," *The Nineteenth-Century Writer and His Audience: Selected Problems in Theory, Form, and Content*, ed. Harold Orel and
George J. Worth (Lawrence: University of Kansas Publications, 1969).

8. The supposed descent of comedy from ancient popular rituals is traced
notably by Cornford, *The Origin of Attic Comedy* and by C. L. Barber, *Shakespeare's Festive Comedy*.

9. For confoundings of comedy and realism, see, for example, Levine, 183;
Feibelman, 272; Watts, 193; Moore, passim.

10. For a brief historical survey of attacks on laughter, see Morreall, 85–88.

11. Vasey is mentioned in Morreall, 88. For a discussion of Acton, see Marcus, chap. 1.

12. Freud makes much the same argument in his analysis of smutty jokes,

which are designed, he says, to retrieve the pleasure of repressed impulses (*Jokes*, 101).

13. For similar objections to defining comedy with reference to laughter, see Heilman, 17; Rodway, 11; Knights, 433; Amur, 4ff. A. N. Kaul mounts an especially determined attack on "the laughter theory" (the idea that laughter is integral to comedy), which, he claims, reduces comedy to a mere succession of jokes, themselves necessarily incidental and spontaneous and thus incompatible with the concept of a unified comic action (pp. 16–17).

14. "Comedy," says James K. Feibelman, "is an intellectual affair, and deals chiefly with logic" ("Meaning," 471). See Martin for an account of the gradual acceptance among Victorian theorists of "intellect as the basis of comedy" (p. vii).

15. *Marginalia*, PR 2601 G6, IV.182.

16. Puck's phrase is cited by Helen Gardner in support of her argument that "fantasy is the natural instrument of comedy" (pp. 21–22).

17. Comedies may of course contain purely destructive, belittling humor, too, the kind described by "superiority theories" of laughter such as Bergson's, but it can hardly become dominant without severely disrupting comic structure.

CHAPTER 2   TROLLOPE AND "THE GOOD THINGS OF THIS WORLD"

1. Shirley Robin Letwin acutely describes Trollope as an antagonist of the dominant Western moral tradition equating virtue with "emancipation from the material world" (p. 39). The gentleman, she says, is "committed to pursuing the pleasures of life on earth" (p. 216).

2. One wonders how much of the long tradition of dismissing Trollope's claims as a serious novelist can be attributed ultimately to resentment of the sociopolitical values that his novels thus seem to reflect. A recent book by Bill Overton, *The Unofficial Trollope*, makes this resentment explicit. According to Overton, Trollope vitiates himself artistically by his failure to give a negative analysis of ruling-class ideology, by his seeming to reinforce rather than to assault a social status quo the illegitimacy of which seems to Overton too self-evident to require any demonstration. See especially pp. 152–93.

3. Coral Lansbury, 39–41 and passim, discusses Trollope's hunting scenes from a different perspective from mine, arguing that they represent "testing-places for popularity and success" (p. 98).

4. See Letwin, 63.

5. See, for example, Bakhtin, *Rabelais and His World*.

6. See also Trollope's declaration in "Higher Education of Women" that "amusements do not really amuse, that recreation ceases to recreate, and that play itself becomes worse than work, harder than work, when the search after them is made the one employment of life" (p. 85).

7. Note, for example, the nearly identical scenes of fathers receiving their sons in *Barnaby Rudge*, chap. 15 and *Phineas Redux*, chap. 21.

8. See Kincaid, 90, for a brief discussion of seasonal effects in *The Belton Estate*.

CHAPTER 3   CHARM AND DESIRE

1. For a brief discussion of the superior role of women in comedy, see Charney, 90–91.

2. *Marginalia*, PR 2421 D8 1842, Copy 2, As. Col., III.215.

3. Ibid., vol. XI, endleaf.

4. Ibid., VIII.206.

5. Philip Collins, "Business and Bosoms," 302–8, gives a lengthy inventory of Trollope's descriptions of women's breasts, which come in his fiction in every possible size and shape.

6. Nor does it disqualify her to have an eroticized sensibility of her own, as Juliet McMaster has persuasively shown. Trollope's women, she says, "are sensual, and deeply moved by the physical attributes of their men" (p. 172).

7. Trollope declares in "Higher Education of Women" that "the woman's privilege" relative to man is a "quicker appreciation and more sparkling intelligence" (p. 73).

8. A character like Ralph strongly qualifies Coral Lansbury s argument that in Trollope's view "popularity . . . is always derived from moral excellence" (p. 76).

9. As Juliet McMaster observes in her discussion of Can You Forgive Her?, "a great part of the attraction" of ne'er-do-well men for Trollope's women "is that life with them would involve danger and self-sacrifice" (p. 24).

10. See Polhemus, The Changing World, 117–18, for an intriguing discussion of the ways in which women could employ the idealized love code to subjugate men.

11. See, for example, Freud, "A Special Type of Choice," 166–67. For a general study of the pattern of "triangular" desire in modern fiction, though without any mention of Trollope, see Girard, Deceit, Desire, and the Novel.

12. "In Trollope's world," says Coral Lansbury, "the only relationship that requires no compromise is friendship" (p. 169).

CHAPTER 4   COMIC DESIGN AND "THE IMPRESSION OF LIFE"

1. Robert Newsom, citing Scholes and Kellogg's analysis in The Nature of Narrative of the novel as an unstable amalgam of history and romance, makes much the same point with reference to the role of romance elements in modern realism. Even novels aiming "to smash romantic illusions," he argues, are obliged "initially to sustain them as well" (p. 148).

2. See Walter M. Kendrick's extended discussion of Trollope's disavowal of plot (pp. 19, 27–29, and passim).

3. In his thoughtful essay on The Last Chronicle of Barset, William A. West identifies "large, loose plots" (p. 130) as characteristic not of realism but of comedy—a view that seems directly to contradict my own. West, however, blurs his argument by using "loose plot," "complex plot" and "multiple plot" as interchangeable terms. It is true, as he argues, that comedies allow more complexity of plot than do tragedies, that they need not be so strongly focused on a single main action, and that they allow the logic of cause and effect to be freely overturned by improbabilities; but this is not the kind of "looseness" in the sense of formal shapelessness that apRoberts, the North British Review writer and others identify with realism. Comic complexity normally emphasizes the impression of geometrical form rather than minimizing it.

Proceeding with his argument, West approvingly cites Frye's declaration (Anatomy, 170) that "in striking contrast to tragedy, there can hardly be such a thing as inevitable comedy" (West, 131). But the happy ending of comedy, with young lovers united and killjoys rebuked, would seem to be fully as inevitable as the catastrophic ending of tragedy. In one sense it is more so. A comedy that suddenly swerved into tragedy would be a great anomaly, but tragedy swerving at last (for all its supposed inevitability) into comedy forms a classic genre of early drama, "tragicomedy." *The Last Chronicle* is a modern tragicomedy in this formal, generic sense.

4. The linguist Brian McHale exactly confirms Trollope's point. "All novelistic dialogue," he says, "is conventionalized or stylized to some degree. Straightforward transcription would be intolerable in a novel, since the 'normal non-fluency' of ordinary speech has the appearance of illiteracy in print" (p. 259).

5. For a fuller discussion of these points, see Herbert, "*He Knew He Was Right*."

6. *Marginalia*, PR 2421 D8 1843, Copy 2, As. Col., II.229.

7. The pattern of Trollope's plot here strikingly parallels that of Ibsen's one true comedy, *The League of Youth*, which appeared in the same year in which Trollope wrote *Ralph the Heir* (1869). In Ibsen's play—like *Ralph the Heir*, a tale of electioneering—the adventurer Stensgard is humiliated in act 5 by finding that all three women he has proposed to are engaged to other men. Stensgard, however, is an image of fierce willpower, while Ralph is an image of the reverse.

8. *Marginalia*, PR 2421 D8 1843, Copy 2, As. Col., VIII.206.

CHAPTER 5   TRAGIC FIXITY, COMIC RIPENING

1. *The Works of Beaumont and Fletcher*, 11 vols., ed. Alexander Dyce (London: Moxon, 1843–46), 10:111.

2. Samuel Butler uses the same metaphor of the personality as a developing embryo in *The Way of All Flesh* (chap. 53), stressing, however, the process of individual evolution rather than the persistence of "constant traits" from one stage to the next.

3. Cf. Kendrick's discussion of change in Trollope: pp. 119–20, 127.

4. *Marginalia*, PR 2700 1805 As. Col., III.475.

5. In *An Old Man's Love* (chap. 2), Trollope's narrator insists at some length that faces are in fact reliable signs of character.

6. *The Mayor of Casterbridge*, chap. 17. The phrase is quoted from Novalis.

7. In other novels, "Glasslough" is "Grasslough" and "Longstaff" is "Longestaffe."

CHAPTER 6   COMIC IMPERFECTION

1. Cf. Trollope's *Autobiography*, 124: "No novel is anything . . . unless the reader can sympathize with the characters whose names he finds upon the page. . . . Truth let there be; truth of description, truth of character."

2. Walter M. Kendrick cogently observes that in Trollope's theory of fiction "the feeling of reality is inseparable from the action of sympathy" (*The Novel-Machine*, 25). He fails to take into account what I have stressed: the severe anomalies that this theory entailed when put into practice.

3. See Skilton, 86, for a discussion of the contemporary charge of "vulgarity" against Trollope.

4. It is worth noting his readiness to respond to such effects, as we see, for example, in his high praise for Thackeray's *Barry Lyndon*, the main principle of which, according to Trollope, is the author's irresistible sympathy for his utterly dissolute rogue-hero, a sympathy that reflects itself in the "lilt, if I may so call it, in the progress of the narrative" (*Thackeray*, 74).

5. My view here is very much in the spirit of Ruth apRoberts's discussion of

Trollope's "situation ethics," though I find his novels both more laden with moral tension and also more grounded in fixed moral standards than she allows.

6. See Cadbury, "Character and the Mock Heroic in *Barchester Towers*."

7. Cf. the reading of this scene by U. C. Knoepflmacher, who takes it to be a humorless condemnation of the archdeacon's "sinful" character (pp. 20–23). R. M. Polhemus, on the other hand, sees the humor (*The Changing World*, 37).

CHAPTER 7   *The Way We Live Now*: Puritanism, Laughter, Make-Believe

1. Other critics similarly praise Roger for being Trollope's "true gentleman" (Letwin, 262), "a stable guardian of values" (Tanner, 263), "Trollope's spokesman" and "one of his two or three decent figures" in *The Way We Live Now* (Rosenberg, 142). A. O. J. Cockshut notes that this paragon does seem an awful prig, an effect, he says, "which was certainly not intended" (p. 208).

2. Robert Tracy's stern gloss on this speech of the grievously victimized Mrs. Hurtle: "She rejects the values of an ordered and interdependent society in favor of that individualism which Trollope presents as inimical to order" (*Trollope's Later Novels*, 173). If anything is recklessly individualistic and inimical to order in this situation, it is obviously Paul's capricious breaking of an honorable engagement of marriage that was his own idea to begin with. All Mrs. Hurtle says is that prejudiced bullies should not, in a decent society, be able to run roughshod over the helpless.

3. Trollope was devoted to Molière, whose plays he knew intimately from childhood, and he considered the character of Alceste to be "the best of Molière" (*Letters*, 954). See also Harvey, 12.

4. "I know no personage in the British drama," Trollope remarked in his notes to the play, "better adapted to bring out the power of a great dramatist" (*Marginalia*, PR 2700 1805 As. Col., III.590).

5. *Marginalia*, PR 2700 1805 As. Col., IV.16.

6. See Kincaid, 165n; Edwards, 169, 181; Harvey, 125, 137.

7. Fisker has a particular original in Dickens's flamboyant rascal Montague Tigg in *Martin Chuzzlewit*, the proprietor of a bogus insurance company, the Anglo-Bengalee, which in its name and especially its sheer unreality evokes the South Central Pacific and Mexican Railway.

CHAPTER 8   *Ayala's Angel*: Folly and Scarce Resources

1. Robert Tracy, for example, considers *Ayala* inconsequential, fit reading for the reader "who seeks only to be charmed" (p. 251). Even Robert M. Polhemus, who elsewhere shows considerable sensitivity to comic values, dismisses the book as the product of "an incoherent, tired imagination" (*The Changing World*, 219). The novel clearly needs a full-dress study to help redeem it from verdicts like these.

2. Just as the sale of luxury consumer goods like Mercedes-Benzes and gourmet ice cream always surges, we are told, in periods of economic recession.

Works Cited

Altick, Richard D. *The English Common Reader: A Social History of the Mass Reading Public 1800–1900*. Chicago and London: University of Chicago Press, 1957.

Amur, G. S. *The Concept of Comedy: A Re-Statement*. Karnatak University Research Series 4. Dharwar: Karnatak University, 1963.

apRoberts, Ruth. *The Moral Trollope*. Athens, Ohio: Ohio University Press, 1971.

Arnold, Matthew. *Culture and Anarchy*. Edited by J. Dover Wilson. Cambridge: Cambridge University Press, 1966.

Austen, Jane. *Pride and Prejudice*. Boston: Houghton Mifflin, 1956.

Bakhtin, Mikhail. *Rabelais and His World*. Translated by Helene Iswolsky. Cambridge, Mass. and London: MIT Press, 1968.

Balzac, Honoré de. *Père Goriot*. Translated by Henry Reed. New York: Signet, 1962.

Barber, C. L. *Shakespeare's Festive Comedy: A Study of Dramatic Form and its Relation to Social Custom*. Cleveland and New York: Meridian, 1963.

Barickman, Richard, Susan MacDonald, and Myra Stark. *Corrupt Relations: Dickens, Thackeray, Trollope, Collins, and the Victorian Sexual System*. New York: Columbia University Press, 1982.

Barthes, Roland. *S/Z*. Translated by Richard Miller. New York: Hill and Wang, 1974.

Baudelaire, Charles. "On the Essence of Laughter, and, in General, on the Comic in the Plastic Arts." Translated by Jonathan Mayne. In *Comedy: Meaning and Form*, edited by Robert W. Corrigan, 448–65. San Francisco: Chandler, 1965.

Beaumont, Francis. *The Works of Beaumont and Fletcher*. 14 vols. Edited by Henry Weber. Edinburgh: Ballantyne, 1812.

Becker, George J. *Realism in Modern Literature*. New York: Ungar, 1980.

Bergson, Henri. "Laughter." In *Comedy*, edited by Wylie Sypher, 61–190. Garden City: Doubleday, 1956.

Booth, Bradford A. *Anthony Trollope: Aspects of His Life and Art*. Bloomington: Indiana University Press, 1958.

Bowen, Elizabeth. "Introduction." In *Doctor Thorne*, by Anthony Trollope. Boston: Houghton Mifflin, 1959.

Bradford, Gamaliel. "Trollope and the Osler Treatment." *The Nation* 80 (8 June 1905):458.

Cadbury, William. "Character and the Mock Heroic in *Barchester Towers*." *Texas Studies in Literature and Language* 5 (1963–64):509–19.

Carroll, Lewis (C. L. Dodgson). *Alice's Adventures in Wonderland* and *Through the Looking-Glass*. New York and Toronto: Signet, 1960.

Castle, Terry. "Sketch for a History of the English Masquerade 1710–1790." Unpublished MS.

Chapman, George. *The Plays of George Chapman*. Edited by Thomas Marc Parrott. New York: Russell, 1961.

Charney, Maurice. *Comedy High and Low: An Introduction to the Experience of Comedy*. New York: Oxford University Press, 1978.

Cockshut, A. O. J. *Anthony Trollope: A Critical Study*. London: Collins, 1955.

Cohen, Joan. *Form and Realism in Six Novels of Anthony Trollope*. The Hague: Mouton, 1976.

Collier, Jeremy. *A Short View of the Immorality and Profaneness of the English Stage*. Munchen: Fink, 1967.

Collins, Philip. "Business and Bosoms: Some Trollopian Concerns." *Nineteenth-Century Fiction* 37 (1982):383–95.

Congreve, William. *The Comedies of William Congreve*. Edited by Anthony G. Henderson. Cambridge: Cambridge University Press, 1982.

Cook, Albert. *The Dark Voyage and the Golden Mean: A Philosophy of Comedy*. New York: Norton, 1966.

Cornford, Francis M. *The Origin of Attic Comedy*. Cambridge: Cambridge University Press, 1934.

Donaldson, Ian. *The World Upside-Down: Comedy From Jonson to Fielding*. Oxford: Clarendon, 1970.

Douglas, Mary. *Purity and Danger: An Analysis of Concepts of Pollution and Taboo*. London, Boston, and Henley: Routledge, 1979.

Dryden, John. "Preface to *An Evening's Love: or, The Mock Astrologer*." In *Restoration and Eighteenth-Century Comedy*, edited by Scott McMillin, 352–60. New York: Norton, 1973.

Edwards, P. D. *Anthony Trollope, His Art and Scope*. Hassocks: Harvester, 1978.

Eliot, George. *Adam Bede*. Edited by John Paterson. Boston: Houghton Mifflin, 1968.

———. *The George Eliot Letters*. 7 vols. Edited by Gordon S. Haight. New Haven: Yale University Press, 1954.

———. *The Mill on the Floss*. Edited by Gordon S. Haight. Boston: Houghton Mifflin, 1961.

Etherege, George. *The Plays of Sir George Etherege*. Edited by Michael Cordner. Cambridge: Cambridge University Press, 1982.

Farquhar, George. *The Beaux' Stratagem*. Edited by Michael Cordner. London: Benn; New York: Norton, 1976.

Feibelman, James. *In Praise of Comedy: A Study in Its Theory and Practice*. New York: Macmillan, 1939.

Fletcher, John. *The Works of Beaumont and Fletcher*. 14 vols. Edited by Henry Weber. Edinburgh: Ballantyne, 1812.

Ford, Ford Madox. *The English Novel: From the Earliest Days to the Death of Joseph Conrad*. Philadelphia and London: Lippincott, 1929.

Frazer, James George. *The Golden Bough: A Study in Magic and Religion*. New York: Collier, 1963.

Freud, Sigmund. "Creative Writers and Day-Dreaming." *The Standard Edition of the Complete Psychological Works of Sigmund Freud*. 24 vols. Translated and edited by James Strachey, 9:143–53. London: Hogarth, 1955.

———. *Jokes and Their Relation to the Unconscious*. *The Standard Edition*, vol. 8.

———. "A Special Type of Choice of Object Made by Men." *The Standard Edition* 11:165–75.

———. "On the Universal Tendency to Debasement in the Sphere of Love." *The Standard Edition* 11:177–90.

Frye, Northrop. *Anatomy of Criticism*. New York: Atheneum, 1966.

Gardner, Helen. "*As You Like It*." In *More Talking of Shakespeare*, edited by John Garrett, 17–32. New York: Theatre Arts, 1959.

Gay, Peter. *Education of the Senses*. New York and Oxford: Oxford University Press, 1984.

Gilbert, W. S. *The Mikado; or, The Town of Titipu*. In *Plays and Poems of W. S. Gilbert*, edited by Deems Taylor. New York: Random, 1932.

Gindin, James. *Harvest of a Quiet Eye: The Novel of Compassion*. Bloomington and London: Indiana University Press, 1971.

Girard, René. *Deceit, Desire, and the Novel: Self and Other in Literary Structure*. Translated by Yvonne Freccero. Baltimore and London: The Johns Hopkins University Press, 1984.

Gissing, George. *New Grub Street*. Edited by Irving Howe. Boston: Houghton Mifflin, 1962.

Gombrich, E. H. *Art and Illusion: A Study in the Psychology of Pictorial Representation*. Princeton: Princeton University Press, 1969.

Gurewitch, Morton. *Comedy: The Irrational Vision*. Ithaca and London: Cornell University Press, 1975.

Hagan, John H. "*The Duke's Children*: Trollope's Psychological Masterpiece." *Nineteenth-Century Fiction* 13 (1958):1–21.

Hardy, Thomas. *Jude the Obscure*. New York: Signet, 1961.

———. *The Mayor of Casterbridge*. Edited by Robert B. Heilman. Boston: Houghton Mifflin, 1962.

Harvey, Geoffrey. *The Art of Anthony Trollope*. London: Weidenfeld, 1980.

Heilman, Robert Bechtold. *The Ways of the World: Comedy and Society*. Seattle and London: University of Washington Press, 1978.

Henkle, Roger B. *Comedy and Culture: England 1820–1900*. Princeton: Princeton University Press, 1980.

Herbert, Christopher. "*He Knew He Was Right*, Mrs. Lynn Linton, and the Duplicities of Victorian Marriage." *Texas Studies in Literature and Language* 25 (1983):448–69.

Huizinga, Johan. *Homo Ludens: A Study of the Play-Element in Culture*. Boston: Beacon, 1950.

Jonson, Ben. *The Complete Plays of Ben Jonson*. 4 vols. Edited by G. A. Wilkes. Oxford: Clarendon, 1981.

————. "Pleasure Reconciled to Virtue." In *Ben Jonson: Selected Masques*, edited by Stephen Orgel. New Haven and London: Yale University Press, 1970.

Joyce, Stanislaus. *My Brother's Keeper: James Joyce's Early Years*. Edited by Richard Ellmann. New York: Viking, 1958.

Kaul, A. N. *The Action of English Comedy: Studies in the Encounter of Abstraction and Experience from Shakespeare to Shaw*. New Haven: Yale University Press, 1970.

Kendrick, Walter M. *The Novel-Machine: The Theory and Fiction of Anthony Trollope*. Baltimore and London: The Johns Hopkins University Press, 1980.

Ker, W. P. "Anthony Trollope." In *On Modern Literature: Lectures and Addresses by W. P. Ker*, edited by Terence Spencer and James Sutherland, 136–46. Oxford: Clarendon, 1955.

————. "On Comedy." In *On Modern Literature*, 196–209.

Kincaid, James R. *The Novels of Anthony Trollope*. Oxford: Clarendon, 1977.

Kitson Clark, D. *The Making of Victorian England*. New York: Atheneum, 1976.

Knights, L. C. "Notes on Comedy." In *Theories of Comedy*, edited by Paul Lauter, 432–43. Garden City: Doubleday, 1964.

Knoepflmacher, U. C. *Laughter and Despair: Readings in Ten Novels of the Victorian Era*. Berkeley, Los Angeles, London: University of California Press, 1971.

Kronenberger, Louis. *The Thread of Laughter*. New York: Knopf, 1952.

Kuhn, Thomas S. *The Structure of Scientific Revolutions*. 2d ed. Chicago and London: University of Chicago Press, 1970.

Lamb, Charles. "On the Artificial Comedy of the Last Century." In *Theories of Comedy*, edited by Paul Lauter, 295–302. Garden City: Doubleday, 1964.

Langer, Suzanne K. *Feeling and Form*. New York: Scribner's, 1953.

Lansbury, Coral. *The Reasonable Man: Trollope's Legal Fiction*. Princeton: Princeton University Press, 1981.

Lawrence, D. H. *Studies in Classic American Literature*. New York: Viking, 1964.

Lehmann, Benjamin. "Comedy and Laughter." In *Comedy: Meaning and Form*, edited by Robert W. Corrigan, 163–78. San Francisco: Chandler, 1965.

Letwin, Shirley Robin. *The Gentleman in Trollope: Individuality and Moral Conduct*. Cambridge, Mass.: Harvard University Press, 1982.

Levine, George. *The Realistic Imagination: English Fiction from Frankenstein to Lady Chatterly*. Chicago and London: University of Chicago Press, 1981.

McHale, Brian. "Free Indirect Discourse: A Survey of Recent Accounts." *Poetics and Theory of Literature* 3 (1978):249–87.

McMaster, Juliet. *Trollope's Palliser Novels: Theme and Pattern*. New York: Oxford University Press, 1978.

Malinowski, Bronislaw. *Argonauts of the Western Pacific: An Account of Native Enterprise and Adventure in the Archipelagoes of Melanesian New Guinea*. London: Routledge; New York: Dutton, 1932.

Malthus, Thomas Robert. *On Population*. Edited by Gertrude Himmelfarb. New York: Modern Library, 1960.

Marcus, Steven. *The Other Victorians: A Study of Sexuality and Pornography in Mid-Nineteenth-Century England*. London: Corgi, 1969.

Marston, John. *The Malcontent*. Edited by George K. Hunter. London: Methuen, 1975.

Martin, Robert Bernard. *The Triumph of Wit: A Study of Victorian Comic Theory*. Oxford: Clarendon, 1974.

Massinger, Philip. *The Plays and Poems of Philip Massinger*. Edited by Philip Edwards and Colin Gibson. Oxford: Clarendon, 1976.

Mayhew, Henry. *The Morning Chronicle Survey of Labour and the Poor: The Metropolitan Districts*. 6 vols. Firle, Sussex: Caliban, 1980.

Meredith, George. "An Essay on Comedy." In *Comedy*, edited by Wylie Sypher, 3–57. Garden City: Doubleday, 1956.

Middleton, Thomas, and William Rowley. *A Fair Quarrel*. Edited by George R. Price. Lincoln: University of Nebraska Press, 1976.

Mill, John Stuart. *Autobiography*. Edited by Jack Stillinger. Boston: Houghton Mifflin, 1969.

———. *On Liberty*. Edited by Alburey Castell. New York: Appleton-Century-Crofts, 1947.

Miller, J. Hillis. *The Form of Victorian Fiction: Thackeray, Dickens, Trollope, George Eliot, Meredith, and Hardy*. Notre Dame and London: University of Notre Dame Press, 1968.

Mizener, Arthur. "Anthony Trollope: The Palliser Novels." In *From Jane Austen to Joseph Conrad: Essays Collected in Memory of James T. Hillhouse*, edited by Robert C. Rathburn and Martin Steinmann, Jr., 160–76. Minneapolis: University of Minnesota Press, 1958.

Moore, John B. *The Comic and the Realistic in English Drama*. Chicago: University of Chicago Press, 1925.

Morreall, John. *Taking Laughter Seriously*. Albany: State University of New York Press, 1983.

Newman, John Henry. *Apologia Pro Vita Sua*. Edited by A. Dwight Culler. Boston: Houghton Mifflin, 1956.

Newsom, Robert. *Dickens on the Romantic Side of Familiar Things: "Bleak House" and the Novel Tradition*. New York: Columbia University Press, 1977.

O'Connor, Frank. *The Mirror in the Roadway: A Study of the Modern Novel*. New York: Knopf, 1964.

Olson, Elder. *The Theory of Comedy*. Bloomington and London: Indiana University Press, 1968.

Ortega y Gasset, José. *The Dehumanization of Art and Notes on the Novel*. Translated by Helene Weyl. Princeton: Princeton University Press, 1948.

Overton, Bill. *The Unofficial Trollope*. Brighton, Sussex: Harvester; Totowa, N. J.: Barnes & Noble, 1982.

Perkin, Harold. *The Origins of Modern English Society 1780–1880*. London and Henley: Routledge, 1969.

Polhemus, Robert M. "Being in Love in *Phineas Finn/Phineas Redux*: Desire, Devotion, Consolation." *Nineteenth-Century Fiction* 37 (1982):383–95.

———. *The Changing World of Anthony Trollope*. Berkeley and Los Angeles: University of California Press, 1968.

———. *Comic Faith: The Great Tradition From Austen to Joyce*. Chicago and London: University of Chicago Press, 1980.

Potts, L. J. *Comedy*. London: Hutchinson, 1963.

Praz, Mario. *The Hero in Eclipse in Victorian Fiction*. Translated by Agnes David-son. London, New York, Toronto: Oxford University Press, 1956.

Proust, Marcel. *Remembrance of Things Past*. 2 vols. Translated by C. K. Scott Moncrieff. New York: Random, 1934.

Qualls, Barry V. *The Secular Pilgrims of Victorian Fiction: The Novel as Book of Life*. Cambridge: Cambridge University Press, 1982.

Robertson, Tom. *Plays by Tom Robertson*. Edited by William Tydeman. Cam-bridge: Cambridge University Press, 1982.

Rodway, Allan. *English Comedy: Its Role and Nature from Chaucer to the Present Day*. London: Chatto and Windus, 1975.

Rosenberg, Edgar. *From Shylock to Svengali: Jewish Stereotypes in English Fiction*. Stanford: Stanford University Press, 1960.

Scholes, Robert, and Robert Kellogg. *The Nature of Narrative*. London, Oxford, New York: Oxford University Press, 1976.

Scott, Walter. *The Heart of Mid-Lothian*. London and New York: Everyman's, 1975.

Seltzer, Mark. *Henry James and the Art of Power*. Ithaca and London: Cornell University Press, 1984.

Shakespeare, William. *William Shakespeare: The Complete Works*. Edited by Peter Alexander. New York: Random, 1952.

Sheridan, Richard Brinsley. *Sheridan: Plays*. Edited by Cecil Price. London, New York, Toronto: Oxford University Press, 1975.

Shirley, James. *The Dramatic Works and Poems of James Shirley*. 6 vols. Edited by William Gifford and Alexander Dyce. London: Murray, 1833.

Skilton, David. *Anthony Trollope and His Contemporaries: A Study in the Theory and Conventions of Mid-Victorian Fiction*. London: Longman, 1972.

Slakey, Roger L. "Melmotte's Death: A Prism of Meaning in *The Way We Live Now*." *ELH* 34 (1967):248–59.

Slights, William W. E. "The Incarnations of Comedy." *University of Toronto Quarterly* 51 (1981):13–27.

Smalley, Donald, ed. *Trollope: The Critical Heritage*. London: Routledge; New York: Barnes and Noble, 1969.

Stang, Richard. *The Theory of the Novel in England 1850–1870*. New York: Co-lumbia University Press; London: Routledge, 1966.

Steele, Richard. *The Plays of Richard Steele*. Edited by Shirley Strum Kenny. Oxford: Clarendon, 1971.

Sypher, Wylie. "The Meanings of Comedy." In *Comedy*, edited by Wylie Sypher, 193–255. Garden City: Doubleday, 1956.

Tanner, Tony. "Trollope's *The Way We Live Now*: Its Modern Significance." *Critical Quarterly* 9 (1967):256–71.

Terry, R. C. *Anthony Trollope: The Artist in Hiding*. Totowa, N.J.: Rowman, 1977.

Thackeray, William Makepeace. "The English Humourists of the Eighteenth Century." *The Works of William Makepeace Thackeray*, Kensington Edition, 26:149–397. New York: Scribner's, 1904.

———. *Vanity Fair: A Novel Without a Hero*. Edited by Geoffrey Tillotson and Kathleen Tillotson. Boston: Houghton Mifflin, 1963.

Tillotson, Kathleen. "The Lighter Reading of the Eighteen-Sixties." In *The Woman in White* by Wilkie Collins, edited by Anthea Trodd, ix–xxvi. Boston: Houghton Mifflin, 1969.

———. *Novels of the Eighteen-Forties*. Oxford: Oxford University Press, 1962.

Todorov, Tzvetan. *The Poetics of Prose*. Translated by Richard Howard. Ithaca: Cornell University Press, 1977.

Tracy, Robert. *Trollope's Later Novels*. Berkeley, Los Angeles, London: University of California Press, 1978.

Trollope, Anthony. *An Autobiography*. London, New York, Toronto: Oxford University Press, 1950.

———. "On English Prose Fiction as a Rational Amusement." In *Four Lectures*, edited by Morris L. Parrish, 94–124. London: Constable, 1938.

———. "Higher Education of Women." In *Four Lectures*, edited by Morris L. Parrish, 67–88. London: Constable, 1938.

———. *The Letters of Anthony Trollope*. 2 vols. Edited by N. John Hall. Stanford: Stanford University Press, 1983.

———. *Thackeray*. English Men of Letters series. New York: Harper, n.d.

Vanbrugh, John. *The Provoked Wife*. Edited by James L. Smith. London and Tonbridge: Benn, 1974.

Van Ghent, Dorothy. *The English Novel: Form and Function*. New York, Evanston, London: Harper, 1961.

Vasey, George. *The Philosophy of Laughter and Smiling*. 2d ed. London: Burns, 1877.

Watt, Ian. *The Rise of the Novel: Studies in Defoe, Richardson and Fielding*. Berkeley and Los Angeles: University of California Press, 1964.

Watts, Harold H. "The Sense of Regain: A Theory of Comedy." In *Comedy: Meaning and Form*, edited by Robert W. Corrigan, 192–97. San Francisco: Chandler, 1965.

Waugh, Evelyn. *Brideshead Revisited: The Sacred and Profane Memories of Captain Charles Ryder*. Boston: Little, Brown, 1945.

Weber, Max. *The Protestant Ethic and the Spirit of Capitalism*. Translated by Talcott Parsons. London: Counterpoint, 1985.

West, William A. "*The Last Chronicle of Barset*: Trollope's Comic Techniques." In *The Classic British Novel*, edited by Howard M. Harper, Jr., and Charles Edge, 121–42. Athens, Ga.: University of Georgia Press, 1972.

Wilde, Oscar. *The Importance of Being Earnest: A Trivial Comedy for Serious People*. Edited by Russell Jackson. London: Benn; New York: Norton, 1980.

Wilkins, George. *The Miseries of Inforced Marriage*. *A Select Collection of Old Plays*. 12 vols. Edited by Robert Dodsley, 5:1–97. London: Prowett, 1825.

Index